# STUDIES IN AMERICAN CULTURE

# STUDIES IN
# American Culture

## *Dominant Ideas and Images*

EDITED BY

JOSEPH J. KWIAT AND MARY C. TURPIE

*University of Minnesota Press*

MINNEAPOLIS

PRINTED IN THE UNITED STATES OF AMERICA AT THE LUND PRESS, INC., MINNEAPOLIS

*Library of Congress Catalog Card Number: 59-15646*

PUBLISHED IN GREAT BRITAIN, INDIA, AND PAKISTAN BY THE OXFORD UNIVERSITY PRESS, LONDON, BOMBAY, AND KARACHI, AND IN CANADA BY THOMAS ALLEN, LTD., TORONTO

*Second printing 1960*

Excerpts from *A Masque of Mercy* by Robert Frost (copyright 1947 by Henry Holt and Company, Inc.) are used by permission of the publisher, Holt. The quotation from *The Liberal Imagination* by Lionel Trilling (copyright 1946 by Lionel Trilling) is used by permission of the publisher, the Viking Press, Inc. The quotation from the Introduction to *Nine Plays* by Eugene O'Neill (copyright 1932 by Liveright) is used by permission of Mrs. O'Neill and Random House.

# *Preface*

THIS book was initiated when Professor Tremaine McDowell announced his premature retirement, due to illness, from the post he had held for thirteen years (1945–1958) as chairman of the Program in American Studies at the University of Minnesota. We planned a volume which would be more than the conventional *Festschrift*. It should give, we felt, a sense of the directions that work in the general field of American culture has been taking within the past decade or so. This period has seen an almost revolutionary academic interest and activity in programs variously known as American Studies or American Civilization or American Culture. We, as co-editors, hoped that Professor McDowell would be able to share with us our effort to take stock of the work that has recently been done and to recognize the problems that still confront the scholar. Unfortunately, he died during the preparation of this volume.

Professor McDowell was one of the chief architects of the American Studies movement in this country. He published in 1948 a book, *American Studies*, on the value of interdisciplinary scholarship and interdisciplinary curricula, and the following year he was founder of the *American Quarterly* at the University of Minnesota. Professor McDowell's influence has been felt abroad not only through his service on the committee to select lecturers in American civilization under the Fulbright act, but also through his many personal contacts with foreign teachers and scholars who are pioneering in the field of American Studies. But perhaps the greatest tribute to the vigor of Professor McDowell's work is the extensive scholarship and teaching in American Studies being carried on by his students throughout the United States.

Our contributors have been, in one way or another, active participants in the Program in American Studies at the University of Minnesota. Former students or colleagues of Professor McDowell's — all of them have helped to shape the Minnesota program and, in turn, have felt the intellectual excitement generated by it. They demonstrate interest in a variety of fields: literary history and criticism; social, intellectual, and aesthetic history; and political, economic, and social theory. Furthermore, they reflect the training they received from a variety of academic institutions: Harvard University, the University of Pennsylvania, Columbia University, the University of Chicago, the University of Iowa, Dartmouth College, Vanderbilt University, and the University of Minnesota; as faculty members they represent, at the moment, the following schools: the University of California, the University of Chicago, Princeton University, Rutgers University, Amherst College, the University of Pennsylvania, and the University of Minnesota. In addition, many of the contributors have lectured on American civilization abroad: in Japan, India, Italy, Belgium, Holland, England, France, Germany, Austria, and the Scandinavian countries. It is entirely appropriate that the final essay in this book should be written by Professor Robert E. Spiller, himself one of the founding fathers of American Studies in this country. In it, he traces the intellectual and academic history of the movement, and interprets the essays in this book in relation to the larger aims of the American Studies enterprise.

We wish to express our gratitude to the editors and publishers of the following journals who granted permission to use in this volume articles originally published by them: *American Quarterly* (the articles by Henry Nash Smith, John W. Ward, and Bernard Bowron, Leo Marx, and Arnold Rose); *Annals* of the American Academy of Political and Social Science (Reuel Denney); *English Studies* (William Van O'Connor); *Die Neueren Sprachen* (Leo Marx); *PMLA* (Joseph J. Kwiat); *Social Research* (David W. Noble); and *Texas Quarterly* (Allen Tate). In several cases the authors revised their papers extensively for book publication. An earlier version of the article by Theodore C. Blegen appeared in *Grass Roots History*, published by the University of Minnesota Press.

We are also indebted to the Graduate School of the University of Minnesota for its cooperation and assistance, and to Mrs. Charlotte Kwiat, Professor Robert C. Rathburn, and our good friends at the University of Minnesota Press, who gave unstintingly of their efforts in seeing the book through publication.

J. J. K. and M. C. T.

# Contents

viii

STUDIES IN AMERICAN CULTURE

# Can "American Studies" Develop a Method?

THE problem of method in American Studies arises because the investigation of American culture, past and present, as a whole does not coincide with the customary field of operations of any established academic discipline. The phrase "as a whole" does not, of course, imply a global attack directed simultaneously toward all the aspects of our culture. The defining characteristic of American Studies is not the size of its problems but the effort to view any given subject of investigation from new perspectives, to take into account as many aspects of it as possible.

In order to illustrate the need for such a shift of perspective, I should like to draw upon my own experience in attempting to interpret Mark Twain. He was a writer and his work belongs to the academic field of American literature. But surely the work of no other writer so clearly needs to be placed in a social setting before it can be fully understood. No other American writer of comparable importance is so unmistakably of the people. He took his materials and his technique from American culture, and he developed in collaboration with his audience. (The artist and his public, he remarked toward the end of his life, "are in a tacit co-partnership.") He served his apprenticeship in newspaper offices; he perfected his style by practicing the art of oral storytelling. His work is an almost uninterrupted commentary on matters uppermost in the minds of his readers, and he had a remarkable ability to objectify their memories and dreams. It would be peculiarly artificial to try to deal with his books as if they were self-contained autonomous universes.

What is then the best way to understand Mark Twain? It is true that much study of his life and work needs to be undertaken along perfectly conventional lines: his dependence upon literary predecessors, for example, has even yet not been fully investigated. But the student of this remarkable career soon finds himself asking questions that lead beyond

3

the usual limits of literary history or criticism. One question, which is probably at bottom anthropological, concerns the matter of taboos governing what may be said, what may be represented, what may be published. Since the appearance of Van Wyck Brooks' *The Ordeal of Mark Twain* (now almost forty years ago) a great deal has been written about the supposed censorship of Mark Twain's work. The subject is relevant to criticism of his books, to the history of American literature, and to the history of American culture. But no one knows very much about it. We do not know to what extent the taboos evident in Mark Twain's work are individual idiosyncrasies and to what extent they were actually (as he often maintained) imposed by the culture. We are even less able to determine whether these canons of propriety were enforced uniformly throughout the society, or whether they varied according to geographical regions (as Bernard De Voto assumes in the chapter on "Cryptorchism" in *Mark Twain's America*) or according to social classes (as is implied in Santayana's celebrated identification of a Genteel Tradition in America).

The literary historian approaches this problem by examining such evidence as the fiction published in magazines and books during the period; correspondence between editors and writers; and book reviews, especially those which comment adversely upon supposed violations of taboos. But the information gathered from these sources needs to be interpreted in the light of a thorough knowledge of class structure, of the stratification of taste according to levels of sophistication, and of the different audiences to which different magazines and publishing houses address themselves. I do not believe, for example, that the usual methods of literary history enable us to explain why Harriet Beecher Stowe's "The True Story of Lady Byron's Life," published in the *Atlantic Monthly* in 1869 under the editorship of William Dean Howells after careful revision by Oliver Wendell Holmes, should have cost the magazine fifteen thousand subscribers — more than one-fourth of its list. The incident suggests that the public which read books (and literary magazines, among which the *Atlantic* enjoyed the highest status) had an appreciably stricter sense of decorum than did Howells and Holmes. The *New York Tribune*, spokesman for a larger but still relatively literate segment of public opinion, asserted that *Innocents Abroad* showed "an offensive irreverence for things which other men held sacred." Yet Howells published a highly favorable review of *Innocents Abroad* in the

4

*Atlantic*. At the other end of the spectrum of tastes, or of degrees of sophistication, *Innocents Abroad* had an enormous sale among people who seldom read anything except newspapers. Perhaps the exaggerated concern for literary propriety came neither from the extreme highbrows nor from the public at large but from a kind of upper-middlebrow audience defined by the subscription lists of the literary magazines. If there were regional differences among segments of this audience, they have not been clearly defined.

In any event, during the 1870's Mark Twain had a complex problem of adaptation to his various audiences. Howells was introducing him to the world of polite letters through the pages of the *Atlantic*. The canvassers for the American Publishing Company were selling tens of thousands of his books to quite unliterary purchasers. On the lecture platform Mark Twain himself was in direct contact with large miscellaneous audiences — in the Middle West, in the East, and (as early as 1872) in England. He was, in fact, one of the pioneers in the discovery and the formation of the mass audience which is so conspicuous in the twentieth century. In these circumstances, he could obviously not have been the free creative artist in the Romantic mode that seems to have been Brooks' ideal. The autonomy of Mark Twain's works was impaired before they were written, and by forces that were in large part internalized in the author. It does not take us very far to conclude, as Brooks did, that this is a scandal. We must recognize that the inhibitions on literary expression (that is, the demands of various special audiences and of the embryonic mass audience) were a complex trait of the culture in which Mark Twain lived. We need to understand them in order to understand Mark Twain's work. We also need to understand them in order to understand the culture.

Indeed, it may turn out that one of the distinctive fields of American Studies is precisely this ambiguous relation between works of art and the culture in which they occur. Certainly the student of Mark Twain is confronted at every turn with problems arising in this area. Let me cite another example. In his early work, especially in *Innocents Abroad* and *Roughing It*, Mark Twain uses at least three distinct prose styles. One of these is a vernacular style, based on the everyday speech of men with little formal education — rivermen, stagecoach drivers, prospectors. The second is patterned on the ornate, elevated rhetoric of the pulpit and of political oratory in the manner of Daniel Webster. The third is a direct, unpretentious style representing the impersonal attitude of the skilled reporter. The vernacular style is of course appropriate when it represents the speech of characters with low status. The narrator reports this speech with evident sympathy and delight. More significantly, he often uses vernacular phrases himself in a way that identifies him with the Boys, men beyond the pale of polite society who are hostile to its official values. The elevated style embodies an aspiration toward genteel culture, for which indeed it serves as a matrix; the narrator often uses it with perfect seriousness, yet he also often burlesques it. The direct style is apparently felt as being neutral, as being somehow outside the hierarchy of classes. The relation of these styles to one another, and Mark Twain's subsequent development (never complete) toward a distinctive personal idiom, are delicate indices to his perception of differences among social classes, of his own place in the status system, and of the status of the audience he believes himself to be addressing.

An examination of these aspects of Mark Twain's style requires a careful discrimination between attitudes toward social status that he has taken over unconsciously from the culture, and attitudes that spring from his conscious recognition of social stratification and of his place within the status system. It is possible, for example, that his success in creating a satisfactory style depended on his achievement of a personal autonomy — an achievement that was intermittent rather than accomplished once and for all. Furthermore, we have to recognize drastic changes in Mark Twain's relation to the status system at different periods of his career. Especially in the five or six years immediately preceding his marriage in 1870, and for a year or two after it, he shows the signs of rapid upward social mobility, and this movement along the dimension of social status is inextricably involved with his development as a writer. Thus almost concurrently he moved from California to the East Coast; he ceased being a newspaper correspondent to become a platform "lecturer," a contributor to literary magazines (including the *Atlantic*), a writer of books, and even a dramatist; after several years of a hand-to-mouth Bohemian existence he began to receive a large income from his writing; and despite the perfectly rational misgivings of the Langdon family, he married Livy. He made his celebrated efforts at reform by trying to give up liquor and profanity, and to become a Christian as that term was understood in Elmira. He built his expensive house in Hartford. In place of Steve Gillis, Joe Goodman, and the members of the San Francisco Minstrel Troupe, he acquired as friends the Reverend Joseph Twichell, Charles Dudley Warner, and William Dean Howells. These biographical facts point in two directions: toward American culture (or the varieties of American regional subcultures) at the end of the Civil War, and toward the literary development recorded in Mark Twain's writings. The problem is at once biographical, historical, sociological, and literary.

Mark Twain's attitudes toward American society found expression not only in his style, but in the use of recurrent figures or types of character: in his early work, for example, what has been called the vernacular character (most fully illustrated in Huck Finn); in his later work, a figure that might be called the transcendent character (the best illustration being Young Satan in *The Mysterious Stranger*). These figures occur in many different guises over a long period of time. They are persistent themes in Mark Twain's writing, and they exert a strong influence on the shaping of plots in his works of fiction, on his imagery, and especially on his language (what would *Huckleberry Finn* be if the language were altered?). Both figures embody the author's attitudes toward society, or rather his reading of social situations. The vernacular character is, so to speak, outside society because he is beneath it; the transcendent character is outside society because he is above it. There are strong hints here of Mark Twain's own alienation from the society. His principal problem as a novelist was how to conceive of significant action for characters whose relation to society was so special. The problem was evidently forced upon him by the culture of late nineteenth-century America. It lies at the center of his literary development, yet it cannot be adequately dealt with by literary methods alone. What is needed is a method of analysis that is at once literary (for one must begin with an analytical reading of the texts that takes into account structure, imagery, diction, and the like) and sociological (for many of the forces at work in the fiction are clearly of social origin). Such an analysis would not only take us much farther into Mark Twain's fictive universe than criticism has gone in the past; it would also give us a new insight into American society of the late nineteenth century, for the vernacular figure and the transcendent figure are not peculiar to Mark Twain. They were widely current in American literature and thought; they are cultural, not merely private and individual, images.

The final problem I shall mention that is posed by Mark Twain's career is his relation to the established role of the Man of Letters, the Author, as that role had been defined by New England in the place accorded Emerson, Longfellow, Lowell, Holmes, and so on. This role, one of the conspicuous features of nineteenth-century American culture, was undergoing rapid change during Mark Twain's lifetime, and by the time of his death it had, I think, all but disappeared. In our own day the figure of the Alienated Artist has to some extent taken the place of the figure of the Man of Letters. Mark Twain felt the impact of the social forces that created both the older and the newer role of the artist in America, and at the same time his unprecedented popularity gave tantalizing glimpses of yet another role for the artist — that of the darling of the mass audience, a poker-faced bard whose jokes concealed his Whitmanian function of bringing the great democracy to knowledge of itself. This last role was perhaps never more than a possibility, but the partial extent to which it was realized defines one dimension of the unique achievement of *Life on the Mississippi*, *Huckleberry Finn*, and *A Connecticut Yankee*. After the 1880's the pressures of personal misfortune and even more importantly of cultural change prevented this kind of achievement. *Pudd'nhead Wilson*, *The Mysterious Stranger*, and the lesser works of Mark Twain's last two decades are written from the perspective of alienation (an alienation which, it should be pointed out, was accompanied by increasing fame and popularity). To explain what happened to Mark Twain after *Huckleberry Finn* has long been a capital problem of criticism. It is an equally important problem of cultural history, and neither can be solved without full exploration of the other. To find out what was happening to the man and to the society we have to ask questions which lead simultaneously to literary analysis and to analysis of social change.

Yet I must confess that the inquiries I have described are largely hypothetical. The student who tries to explore American culture even in this limited fashion by drawing upon the techniques of literary criticism and of the social sciences soon encounters difficulties.

The difficulties are due in part to the trend of literary studies in this country during the past two or three decades, which has led them away from rather than toward the social sciences. Just recently there are signs of a major shift of direction in literary criticism which may conceivably lead to more interest in the social setting of works of art. Such a change of direction would be most welcome. The techniques of anal-

8

ysis that have been developed by recent literary criticism should ultimately make it possible to deal with the relation between literature and culture at a much more profound level than has been attainable in the past. But change of this sort does not occur overnight, and the dominant force in literary studies is likely for some time yet to continue to be what we familiarly know as the New Criticism. This means that, in general, the guiding principle will be a concern for the autonomy of the work of art.

It would be foolish and, for most of us, ungrateful to deny the solid accomplishments of the New Criticism. Like all literary revolutions, this one proposed to *écraser l'infâme*: it set about purifying criticism from the contamination of everything that was not literary. Again like other revolutions, the New Criticism brought with it a remarkable *élan*. It improved the morale of literary studies. It gave to scholarship and criticism a new penetration and intensity, and it markedly raised the level of literary instruction in American colleges and universities.

But these results were achieved only at a certain cost. The New Criticism has made it extraordinarily difficult to relate literature to the culture within which it occurs and of which it is indisputably a part. From the beginnings of the movement in the work of Ezra Pound and T. S. Eliot, it has been closely related to the idea of the artist's alienation. The determination to maintain the purity of literature has implied a strongly negative attitude toward society, which within this tradition is habitually viewed as irredeemably Philistine and depraved: in Eliot's phrase, a "panorama of futility and anarchy." Although the actual techniques were largely invented and applied by other men, the master image of the movement has been Eliot's *The Waste Land*, and the critical undertaking has been strongly influenced by Eliot's idea of literature as a timeless order of eternal objects. This order he calls tradition, but it is very different from the usual conception of tradition because it is outside time and thus unhistorical or even antihistorical.

The pioneer technician of the New Criticism, I. A. Richards, had a somewhat different set of assumptions — he was at the outset, during the 1920's when he exerted his greatest influence on literary studies, an avowed Benthamite. His effort to state the doctrine of pure literature in positivist terms seems at first glance quite remote from the ideas of Pound and Eliot. But the effect of his teaching was essentially the same. Although he has now modified his original distinction between the statements of science, capable of being verified by empirical tests, and the pseudo-statements of poetry, which seem to be verifiable propositions but actually have no referent outside themselves, it has had great influence. And it separates art from society just as drastically as does Eliot's supernaturalism or Pound's denunciations of the "old bitch gone in the teeth," the "botched civilization."

Despite the sincere desire of some of the leaders in the movement to recognize the intimate relation between a work of art and its social setting, the effect of the New Criticism in practice has been to establish an apparently impassable chasm between the facts of our existence in contemporary society and the values of art. In this respect, the philosophical position of the New Criticism seems to me to bear a striking resemblance to Edgar Allan Poe's conception that art belongs to a nonempirical realm of "ideality" totally divorced from the sordid or commonplace facts of everyday life. The root of the matter is the belief in an extreme dualism of nature and spirit. If society is taken to be a part of the natural order, and art is assigned to the realm of spirit, it becomes impossible to relate art (except negatively) to the actual culture within which it occurs.

We are no better off if we turn to the social sciences for help in seeing the culture as a whole. We merely find society without art instead of art without society. The literary critic would cut aesthetic value loose from social fact; the social scientist, despite his theoretical recognition that art is an important aspect of culture, uses techniques of research which make it difficult or impossible for him to deal with the states of consciousness embodied in serious art.

To a student of literature, the social scientists seem to proceed ordinarily as if certain tangible values inherent in society were the only values that need to be taken into account. They find their reality in observed fact, and like all other scholars they have defined facts as the data which their methods of inquiry enable them to discover and record. The extreme form of this tendency is the emphasis on quantification, on the use of data susceptible of statistical treatment. The sociological studies of literature which I have encountered characteristically involve a "content analysis" of large numbers of works of popular fiction or drama. The assumption on which they are based is, in the words of one such study, that popular literature "can be regarded as a case of 'social fantasy'— that the psychological constellations" in such material "indicate sensitive areas in the personalities of those for whom the work has appeal; their needs, assumptions and values are expressed ('projected')" in the play or novel or short story. Popular literature is used as if it were a body of material resulting from a series of projective psychological tests. For certain purposes this seems to me entirely justified, although I am not sure one can accept Lyman Bryson's contention that "today's popular art did not come out of yesterday's fine art . . . [but] is something developed out of natural social habits and needs by the machine." Popular art is certainly notable for its lack of originality; it is meant to be a homogeneous product identified by brand labels that the customer can count on. Its characters and situations are indeed, as another sociological study maintains, "ubiquitous mass symbols," extremely limited in range at any given moment. The relative homogeneity of popular art lends itself to the quantitative methods of content analysis.

But is nothing of consequence about a culture to be learned from its serious art? I suppose that when we speak of a serious novel, for example, we have in mind a work whose meaning is not exhausted by the identification of stereotyped ideas and attitudes in it. It is serious precisely because it differs in some respects from the mass of popular literature with which it is contemporary and with which, to be sure, it probably has something in common. The serious work has its period flavor but it also has other qualities, and some of these other qualities may be unique. Yet what the serious work uniquely expresses is not on that account unreal, or on that account alone unrepresentative. A description of the culture within which this book of permanent interest was created would be incomplete if we left it out of account. Subtract the work of a few dramatists from what we know of Periclean Athens, or of Elizabethan England, and our image of the culture undergoes a drastic change, quite apart from merely aesthetic considerations.

The procedures of content analysis do not seem to be adapted to the analysis of works of art differing appreciably from popular art. The content that is analyzed is too rudimentary; it is, again by definition, a factor common to large numbers of works, which means a factor that is very far from exhausting the particularity of even a simple work of art. We need a method that can give us access to meanings beyond the range of such a systematic simplification — meanings that are not, so to speak, homogenized. Lacking such a method, the sociological study of the arts will inevitably yield an image of the culture which is truncated.

Contemporary American culture is no doubt frightening enough, but it is made unnecessarily appalling by studies of popular art which take no account of any subtleties beyond the horizon of the mass media. There is more to us than that!

In fact, there is more than that in the sociological findings. Reading the articles in the journals, one may easily forget that after all the same culture which has produced the soap opera has also produced the sociological journals. If the mass culture is there, so also are the observers and interviewers, the statisticians and the appraisers. Only, they have hidden themselves. The man who conducts the content analysis and identifies the obsessive fantasies in the movies describes a world from which freedom is entirely absent and in which consciousness itself is rudimentary. He silently assumes that he and the colleagues to whom he reports his findings monopolize freedom and consciousness. The mores of his craft (borrowed from the natural sciences) encourage him to conceal his own consciousness behind statistical tables, and he seeks to deny his own individuality by a ceremonial avoidance of the first person. A kind of automation is suggested by these devices of rhetoric: the third person and the passive voice seem to establish as the model of the society a self-contained mechanism from which consciousness has been banished. The scientific observer is outside the field of his observations. He simply makes dial-readings.

I have suggested that the rhetoric of the social sciences seems to reflect an effort to minimize the role of consciousness. This observation can be justly extended to other aspects of the attitude toward language that an outsider encounters in reading current scholarship in these fields. Content analysis of works of literature, for example, requires the investigator to leave entirely out of account the actual words of the individual texts. The content which is extracted for counting and comparison with the content of other texts is detached from its original form of expression and thereafter exists (if it exists at all) in the neutral linguistic matrix of paraphrase. Here again, a procedure which may be suitable in dealing with texts lacking distinction of style is inappropriate in dealing with a serious work of literature. For what can be paraphrased is a small part of the whole meaning of such a work. The range of possible human experiences beyond the limits of paraphrasable meaning is the province of imaginative or poetic language. The complex modes of statement which characterize the truly imaginative use of language (and I would be understood here as referring to the different vocabularies of the several arts) are the only instruments we have for embodying and communicating the full content of consciousness.

These more complex meanings are just as real as are the stereotyped fantasies of popular art; in fact, they are more real, because they are more precisely and durably embodied in the medium. And they are part of the culture. A hundred years ago it might have been said that they constitute the whole of culture. We believe differently now, and I trust I have made it clear that I have no intention of trying to reinstate a conception of the arts as existing in a separate aesthetic realm which contains all values. But I believe the social sciences have reacted too strongly against Matthew Arnold's view of culture. A fully adequate science of society will recognize the existence and the importance of the experiences and attitudes with which Arnold was concerned. And this recognition is possible only for one who is aware of the almost infinite subtlety and complexity of imaginative modes of statement. To recognize no serious and accurate function of language except its use as an instrument of precise denotation is to reduce the scope of consciousness and to deny the significance of whole universes of human experience. The result is a mutilated image of man and of culture.

I have described a situation in which, as it seems to me, the characteristic methods of literary criticism and the social sciences exhibit, each in its own way, serious shortcomings from the standpoint of the enterprise of understanding American culture as a whole. The social sciences seem to me to assume too hastily that value is to be found only in social experience, in group behavior, in institutions, in man as an average member of society. Current literary criticism assumes, also too hastily, that value lies outside society, in works of art which exist on a plane remote from the Waste Land of our actual experience. I have sincere respect for the accomplishments of American scholarship in all these areas, and I recognize that these accomplishments have been made possible only by the rigorous narrowing of fields of inquiry, by the specialization of interests that has been so marked a feature of scholarship in this country during the past half-century. On the other hand, I also believe that the desire to study American culture as a whole, which underlies the nascent movement toward American Studies, has valid motives behind it, and that without disturbing sociologists or literary critics in their important

13

undertakings we can properly ask whether a method cannot be found for investigating the whole of the culture.

The concept "culture" seems, in the abstract at least, to embrace the concepts "society" and "art." Why may we not say quite simply that the problem of method in American Studies can be solved by presupposing a value implicit in culture which includes and reconciles the apparently disparate values assumed in the disciplines of, say, literature and sociology? From this point of view, the problem of method in American Studies might seem to find its answer in the already existing field of cultural anthropology. But is this formula more than a verbal solution to the dilemma? The central question is whether cultural anthropology can take account of the full range of meanings available to us in the arts of complex modern societies like our own. From a sketchy acquaintance with some of the scholarship in this field, I gain the impression that when it undertakes the study of complex societies, it tends to resemble sociology, with perhaps a stronger inclination to invoke comparisons between advanced and preliterate cultures. Moreover, cultural anthropology does not seem to differ appreciably from sociology in its assumptions about the relation of fact and value.

I conclude, in short, that no ready-made method for American Studies is in sight. We shall have to develop one for ourselves, and I am afraid that at present we shall have to be content with a very modest program. The best thing we can do, in my opinion, is to conceive of American Studies as a collaboration among men working from within existing academic disciplines but attempting to widen the boundaries imposed by conventional methods of inquiry. This implies a sustained effort of the student of literature to take account of sociological, historical, and anthropological data and methods, and of the sociologist or the historian to take account of the data and methods of scholarship in the fields of the arts. I am optimistic enough to believe that inquiries which have their starting points in various academic departments can converge as they are brought to bear upon a single topic, namely, American culture past and present.

Method in scholarship grows out of practice, or rather out of repeated criticism of practice intended to remedy observed shortcomings. In the inadequacies of answers we have found to our questions we discover clues to the reformulation of the questions, and the reformulated questions in turn suggest new ways of finding answers. If I insist that the development of a method for American Studies is bound up with an effort to resolve the dilemma posed by the dualism which separates social facts from aesthetic values, I do not imagine that a new method can be deduced from philosophical premises. A new method will have to come piecemeal, through a kind of principled opportunism, in the course of daily struggles with our various tasks. No one man will be able to redesign the whole enterprise. What will count is the image in our minds of the structure we believe we are helping to build. Such an image will influence a long series of particular decisions, will determine a tendency over a period of time rather than give us a new apparatus all at once.

From the standpoint of the social sciences the lines of investigation I have mentioned probably seem of limited value because they point to the analysis of specific, individual cases. This is an inevitable consequence of the nature of literary and historical inquiry. But I venture to suggest that individual instances embody whatever uniformities may exist in a culture, and that a really exhaustive knowledge of the concrete case — a work of art, a specific situation, a career — might well lead to the recognition of aspects of the culture which have previously escaped attention. At the very least one might hope for suggestions capable of being formulated as hypotheses and then tested against more extensive evidence. Why is it not conceivable that the masterpiece of literature, or the exceptionally productive career, might turn out to be a valid expression of the culture in ways beyond the scope of stereotyped examples of popular art or merely average life-patterns?

⚬ REUEL DENNEY

# How Americans See Themselves

O N E way of approaching the topic broached in the title is to survey recent "national character" studies of Americans, by Americans.

Clearly this is not the only way. It limits our answers to those given by specialized students of "national character"— and these compose only one among many groups that have something to say about how Americans see themselves. Moreover, since the concept of "national character" is beset by technicalities of definition, the answers will be framed generally in some highly conceptualized view of social structure and culture. They will not necessarily be the answers that would occur to a majority of educated Americans. They will certainly not be expressed in quite the same language that such a group would use.

It must be noted at the outset that not all students of how Americans see themselves are satisfied with the national-character approach. Why they are not satisfied tends to emerge only after a close look at what national-character analysis claims to be getting at. This leads immediately to recognition of the diversity of viewpoints in the field.

We can begin by asking whether observers of the American national character agree with each other in ascribing certain traits to that character. They do. A variety of specialists, despite their differences in aims and methods, arrive at overlapping conclusions. At first sight, the overlaps may be not at all obvious. In the "learned behavior" of Americans — call it their national character — Mead has found a tendency toward watchful waiting; Benedict a high capacity for the moralization of industrial rationality; Adorno and Frenkel-Brunswik a tendency toward political dependence on large power structures; Erikson an insistence on adolescent plasticity; Ruesch and Bateson a tendency toward the collectivization of intimate aspects of life; and Riesman a long-range tendency for moral sanctions to migrate from origins in parents to origins within the social organization of people of one's own age.[1] These sampled conclusions do not entirely overlap. In some cases they quite disagree. What is more, it is clear that some of the ascribed traits might also be true, to a greater or lesser degree, of the character of other nationals, and therefore not distinctively American. Nevertheless, there are some grounds for agreement on traits seen in Americans by most of the observers and seen by the observers as more characteristic of Americans than foreigners.

As I read our sociological students of American character, they appear to agree that American character is, first, much engaged by the need to internalize the human meaning of industrialism; second, organized in such a way that adolescence is more of a crisis in the life cycle than in many other cultures; third, concerned with ambiguity of sexual roles arising from the industrialization of women; and, fourth, engaged in playing out some sort of this-worldly mysticism that resembles, but is not the same as, the moral materialism of early British industrialism. That is to say, the American character is historically unique in the way in which it disposes its attitudes about male and female, work and play, youth and age. If one asks whether these conclusions answer the question "How do most Americans see themselves?" it must be said that they do not. The point of most of our contemporary researches of this sort is that national character is what makes nationals see themselves as they *think* they are. Presumably, it takes time for scholarly appraisals of national character to be popularized, and thus be domesticated in a national belief system.

The term "national character," of course, contains semantic hazards that easily stimulate basic questions from literate Americans not sure of the scope of the term.

The specialist finds it easy to respond, up to a point, to many such questions. National character he defines as something quite different from, though related to, moral character. Character appears *in* attitudes, but is not fully revealed *by* attitudes. Conclusions about national character may be documented by references, say, to the assertion that such and such a child-rearing practice appears to be national in its scope and differential in its effects. National character, the specialist says, is subject to ambiguous definition. The term can refer to group traits A, B, and C, which everyone has some share of, though not equally. It can refer to the preponderance of types A, B, and C in the population,

17

types not universal, but statistically noticeable. It can refer to norms of character toward which all nationals feel themselves drawn, no matter how various their success in modeling themselves on these norms. The specialist is likely to add that while it is important to understand these distinctions, it is stultifying to overwork them.

We find, of course, a great variety of traditions in American writing on the American national character. There is no space in this discussion for the approaches suggested by observers earlier than 1900. It is sufficient to say that many of the sharpest formulations of these years either came from foreign observers or were based on self-analytical reactions of Americans to the remarks of foreign observers. It is possible to speak here only of the self-observation that began at about the time of America's intensified contacts with other nationals during and after World War I. Further, only the studies of specialists in the behavioral sciences can be considered; there is no room to report the observations of weathermen, medical men, journalists, politicians, advertisers, publicists, professors of history, and many other professionals who have had their say on American national character — even though their intuitions or phrases have often suggested to workers in the behavioral sciences the direction in which to look.

By far the most useful history of recent interest in national-character studies on the part of the behavioral sciences is provided by Margaret Mead in her essay "The Study of National Character."[2] She shows there how World War II stimulated policy-makers of the United States to study more concretely than they ever had before the contrasts that appear to distinguish the national character of Americans from that of others. What is more to the point for this discussion is her lucid summary of the approaches. Some writers, as she shows, have emphasized the impact of American child-rearing expectations and practices on the adult — to be especially noted here are Kardiner, Gorer, and Erikson. Others have emphasized the subordination of national "character" to a general pattern of culture — a pattern in which only some of the results are characterological. Such a student is Ruth Benedict. Miss Benedict's remarks on American character tend to emphasize the selectivity of American culture in giving preferential nurture to certain psychological types and certain attitudes toward life. Still other approaches employed in recent years put other questions and get other answers. British-born anthropologist Gregory Bateson's emphasis on the types of social interaction between roles and individuals in the culture comes close to being a "structural" rather than a "characterological" approach. Yet it yields most promising formulations for getting at differences, for example, in the tones of British and American child-parent relationships.

In reviewing these and other angles of attack, Miss Mead suggests that there are three general methods at work. One approach emphasizes study of the patterns of two or more cultures that have had similar historical experiences but appear to display differences in patterning. Another emphasizes the relation between the motivations imparted to the child and the rest of the culture. A third emphasizes study of key "role-relationships" in the culture. It might well be asked whether all of these are studies of national character; or whether some of them are studies chiefly of noncharacterological variables in social organization.

To return to the definition offered earlier in these remarks, it will be assumed here that national character, whatever it may mean in a wider sense, denotes specifically the total "learned behavior" of the people who are the object of study. To speak of national character in these terms may mean, as the British psychologist Ginsberg has said, to speak either of common traits generally distributed or recognizable patterns of behavior in the group as a whole—or to speak of both at the same time. In this paper, as in *The Lonely Crowd*, the attempt will be made to hew closer to the first definition. While it is conceded that data about "culture pattern" and "social structure" are indispensable in discussing "character," "character" itself is taken as a unique variable. This position is clearly dependent on three important assumptions.

The first assumption is that we are not talking about constitutional personality types, or about their national distribution. To be able to talk about the presence or absence of given personality types—whether one uses typologies suggested by Freud, Jung, Adler, or others—is nevertheless indispensable to the task. It is the necessary condition for discriminating these relatively "unlearned" aspects of the person from his "learned" or characterological aspects. The second assumption is that a certain homogeneity over space and time can be found in the learned behavior of the nationals of a given country. Oceans of ink have been spilled over the shape and degree of that homogeneity. The position taken here is that such homogeneity need not add up to very much to make its point. National character is not studied with the hope of proving a vast difference between the nationals of countries A and B; it is examined with the hope of finding (or conscientiously not finding) marginal differences between many, perhaps most, of the nationals of countries A and B. The third assumption is that this "certain homogeneity" cannot be exhaustively explained by reference to noncharacterological concepts of the society such as social structure, culture, and world view.

It should be noticed that we possess, in Ralph Linton's essay on "The Concept of National Character," [3] a most coherent statement of the approach that emphasizes the distribution of certain types of "personality" in the society. Linton makes it clear, in this paper, that he and Kardiner, in their cooperative investigations, distinguish between the "total personality" of an individual and what they call his "basic personality." It is the latter term that they use to denote the general coherence of personality throughout cultural types, or a whole culture, which can also bear the name "national character." This approach, like all the others, tends to turn up data that are best expressed in its own vocabulary. This itself makes more clear truisms which should be almost glaringly obvious by this point: the terms "the individual" and "the society" are complementary terms; either tends to get defined in terms of the other; national-character studies can be discriminated from each other according to the way they manipulate emphasis on one complementary term or the other, in their vocabulary.

If we think of the research position having been stated in this way, we can imagine that "the American being studied" might rejoin as follows: "I am quite aware, from my reading of the newspaper, radio listening, television viewing, and so on, that American character seems disposed toward distinctive definitions of male and female, work and play, youth and age. In fact, my everyday experience, matched against whatever I can learn about non-Americans, makes me sure that this is so. What more is it that you have found out that I do not know?"

The answer might run along the following lines.

All of us, as Americans, accept the machine so readily that we do not realize the unique qualities of our historic encounter with it. We were the first nation for whom the machine did not mean a new accumulation of that oldest of miseries: overwork on top of undernourishment. We have paid for this triumph by meeting the machine at a different, higher level of encounter. It did not differentiate us into "powerful" and "powerless"; it conformed us into the "powerful-powerless." A strain of doubt about industrialization is involved in our anxiety about conformism at all social levels of the United States, among both men and women, among both young and old. The basic imagery of this point is amply demonstrated, I think, in Rhoda Métraux's study[4] of the interchangeability of terms used to describe the human being and the machine in the United States. It could be documented further by a study of advertising imagery, with the man-shaped machines by Artzybasheff at one end of the scale of hybrids and the Absorbine Jr. puppet-man at the other end.

Of course, this means a variety of things. It means that the American winces if he sees a man doing a machine's work — as when he sees a Chicago Negro hand-shoveling coal for lack of a portable conveyor belt. It means also, at the other extreme of viewpoint and the business cycle, that the American sometimes winces if he sees a machine doing a man's work. This is true of some business executives who visit the Massachusetts Institute of Technology and see computers making certain kinds of decisions that they have been accustomed to make. It means that some machines are outmoded while men who know no other way of making a living than tending them are still alive and in need of jobs. And it means that some kinds of jobs and workers are suddenly ennobled by new machines — as when the street sweeper rises to glory by being presented with the wheel of a $15,000 automatic machine as fine as the ones that labor artistocrats like "cat skinners" use. In a country where children are as a matter of course trained by science fiction to use machines that have not yet been invented, many of the seventy-million work force live at the edge of a technology which is destroying their occupational role by building their skills into machines.

If this seems a far cry from conclusions about the American character arrived at by the specialists I have mentioned, let us look more closely. Erik H. Erikson has made the point that the American male is strenuously taught to "leave home." He adds that a boy's play with machines (Ben Rogers' fantasy, in *Tom Sawyer*, of being both steamboat captain and steamboat) is part of the process. Max Weber[5] and Ruth Benedict have made the point that the American's high capacity for translating the Puritan ethos and industrial teamwork into moral terms is connected with his belief in the ultimate "rightness" of rapid capital formation. Margaret Mead's study of the strain of watchful waiting and calculated risk-taking in the American is at least related to the domination in our public imagery of mechanical metaphors. Geoffrey Gorer,[6] a British observer, has made the point that the machines, services, and products of the market tend to acquire a symbolic aura in which biological and mechanical functions are overlaid. David Riesman, Nathan Glazer, and I (in *The Lonely Crowd*) concluded about American child-rearing that it teaches children, in effect, to regard themselves as interchangeable parts of a social process, as commodities possessing some of the "substitutability"— and "marginal differentiation"— of goods in exchange. This, to be sure, was part of a wider view which saw American character as reacting not merely to industrialism but to industrial abundance.

These observations on industrialism would be part of the answer to the "American being studied." Of importance also are the views of the behavioral scientists on age. When F. Scott Fitzgerald said that "there are no second acts in American lives," he was probably referring to a schema like this: Act One, Adolescence; Act Three, Success or Failure. The European drama might be summarized as Act One, Youth; Act Two, Success or Failure; Act Three, Gravy or Regrets. A good deal of anthropological attention has been paid to the question of whether the so-called storminess of American adolescence is unique. It has been argued by as good an authority as Margaret Mead that, in effect, the American adolescent is stunned by the miseries of the American sexual system, both in fact and in prospect. This may be true. American adolescents tend to betray surprise that their parents have any guts left in them at all and this may be an unconscious tribute to what they imagine to be supertoughness on the part of their parents in surviving a life experience with the American love and money game. On the other hand, successive generations of American adolescents have a way of palming themselves off as cool compared with their parents, and so induce in the older generation the suspicion that if *they* were stormy, they were fools.

The argument is, generally, that while many other cultures make puberty crisis a crisis, Americans know how to make it a nightmare. It is argued that class aspects of the public school and social mobility system, neurotic patterns in the American middle-class family, the prospective industrialization of adolescent women, the feminine protest mother, and a variety of other factors add up to a conscientious pursuit of unhappiness where adolescent life is concerned. Talcott Parsons,[7] for example, has shown that the American girl starts, in her early years, with a high sense of identity and then is forced to forsake some of the identity and its status; while, on the other hand, the boy starts with a very vaguely defined sense of himself and then comes into a large, sudden windfall of prestige when he puts on long pants and is identified as a prospective free agent and all-round-doer. Again, it has been effectively argued that the ambiguity of social and occupational roles in prospect for adolescents in a society that keeps them out of the labor market for a long time, is influential.

Without being sure how this all adds up, a student of American character may say, as he usually does, that the American is more American in his adolescence than at any other time in his life. Another way of putting this is to say that in later life the American is most American when he shows traces of an adolescence not left behind.

It seems to me that most theories place perhaps too much importance on institutional details. The observers of adolescence are, after all, the nonadolescents. Statistics show that there have been more and more of these, living to riper and riper years, for the last couple of generations. It must be noted too that most youths seem in retrospect misspent. We have, then, more and more people thinking more and more about adolescence in this way than ever before. This sets up a communication pressure on youth which makes it unlikely that any will claim to be happy while he stands a chance of getting something out of appearing to be unhappy. The audience is too good to resist.

If one is tempted to ask what this has to do with national character, then the answer might be somewhat as follows. National character, by most of the definitions we have considered, sees people of different cultures as developing their life expectations, and their age-graded attitudes, in distinctive ways. Some of these traits might best be studied by acquiring greater knowledge of how the age and kinship system works. Some might best be studied by viewing them as aspects of ideology, rather than behavior in response to social structure. In either of these cases, one could up to a certain point neglect character as a dynamic variable. In the last analysis, however, the student of national character would insist that the expectations spoken of here do not exist as mere structural or ideological reflexes. They are "interpreted" in some way, by individuals and by groups — and the way in which they are interpreted shows that they are interpreted by "character" going about its work. The dynamism of "character" helps to explain things that cannot be explained by references to ideology, social structure, or individual personality.

It should be quite apparent from these remarks that these specialists

23

in the behavioral sciences who have shown an interest in American national character are working with concepts that are far from being completely diffused in American public opinion. How do Americans at large see themselves? They seem to see themselves through their reflection in primary group life with the family, and through the reflections that come back to them from the wider institutions of their social life, including the media of communication. They see themselves, of course, through the spectacles of ideology and of differential social perception — in the first instance seeing things as they ought to be and in the second as they think they must be, in fact. The degree to which the general American public asks itself the self-identifying questions asked by the specialists mentioned in this paper is largely a function of the mass media and of the public's education. The work of the behavioralists in national-character studies has been rather well reported, as a whole — but not widely and intensively reported. It is fair to say that the more popularized approaches to national character in recent years have been a rather narrow selection of what the scholarly world offers.

Let us take, for illustration, a quick view of some of the popularly distributed theories of national character. A prime example might be found in the "diaper-ology" of Philip Wylie. His well-known emphasis on the dubious aspects of the mother-son relationship in the United States has been a most popular source of self-interpretation for Americans in the last fifteen years. Another popular source of folk notions about the national character might be said to exist in such a self-selling piece of fiction as Ayn Rand's *The Fountainhead*. Here we find a kind of popular diagnosis of American national character as suffering from a lack of respect for individuality and genius — a best seller that fictionally dramatizes the strain of conformity in American national character. On still a different front, we have seen the people of the United States, during the last twenty years or so, subjected to large-scale campaigns for tolerance. The assumption about national character that appears to lie behind these drives is not easy to condense in a few words. Nevertheless, it seems to be assumed that Americans will respond to preaching for tolerance because of a trained distaste for unfair play, because of a feeling that prejudices hamper the general welfare — and because of considerable reserves of social guilt.

Such a quick view of certain popular mechanisms of self-estimation and self-definition is not intended to sharpen distinctions between "expert" studies of national character and others. The identities in concern are more interesting, perhaps, than the disparities. In the social history of the last twenty-five years, indeed, one can discover, if one wants to, a blending of the voices of the intellectual, on the one hand, and of the general public, on the other, on the theme of national character. Neither is quite sure that such a thing exists in some highly definable sense. Both are sure that it is "better" than many intellectuals thought it was two decades ago. If there is such a thing as national character, then intellectuals today seem to be partaking of some of the faith in it that nonintellectuals have evinced, most of the time, during this troubled century. Along these lines, certain theoretical formulations have been and may continue to be important.

Consider, for example, the emphasis on historical change in *The Lonely Crowd*. This study suggested that one of the more important things about American character was its tendency to change. Instead of searching for modes of social identity and learned behavior that are constant on the American scene, it suggested that systematic shifts from one mode to another be examined. Much of the argument could be expressed in cultural or structural or institutional terms. Riesman, Glazer, and I insisted, however, that character is a distinct and dynamic variable. To be burdened with something called a national character is not so threatening if one is persuaded that it contains the possibility of change.

There remain to be suggested a few points about the intellectual origins of character studies, and about the shape they are taking now, in a less pressured stage of development than that during World War II. Back of national-character studies loom the figures of Kant and Hegel, along with such folk nationalists as Herder. Students of characterology have traced certain aspects of the interest in national character to that originally German, and later Continental, interest in "viewpoint" suggested by Kant's subjective categories. The study of national character is a tension point in the study of the relations between the individual, the culture, the society, and the state. Despite its late nineteenth-century tendency to degenerate into international and interethnic abuse, it appears, in the twentieth century, to have added an item of flexibility to the vocabulary of the behavioral sciences.[8] American interest in the application of national-character theories to America itself could be taken as a determination to attempt deeper self-identification than has been open to, or desired by, Americans of past generations.

Some of the formulations of recent years have, indeed, the quality of social science becoming myth — in the good rather than the bad senses of that term. Miss Mead's remark that all Americans are "third generation," for example, has the force of an epic formulation. Is it true? Is it true that even many descendants of the oldest settlers feel themselves connected to their ancestors by roots that are no more deep and mature than the roots of those who are strictly of the "third generation"? Frost says, "The land was ours before we were the land's." We may feel less of this tension than we did a century or two ago; but do we still feel it? Are we *all* that new? If so, no wonder our national character surprises us so much. No wonder it is a topic that so much appeals to us, outside of the technical realm, as an opportunity to talk, not only about what we are, but about what we might be.

### NOTES

[1] See the following volumes: Margaret Mead, *And Keep Your Powder Dry* (New York: William Morrow, 1943). Ruth Benedict, *Patterns of Culture* (Boston: Houghton Mifflin, 1934). T. W. Adorno, Else Frenkel-Brunswik, Daniel J. Levinson, and R. Nevitt Sanford, *The Authoritarian Personality* (New York: Harper and Brothers, 1949). Erik H. Erikson, *Children and Society* (New York: W. W. Norton, 1950). Jurgen Ruesch and Gregory Bateson, *Communication: The Social Matrix of Psychiatry* (New York: W. W. Norton, 1951); see also other papers by Bateson as listed in the bibliography of Margaret Mead and Rhoda Métraux, eds., *The Study of Culture at a Distance* (Chicago: University of Chicago Press, 1953). David Riesman, with Reuel Denney and Nathan Glazer, *The Lonely Crowd* (New Haven, Conn.: Yale University Press, 1950); for further remarks by Riesman on American character and culture, see his *Individualism Reconsidered* (Glencoe, Ill.: The Free Press, 1954).

[2] Margaret Mead, "The Study of National Character," in Daniel Lerner and Harold Lasswell, eds., *The Policy Sciences* (Stanford, Calif.: Stanford University Press, 1951), a Hoover Institute Study. See also Ralph Linton, *The Cultural Background of Personality* (New York: D. Appleton-Century, 1945); Abram Kardiner, *Psychological Frontiers of Society* (New York: Columbia University Press, 1945).

[3] Ralph Linton, "The Concept of National Character," in Alfred H. Stanton and Stewart E. Perry, eds., *Personality and Political Crisis* (Glencoe, Ill.: The Free Press, 1951). Compare the approach of Margaret Mead, in articles listed in the bibliography of Mead and Métraux, eds., *The Study of Culture at a Distance*.

[4] Rhoda Métraux, "Resonance in Imagery," in Mead and Métraux, eds., *The Study of Culture at a Distance*, pp. 343–364.

[5] See H. H. Gerth and C. Wright Mills, *From Max Weber: Essays in Sociology* (New York: Oxford University Press, 1946).

[6] Geoffrey Gorer, *The American People* (New York: W. W. Norton, 1948).

[7] Talcott Parsons, "Age and Sex in the Social Structure of the United States," *American Sociological Review*, VII (October 1942), 604–616.

[8] See the work of Otto Klineberg, especially "A Science of National Character," *Journal of Social Psychology*, XIX (1944), 147–162, for helpful formulations offered a decade ago.

# The Meaning of Lindbergh's Flight

ON FRIDAY, May 20, 1927, at 7:52 A.M., Charles A. Lindbergh took off in a silver-winged monoplane and flew from the United States to France. With this flight Lindbergh became the first man to fly alone across the Atlantic Ocean. The log of flight 33 of the *Spirit of St. Louis* reads: "Roosevelt Field, Long Island, New York, to Le Bourget Aerodrome, Paris, France. 33 hrs. 30 min." Thus was the fact of Lindbergh's achievement easily put down. But the meaning of Lindbergh's flight lay hidden in the next sentence of the log: "(Fuselage fabric badly torn by souvenir hunters.)"

When Lindbergh landed at Le Bourget he is supposed to have said: "Well, we've done it." A contemporary writer asked, "Did what?" Lindbergh "had no idea of what he had done. He thought he had simply flown from New York to Paris. What he had really done was something far greater. He had fired the imagination of mankind." From the moment of Lindbergh's flight people recognized that something more was involved than the mere fact of the physical leap from New York to Paris. "Lindbergh," wrote John Erskine, "served as a metaphor." But what the metaphor stood for was not easy to say. The *New York Times* remarked then that "there has been no complete and satisfactory explanation of the enthusiasm and acclaim for Captain Lindbergh." Looking back on the celebration of Lindbergh, one can see now that the American people were trying to understand Lindbergh's flight, to grasp its meaning, and through it, perhaps, to grasp the meaning of their own experience. Was the flight the achievement of a heroic, solitary, unaided individual? Or did the flight represent the triumph of the machine, the success of an industrially organized society? These questions were central to the meaning of Lindbergh's flight. They were also central to the lives of the people who made Lindbergh their hero.

The flight demanded attention in its own right, of course, quite apart from whatever other significance it might have. Lindbergh's story had all the makings of great drama. Since 1919 there had been a standing prize of $25,000 to be awarded to the first aviator who could cross the Atlantic in either direction between the United States and France in a heavier-than-air craft. In the spring of 1927 there promised to be what the *New York Times* called "the most spectacular race ever held — 3600 miles over the open sea to Paris." The scene was dominated by veteran pilots. On the European side were the French aces Nungesser and Coli; on the American side, Commander Richard E. Byrd, in a big tri-motored Fokker monoplane, led a group of contestants. Besides Byrd, who had already flown over the North Pole, there were Commander Davis, flying a ship named in honor of the American Legion which had put up $100,000 to finance his attempt, Clarence Chamberlin, who had already set a world's endurance record of more than fifty-one hours in the air in a Bellanca tri-motored plane, and Captain René Fonck, the French war ace, who had come to America to fly a Sikorsky aircraft. The hero was unheard of and unknown. He was on the West Coast supervising the construction of a single-engined plane to cost only $10,000.

Then fate played its part. It seemed impossible that Lindbergh could get his plane built and east to New York in time to challenge his better equipped and more famous rivals. But in quick succession a series of disasters cleared his path. On April 16, Commander Byrd's *America* crashed on its test flight, crushing the leg of Floyd Bennett who was one of the crew and injuring Byrd's hand and wrist. On April 24, Clarence Chamberlin cracked up in his Bellanca, not seriously, but enough to delay his plans. Then on April 26, Commander Davis and his co-pilot lost their lives as the *American Legion* crashed on its final test flight. In ten days, accidents had stopped all of Lindbergh's American rivals. Nungesser and Coli, however, took off in their romantically named ship, the *White Bird*, from Le Bourget on May 8. The world waited and Lindbergh, still on the West Coast, decided to try to fly the Pacific. But Nungesser and Coli were never seen again. As rumors filled the newspapers, as reports came in that the *White Bird* was seen over Newfoundland, over Boston, over the Atlantic, it soon became apparent that Nungesser and Coli had failed, dropping to their death in some unknown grave. Disaster had touched every ship entered in the transatlantic race.

Now, with the stage cleared, Lindbergh entered. He swooped across the continent in two great strides, landing only at St. Louis. The first leg of his flight established a new distance record but all eyes were on the Atlantic and the feat received little notice. Curiously, the first time Lindbergh appeared in the headlines of the New York papers was Friday the thirteenth. By this time Byrd and Chamberlin were ready once again but the weather had closed in and kept all planes on the ground. Then, after a week of fretful waiting, on the night of May 19, on the way into New York to see *Rio Rita*, Lindbergh received a report that the weather was breaking over the ocean. He hurried back to Roosevelt Field to haul his plane out onto a wet, dripping runway. After mechanics painfully loaded the plane's gas by hand, the wind shifted, as fate played its last trick. A muddy runway and an adverse wind. Whatever the elements, whatever the fates, the decisive act is the hero's, and Lindbergh made his choice. Providing a chorus to the action, the *Herald Tribune* reported that Lindbergh lifted the overloaded plane into the sky "by his indomitable will alone."

The parabola of the action was as clean as the arc of Lindbergh's flight. The drama should have ended with the landing of the *Spirit of St. Louis* at Le Bourget. That is where Lindbergh wanted it to end. In *"We,"* written immediately after the flight, and in *The Spirit of St. Louis,* written twenty-six years later, Lindbergh chose to end his accounts there. But the flight turned out to be only the first act in the part Lindbergh was to play.

Lindbergh was so innocent of his future that on his flight he carried letters of introduction. The hysterical response, first of the French and then of his own countrymen, had been no part of his careful plans. In *"We,"* after Lindbergh's narrative of the flight, the publisher wrote: "When Lindbergh came to tell the story of his welcome at Paris, London, Brussels, Washington, New York, and St. Louis he found himself up against a tougher problem than flying the Atlantic." So another writer completed the account in the third person. He suggested that "the reason Lindbergh's story is different is that when his plane came to a halt on Le Bourget field that black night in Paris, Lindbergh the man kept on going. The phenomenon of Lindbergh took its start with his flight across the ocean; but in its entirety it was almost as distinct from that flight as though he had never flown at all."

Lindbergh's private life ended with his flight to Paris. The drama was no longer his, it was the public's. "The outburst of unanimous acclaim was at once personal and symbolic," said the American *Review of Reviews*. From the moment of success there were two Lindberghs, the private Lindbergh and the public Lindbergh. The latter was the construction of the imagination of Lindbergh's time, fastened onto an unwilling person. The tragedy of Lindbergh's career is that he could never accept the role assigned him. He always believed he might keep his two lives separate. But from the moment he landed at Le Bourget, Lindbergh became, as the *New Republic* noted, "*ours* . . . He is no longer permitted to be himself. He is us personified. He is the United States." Ambassador Herrick introduced Lindbergh to the French, saying, "This young man from out of the West brings you better than anything else the spirit of America," and wired to President Coolidge, "Had we searched all America we could not have found a better type than young Lindbergh to represent the spirit and high purpose of our people." This was Lindbergh's fate, to be a type. A writer in the *North American Review* felt that Lindbergh represented "the dominant American character," he "images the best" about the United States. And an ecstatic female in the *American Magazine*, who began by saying that Lindbergh "is a sort of symbol. . . . He is the dream that is in our hearts," concluded that the American public responded so wildly to Lindbergh because of "the thrill of possessing, in him, our dream of what *we* really and truly want to be." The act of possession was so complete that articles since have attempted to discover the "real" Lindbergh, that enigmatic and taciturn figure behind the public mask. But it is no less difficult to discern the features of the public Lindbergh, that symbolic figure who presented to the imagination of his time all the yearnings of its dream for itself.

Lindbergh's flight came at the end of a decade marked by social and political corruption and by a sense of moral loss. The heady idealism of World War I had been succeeded by a deep cynicism as to the war's real purpose. The naive belief that virtue could be legislated was violated by the vast discrepancy between the law and the social habits of prohibition. A philosophy of relativism had become the uneasy rationale of a nation which had formerly believed in moral absolutes. The newspapers agreed that Lindbergh's chief worth was his spiritual and moral value. His story was held to be "in striking contrast with the sordid unhallowed themes that have for months steeped the imaginations and thinking of the people." Or, as another had it, "there is good reason why people should hail Lindbergh and give him honor. He stands out in a grubby world as an inspiration."

Lindbergh gave the American people a glimpse of what they liked to think themselves to be at a time when they feared they had deserted their own vision of themselves. The grubbiness of the twenties had a good deal to do with the shining quality of Lindbergh's success, especially when one remembers that Lindbergh's flight was not as unexampled as our national memory would have it. The Atlantic was not unconquered when Lindbergh flew. A British dirigible had twice crossed the Atlantic before 1919 and on May 8 of that year three naval seaplanes left Rockaway, New York, and one, the NC-4 manned by a crew of five, got through to Plymouth, England. A month later, Captain John Alcock, an Englishman, with Arthur W. Browne, an American, flew the first heavier-than-air land plane across the Atlantic nonstop, from Newfoundland to Ireland, to win twice the money Lindbergh did, a prize of $50,000 offered by the *London Daily Mail*. Alcock and Browne's misfortune was to land in a soft and somnolent Irish peat bog instead of before the cheering thousands of London or Paris. Or perhaps they should have flown in 1927.

The wild medley of public acclaim and the homeric strivings of editors make one realize that the response to Lindbergh involved a mass ritual in which America celebrated itself more than it celebrated Lindbergh. Lindbergh's flight was the occasion of a public act of regeneration in which the nation momentarily rededicated itself to something, the loss of which was keenly felt. It was said again and again that "Lindy" taught America "to lift its eyes up to Heaven." Heywood Broun, in his column in the *New York World*, wrote that this "tall young man raised up and let us see the potentialities of the human spirit." Broun felt that the flight proved that, though "we are small and fragile," it "isn't true that there is no health in us." Lindbergh's flight provided the moment, but the meaning of the flight is to be found in the deep and pervasive need for renewal which the flight brought to the surface of public feeling. When Lindbergh appeared at the nation's capital, the *Washington Post* observed, "He was given that frenzied acclaim which comes from the depths of the people." In New York, where four million people saw him, a reporter wrote that the dense and vociferous crowds were swept, as Lindbergh passed, "with an emotion tense and inflammable." The *Literary Digest* suggested that the explanation of the hero-worship of Lindbergh would "throw an interesting light on the psychology of our times and of the American people."

The *Nation* noted about Lindbergh that "there was something lyric as well as heroic about the apparition of this young Lochinvar who suddenly came out of the West and who flew all unarmed and all alone. It is the kind of stuff which the ancient Greeks would have worked into a myth and the medieval Scots into a border ballad. . . . But what we have in the case of Lindbergh is an actual, an heroic and an exhaustively exposed experience which exists by suggestion in the form of poetry." The *Nation* quickly qualified its statement by observing that reporters were as far as possible from being poets and concluded that the discrepancy between the fact and the celebration of it was not poetry, perhaps, but "magic on a vast scale." Yet the *Nation* might have clung to its insight that the public meaning of Lindbergh's flight was somehow poetic. The vast publicity about Lindbergh corresponds in one vital particular with the poetic vision. Poetry, said William Butler Yeats, contains opposites; so did Lindbergh. Lindbergh did not mean one thing, he meant many things. The image of itself which America contemplated in the public person of Lindbergh was full of conflict; it was in a word, dramatic.

To heighten the drama, Lindbergh did it alone. He was the "lone eagle" and a full exploration of that fact takes one deep into the emotional meaning of his success. Not only the *Nation* found Sir Walter Scott's lines on Lochinvar appropriate: "he rode all unarmed and he rode all alone." Newspapers and magazines were deluged with amateur poems that vindicated one rhymester's wry comment,

> Go conquer the perils
> That lurk in the skies —
> And you'll get bum poems
> Right up to your eyes.

The *New York Times,* which alone received more than two hundred poems, observed in trying to summarize the poetic deluge that "the fact that he flew alone made the strongest impression." Another favorite tribute was Kipling's "The Winners," with its refrain, "He travels the fastest who travels alone." The others who had conquered the Atlantic, and those like Byrd and Chamberlin who were trying at the same time, were not traveling alone and they hardly rode unarmed. Other than Lindbergh, all the contestants in the transatlantic race had unlimited backing and access to the best planes, and all were working in teams, carrying at least one co-pilot to share the long burden of flying the plane. So a writer in the *New York Sun*, in a poem called "The Flying Fool," a nickname that Lindbergh despised, celebrated Lindbergh's flight:

> . . . no kingly plane for him;
> No endless data, comrades, moneyed chums;
> No boards, no councils, no directors grim —
> He plans ALONE . . . and takes luck as it comes.

Upon second thought, it must seem strange that the long-distance flight of an airplane, the achievement of a highly advanced and organized technology, should be the occasion for hymns of praise to the solitary unaided man. Yet the National Geographic Society, when it presented a medal to Lindbergh, wrote on the presentation scroll, "Courage, when it goes alone, has ever caught men's imaginations," and compared Lindbergh to Robinson Crusoe and the trailmakers in our own West. But Lindbergh and Robinson Crusoe, the one in his helmet and fur-lined flying coat and the other in his wild goatskins, do not easily coexist. Even if Robinson Crusoe did have a tidy capital investment in the form of a well-stocked shipwreck, he still did not have a $10,000 machine under him.

Lindbergh, in nearly every remark about his flight and in his own writings about it, resisted the tendency to exploit the flight as the achievement of an individual. He never said "I," he always said "We." The plane was not to go unrecognized. Nevertheless, there persisted a tendency to seize upon the flight as a way of celebrating the self-sufficient individual, so that among many others an Ohio newspaper could describe Lindbergh as this "self-contained, self-reliant, courageous young man [who] ranks among the great pioneers of history." The strategy here was a common one, to make Lindbergh a "pioneer" and thus to link him with a long and vital tradition of individualism in the American experience. Colonel Theodore Roosevelt, himself the son of a famous exponent of self-reliance, said to reporters at his home in Oyster Bay that "Captain Lindbergh personifies the daring of youth. Daniel Boone, David Crocket [*sic*], and men of that type played a lone hand and made America. Lindbergh is their lineal descendant." In *Outlook* magazine, immediately below an enthusiastic endorsement of Lindbergh's own remarks on the importance of his machine and his scientific instruments, there was this statement: "Charles Lindbergh is the heir of all that we like to think is best in America. He is of the stuff out of which have been made the pioneers that opened up the wilderness, first on the Atlantic coast, and then in our great West. His are the qualities which we, as a people, must nourish." It is in this mood that one suspects it was important that Lindbergh came out of the West and rode all alone.

Another common metaphor in the attempt to place Lindbergh's exploit was to say that he had opened a new "frontier." To speak of the air as a "frontier" was to invoke an interpretation of the meaning of American history which had sources deep in American experience, but the frontier of the airplane is hardly the frontier of the trailmakers of the old West. Rather than an escape into the self-sufficient simplicity of the American past, the machine which made Lindbergh's flight possible represented an advance into a complex industrial present. The difficulty lay in using an instance of modern life to celebrate the virtues of the past, to use an extreme development of an urban industrial society to insist upon the significance of the frontier in American life.

A little more than a month after Lindbergh's flight, Joseph K. Hart in *Survey* magazine reached back to Walt Whitman's poem for the title of an article on Lindbergh: "O Pioneer." A school had made Lindbergh an honorary alumnus but Hart protested there was little available evidence "that he was educated in *schools*." "We must look elsewhere for our explanation," Hart wrote, and he looked to the experience of Lindbergh's youth when "everything that he ever did . . . he did by himself. He lived more to himself than most boys." And, of course, Lindbergh lived to himself in the only place conceivably possible, in the world of nature, on a Minnesota farm. "There he developed in the companionship of woods and fields, animals and machines, his audaciously natural and simple personality." The word "machines" jars as it intrudes into Hart's idyllic pastoral landscape and betrays Hart's difficulty in relating the setting of nature upon which he wishes to insist with the fact that its product spent his whole life tinkering with machines, from motorcycles to airplanes. But except for that one word, Hart proceeds in uncritical nostalgia to show that "a lone trip across the Atlantic was not impossible for a boy who had grown up in the solitude of the woods and waters." If Lindbergh was "clear-headed, naif, untrained in the ways of cities," it was because he had "that 'natural simplicity' which Fenimore Cooper used to attribute to the pioneer hero of his Leatherstocking Tales." Hart rejected the notion that any student "bent to all the conformities" of formal training could have done what Lindbergh did.

34

"Must we not admit," he asked, "that this pioneering urge remained to this audacious youth because he had never submitted completely to the repressions of the world and its jealous institutions?"

Only those who insist on reason will find it strange that Hart should use the industrial achievement of the airplane to reject the urban, institutionalized world of industrialism. Hart was dealing with something other than reason; he was dealing with the emotion evoked by Lindbergh's solitude. He recognized that people wished to call Lindbergh a "genius" because that "would release him from the ordinary rules of existence." That way, "we could rejoice with him in his triumph, and then go back to the contracted routines of our institutional ways [because] ninety-nine percent of us must be content to be shaped and moulded by the routine ways and forms of the world to the routine tasks of life." It is in the word "must" that the pathos of this interpretation of the phenomenon of Lindbergh lies. The world had changed from the open society of the pioneer to the close-knit, interdependent world of a modern machine-oriented civilization. The institutions of a highly corporate industrial society existed as a constant reproach to a people who liked to believe that the meaning of its experience was embodied in the formless, independent life of the frontier. Like Thomas Jefferson, who identified American virtue with nature and saw the city as a "great sore" on the public body, Hart concluded that "certainly, in the response that the world — especially the world of great cities — has made to the performance of this midwestern boy, we can read of the homesickness of the human soul, immured in city canyons and routine tasks, for the freer world of youth, for the open spaces of the pioneer, for the joy of battling with nature and clean storms once more on the frontiers of the earth."

The social actuality which made the adulation of Lindbergh possible had its own irony for the notion that America's strength lay in its simple uncomplicated beginnings. For the public response to Lindbergh to have reached the proportions it did, the world had by necessity to be the intricately developed world of modern mass communications. But more than irony was involved. Ultimately, the emotion attached to Lindbergh's flight involved no less than a whole theory about American history. By singling out the fact that Lindbergh rode alone, and by naming him a pioneer of the frontier, the public projected its sense that the source of America's strength lay somewhere in the past and that Lindbergh somehow meant that America must look backward in time to rediscover some lost virtue. The mood was nostalgic and American history was read as a decline, a decline measured in terms of America's advance into an urban, institutionalized way of life which made solitary achievement increasingly beyond the reach of ninety-nine per cent of the people. Because Lindbergh's ancestors were Norse, it was easy to call him a "Viking" and extend the emotion far into the past when all frontiers were open. He became the "Columbus" of another new world to conquer as well as the "Lochinvar" who rode all alone. But there was always the brute, irreducible fact that Lindbergh's exploit was a victory of the machine over the barriers of nature. If the only response to Lindbergh had been a retreat to the past, we would be involved with a mass cultural neurosis, the inability of America to accept reality, the reality of the world in which it lived. But there was another aspect, one in which the public celebrated the machine and the highly organized society of which it was a product. The response to Lindbergh reveals that the American people were deeply torn between conflicting interpretations of their own experience. By calling Lindbergh a pioneer, the people could read into American history the necessity of turning back to the frontier past. Yet the people could also read American history in terms of progress into the industrial future. They could do this by emphasizing the machine which was involved in Lindbergh's flight.

Lindbergh came back from Europe in an American man-of-war, the cruiser *Memphis*. It seems he had contemplated flying on, around the whole world perhaps, but less adventurous heads prevailed and dictated a surer mode of travel for so valuable a piece of public property. The *New Republic* protested against bringing America's hero of romance home in a warship. If he had returned on a great liner, that would have been one thing. "One's first trip on an oceanliner is a great adventure — the novelty of it, the many people of all kinds and conditions, floating for a week in a tiny compact world of their own." But to return on the *Memphis*, "to be put on a gray battleship with a collection of people all of the same stripe, in a kind of ship that has as much relation to the life of the sea as a Ford factory has! We might as well have put him in a pneumatic tube and shot him across the Atlantic." The interesting thing about the *New Republic*'s protest against the unromantic, regimented life of a warship is that the image it found appropriate was the Ford assembly line. It was this reaction against the discipline of a mechanized society that probably led to the nostalgic image of Lindbergh as a remnant of a past when romance was possible for the individual, when life held novelty and society was variegated rather than uniform. But what the Ford assembly line represents, a society committed to the path of full mechanization, was what lay behind Lindbergh's romantic success. A long piece in the Sunday *New York Times*, "Lindbergh Symbolizes the Genius of America," reminded its readers of the too obvious fact that "without an airplane he could not have flown at all." Lindbergh "is, indeed, the Icarus of the twentieth century; not himself an inventor of his own wings, but a son of that omnipotent Daedalus whose ingenuity has created the modern world." The point was that modern America was the creation of modern industry. Lindbergh "reveres his 'ship' as a noble expression of mechanical wisdom. . . . Yet in this reverence . . . Lindbergh is not an exception. What he means by the Spirit of St. Louis is really the spirit of America. The mechanical genius, which is discerned in Henry Ford as well as in Charles A. Lindbergh, is in the very atmosphere of [the] country." In contrast to a sentiment that feared the enforced discipline of the machine there existed an attitude of reverence for its power.

Lindbergh led the way in the celebration of the machine, not only implicitly by including his plane when he said, "we," but by direct statement. In Paris he told newspapermen, "You fellows have not said enough about that wonderful motor." Rarely have two more taciturn figures confronted one another than when Lindbergh returned to Washington and Calvin Coolidge pinned the Distinguished Flying Cross on him, but in his brief remarks Coolidge found room to express his particular delight that Lindbergh should have given equal credit to the airplane. "For we are proud," said the President, "that in every particular this silent partner represented American genius and industry. I am told that more than 100 separate companies furnished materials, parts or service in its construction."

The flight was not the heroic lone success of a single daring individual, but the climax of the cooperative effort of an elaborately interlocked technology. The day after Coolidge's speech, Lindbergh said at another ceremony in Washington that the honor should "not go to the pilot alone but to American science and genius which had given years of study to the advancement of aeronautics." "Some things," he said, "should be taken into due consideration in connection with our flight that have not heretofore been given due weight. That is just what made this flight possible. It was not the act of a single pilot. It was the culmination of

37

twenty years of aeronautical research and the assembling together of all that was practicable and best in American aviation." The flight, concluded Lindbergh, "represented American industry."

The worship of the machine which was embodied in the public's response to Lindbergh exalted those very aspects which were denigrated in the celebration of the flight as the work of a heroic individual. Organization and careful method were what lay behind the flight, not individual self-sufficiency and daring romance. One magazine hailed the flight as a "triumph of mechanical engineering." It is not to be forgotten that this era is the work not so much of brave aviators as of engineers, who have through patient and protracted effort been steadily improving the construction of airplanes." The lesson to be learned from Lindbergh's flight, thought a writer in the *Independent*, "is that the splendid human and material aspects of America need to be organized for the ordinary, matter of fact service of society." The machine meant organization, the careful rationalization of activity of a Ford assembly line, it meant planning, and, if it meant the loss of spontaneous individual action, it meant the material betterment of society. Lindbergh meant not a retreat to the free life of the frontier past but an emergence into the time when "the machine began to take first place in the public mind — the machine and the organization that made its operation possible on a large scale." A poet on this side of the matter wrote, "All day I felt the pull / Of the steel miracle." The machine was not a devilish engine which would enthrall mankind, it was the instrument which would lead to a new paradise. But the direction of history implicit in the machine was toward the future, not the past; the meaning of history was progress, not decline, and America should not lose faith in the future betterment of society. An address by a Harvard professor, picked up by the *Magazine of Business*, made all this explicit. "We commonly take Social Progress for granted," said Edwin F. Gay, "but the doctrine of Social Progress is one of the great revolutionary ideas which have powerfully affected our modern world." The idea, however, "may be in danger of becoming a commonplace or a butt of criticism." The speaker recognized why this might be. America was "worn and disillusioned after the Great War." Logically, contentment should have gone with so optimistic a creed, yet the American people were losing faith. So Lindbergh filled an emotional need even where a need should have been lacking. "He has come like a shining vision to revive the hope of mankind." The high ideals of faith in progress had almost come to seem like hollow words to us — but now here he is, emblematic of heroes yet to inhabit this world. Our belief in Social Progress is justified symbolically in him."

It is a long flight from New York to Paris; it is a still longer flight from the fact of Lindbergh's achievement to the burden imposed upon it by the imagination of his time. But it is in that further flight that lies the full meaning of Lindbergh. His role was finally a double one. His flight provided an opportunity for the people to project their own emotions into his act and their emotions involved finally two attitudes toward the meaning of their own experience. One view had it that America represented a brief escape from the course of history, an emergence into a new and open world with the self-sufficient individual at its center. The other said that America represented a stage in historical evolution and that its fulfillment lay in the development of society. For one, the meaning of America lay in the past; for the other in the future. For one, the American ideal was an escape from institutions, from the forms of society, and from limitations put upon the free individual; for the other, the American ideal was the elaboration of the complex institutions which made modern society possible, an acceptance of the discipline of the machine, and the achievement of the individual within a context of which he was only a part. The two views were contradictory but both were possible and both were present in the public's reaction to Lindbergh's flight.

The issue of the *New York Times* which had announced the arrival of Lindbergh in Paris, and whose front pages were covered with the story of his exploit, also carried in its magazine section an article by the famed British philosopher Bertrand Russell. The magazine had of course been made up too far in advance to take advantage of the news about Lindbergh. Yet, in a prophetic way, Russell's article was about Lindbergh. Russell hailed the rise to power of the United States because he felt that in the "new life that is America's" in the twentieth century "the new outlook appropriate to machinery [would] become more completely dominant than in the old world." Russell sensed that some might be unwilling to accept the machine, but "whether we like this new outlook or not," he wrote, "is of little importance." Why one might not was obvious. A society built on the machine, said Russell, meant "the diminution in the value and independence of the individual. Great enterprises tend more and more to be collective, and in an industrialized world the

39

interference of the community with the individual must be more intense." Russell realized that while the cooperative effort involved in machine technology makes man collectively more lordly, it makes the individual more submissive. "I do not see how it is to be avoided," he concluded.

People are not philosophers. They did not see how the conflict between a machine society and the free individual was to be avoided either. But neither were they ready to accept the philosopher's statement of the problem. In Lindbergh, the people celebrated both the self-sufficient individual and the machine. Americans still celebrate both. We cherish the individualism of the American creed at the same time that we worship the machine which increasingly enforces collectivized behavior. Whether we can have both, the freedom of the individual and the power of an organized society, is a question that still haunts our minds. To resolve the conflict that is present in America's celebration of Lindbergh in 1927 is still the task of America.

✖ MULFORD Q. SIBLEY

# Oneida's Challenge to American Culture

THE quest for community — and for the fulfillment of personality which accompanies it — has constituted a central theme in American culture and politics.

The search has taken two forms. According to one, the discovery of community — or its rediscovery — must be essentially the result of large-scale politics reordering the whole society. Thus countless reform movements have endeavored through political action to transform the very basis of the general social order. Professed Jeffersonians have sought to emancipate Americans from subservience to industrialism and centralization; socialists have looked forward to the destruction of capitalism; and assorted money reformers have seen the clue to community in a radical transformation of the currency system.

The second form of the quest for community — the communitarian — is the one with which we shall be primarily concerned here. Attacking many of the premises which constitute the foundations of mass reform movements, communitarianism seeks to achieve community through varying degrees of withdrawal from the mainstream of society and to solve the perennial problems of any culture on a small scale. It flourished in the United States most vigorously during the middle years of the nineteenth century. But even in our own day, when communitarianism has tended to be snuffed out by the imperatives of a mass society, there have been notable attempts to revive it. One might mention, for example, the experiments of the American Bruderhof communities, the Macedonia Community in Georgia founded by a group of conscientious objectors, and the well-known southern Koinonia venture.

As recent studies like that of Mark Holloway[1] stress impressively, the communitarian approach to the problem of community has developed in the United States distinctively "American" emphases. While the experiments have often been inspired by European thinkers, circumstances in the United States have soon stamped them with the hallmarks of American culture.

Communitarian experiments can be variously classified, but one significant basis would be to divide them into those which maintain a large measure of private "property" in material goods and those which tend to be communist in orientation. Such a categorization must, of course, be rather rough; for the extent of communism is a matter of degree and even basically noncommunist experiments usually pay tribute in some measure to the idea of communal ownership and administration. The essentially noncommunist "single-tax" colony at Fairhope, Alabama, might be cited as an example.[2] Here an attempt is made to approximate community ownership of land, but property in other material goods — both producers' and consumers' — tends to be private.

The more completely communist communitarian ventures have often appealed to Americans — curiously enough, in view of the general ideological biases of American culture. Indeed, one of the keenest students of American communitarian experiments, writing at the turn of the twentieth century, could assert, in words which have a strange ring today, that "As all roads led to Rome, so all paths of human progress, all material, social, moral, intellectual and spiritual improvement, lead to communism as the final goal."[3] These words were written, of course, before the term "communism" had become an epithet of opprobrium. Yet perhaps no word in the language better describes the thrust of those withdrawn groups which seek community through collective control and complete mutual sharing, on the basis of need, of at least the material goods of life. They strive after the goal which Marxist ideology professes to see approaching for humanity as a whole.

Although there have been many excellent historical and descriptive studies of both communist and noncommunist communities in the United States,[4] a full understanding of their significance and place in American culture as a whole, and of such special topics as the relation of community and personality, is perhaps not yet possible. There is room and need for studies that explore on a more modest scale various of the social, economic, and philosophical questions that arise in communitarian ventures. Often a single experiment will pose these questions in dramatic form, providing a sharpened view of the larger issue. One such experiment was that which took place at Oneida, New York, during the nineteenth century. No other communitarian venture in the entire range of American development has been more significant. The experiment in many respects remains as topical as the latest radio news report, although it flourished a hundred years ago.

The issues central to a discussion of Oneida must be considered in both their universal and their peculiarly American aspects. In the first place, any quest for a more adequate level of community must develop some system of beliefs; and the very consciousness of the quest will reflect an awareness of the attenuated belief schemes in the general society. It must, secondly, manage to suggest how the functions which any economy has to perform can be carried out. Third, it must grapple with the problem of sex in its many manifestations. Fourth, it must recognize the issues involved in procreation and develop a community attitude toward the future generation. Finally it must wrestle with the problem of governance.

In its treatment of these problems which arise in any culture, Oneida, while not without precedent in some respects, was unique in many others. On the continuum between noncommunist and communist ideal types, it would be about as close to the communist as any historical community.

Although it would be a mistake to think of the Oneida experiment as simply the "lengthened shadow of a man," in Emerson's phrase, it remains true that the initiator, John Humphrey Noyes, provides an indispensable key to an understanding of the venture. From his early adulthood to his death in 1886, he was a prophet of no mean powers; a pioneer in the study of the erotic aspects of community life; a keen student of human psychology; a revolutionist; and a man whose views stand in judgment on both nineteenth and twentieth centuries. Noyes grew up in a New England home and all the well-known factors of early nineteenth-century New England culture affected his development. Originally committed to the bar, he revolted against the conservative bias of the law. Converted during the evangelical fervor of the thirties, he entered upon theological studies only to rebel against them in the name of religious "perfectionism."

His quest for an acceptable body of religious beliefs directed his steps down many odd paths and eventually led him to concern about society and to the political issues of his day. With Garrison, he pioneered as a leader of the peace movement as well as a stimulator of the antislavery crusade. With Garrison, too, he decided to "secede" from a society which could support slavery and condone the Mexican War. How revolutionize this society? This became the central question which Noyes attempted to answer; and for the remainder of his life he struggled with the problem, never giving up hope even after the cherished experiment at Oneida had begun to depart from the principles which he deemed essential.

The religious heresy of Oneida was reflected in its semi-Manichaeanism, combined with the peculiar "perfectionism" which Noyes derived in part from his reading of John Wesley on complete sanctification. As Manichees, the Oneidans held that evil was an uncreated force in the universe. The goodness of God was thus preserved and with it the belief that, given the cooperation of men, He will eventually triumph over the machinations of the uncreated devil. But the Oneidans, unlike the original Manichees, did not think of "matter" as reflecting the devil: practical souls that they were, they saw the material world as a reflection of God's glory and a means for men's perfection.

Noyes held that men are perfectible, that they can and do grow in religious insight, and that even death may eventually be overcome. Because the Second Coming of Christ had already occurred in 70 A.D., with the fall of Jerusalem, all external religious rites became irrelevant after that date. Hence Oneida Perfectionists were freed from ritual; and the call of Micah to an ethically oriented religious faith was taken literally.

In contrast to so much American Protestantism, which has accented the notion of individual salvation and the conception of individual immortality, Oneida stressed the concrete, earthy facts of human relations as the stuff out of which religious experience arises. It was Hebraic rather than Neoplatonic in its outlook. Hence it could brook no thought of a "separation" of church from state, for in its view temporals and spirituals were interwoven. Time and eternity were phases of the same stuff. As a community it conceived itself as seceded from the political society of the United States, even though bound by many American cultural antecedents.

Just as church and state were one, so Oneida could see no conflict between "religion" and "science" — and that in a day when Americans were beginning to be exercised about the problem. The American chemist Draper, for example,[5] and later on Andrew White[6] were to make much of the alleged battle between religion or "superstition" and science or "enlightenment." For the Oneidans, on the contrary, the explanation of both natural and human phenomena — the task of science — could never run counter to the faith in perfectibility which lies beyond science. Indeed, it was quite the reverse: the development of science was in itself a kind of revelation. Thus it is significant that at the time when many Americans were trembling lest the gods of yore be deposed by the brash speculations of the Darwinians, the Oneidans were welcoming *The Origin of Species* and even the allegedly atheistic volumes of Herbert Spencer.

American communitarian experiments have generally fallen into two classes with respect to their position on moral and social progress. On the one hand, there have been those communities which despair of general moral progress — groups like the withdrawn Amish and the Hutterite societies — and think of themselves as removed from the general stream of human events. They seek to preserve their way of life intact and believe that any "worldly" cultural influences should be excluded as likely to impair their own integration.

The reverse position was reflected at Oneida. The prevalent belief was that Oneida constituted but the first communitarian communist society and that others would rapidly follow until the whole of humanity would be socially redeemed.[7] Indeed, there was a point in Noyes' career, just after the foundation of Oneida in 1848, when he firmly believed in a swift end of the traditional historical process: within the twinkling of an eye, so to speak, the whole of America, and then the world, would become communist. He soon gave up this notion. But never did Oneida surrender its faith that it was a new model, which, while ahead of its times, would nevertheless constitute the basis for all future regeneration.

True, its acceptance of external culture was selective. It welcomed science and utilized institutions of higher education, for example, while repudiating the institutions of private property and monogamic marriage. But the selection was not arbitrary; it was based on a consciously held scheme of values.

Just as it was discriminating with respect to the external culture, so it was highly selective in terms of its own membership. Oneida did not make the mistake of New Harmony: it screened its prospective membership carefully, as to both beliefs and character. This accounted for much of its success but also lessened its value as a social laboratory for the testing of hypotheses involving general social reorganization; for the skilled farmers, mechanics, and professional men who came from a New England and Middle States background to build the communist utopia were extraordinary types both intellectually and morally. What might be a successful venture for them would not necessarily demonstrate the feasibility of communism for the heterogeneous masses of the outside world.

As for the economic problem, Oneida rejected the "mixed" economy. Nor did it see any necessary conflict between economic communism, on the one hand, and either freedom or economic efficiency, on the other. Its value system repudiated the notion that the public weal can best be attained by allowing private decisions free play in the market. There was, in fact, no market internally. However, the Community salesmen operated in the external market and the Community itself relied in some measure on hired labor from the outside. Decisions about allocation of resources were made deliberately by the Community governing organ. Distribution was in accordance with the principle of need as determined by each individual, without the intermediation of a money system. The Community placed considerable emphasis on economic progress; and during the course of the experiment both agricultural and industrial costs of production tended to decline.

Oneida was perhaps the most dramatic expression in the American experience of the effort to build economic communism on religious belief. While the prevalent American religious outlook — from early Calvinism to Andrew Carnegie and the twentieth-century generation of Rockefellers — has seen private property in the light of the "trusteeship" theory of responsibility, Oneida denied that private property in either consumers' or producers' goods could be reconciled with the New Testament ethic. Did not Christ command men to be "as one"? Was not the early church at Jerusalem a communist society? It was above all the *spirit* of the New Testament which required communism of material goods, however one might interpret specific texts.

Thus not only capital but also consumers' goods, including even clothing, were "owned" and controlled by the Community as a whole but made available, under general rules, for use by individuals. With respect to consumers' goods, it was argued that, far from destroying or limiting individuality, economic communism actually enhanced it; for each person now had a wide range of choice in shoes, clothes, and other articles and could, moreover, change his items of wearing apparel frequently.

46

While the basic material foundation of the Community was agriculture, important manufacturing enterprises did develop. The Community admitted a member who invented a novel kind of trap, for example, and a whole new industry sprang up. Its salesmen traveled far and wide marketing this device, which was not only more effective but also far more humane than the mechanisms available up to that time. And the trap industry was only one example of initiative under communism.

Already at the time the experiment flowered, the rise of industrialism in America had begun to impose its uniformities on the work patterns of men. Far more than most communitarian communist schemes, Oneida was acutely conscious of the possible deadening effect of certain kinds of work on human personality. It was convinced, moreover, that variety and versatility in work experiences were desiderata of great importance. Noyes, like Marx and Kropotkin as well as contemporary American decentralists like Borsodi,[8] was appalled by the subordination, fragmentation, and monotony to which minute specialization of labor reduces men; and Oneida insisted that each member be afforded an opportunity of gaining a wide variety of labor experiences, even, apparently, at the expense of the god efficiency. Industrial and agricultural positions were rotated; and, where possible, tasks ordinarily regarded as monotonous were turned into social games. During the course of his life at Oneida, one member (who had been a lawyer in "the world") worked as "cook, baker, farm-hand, shop-hand, laundryman, fruit-hand, book-keeper, stoker, pipe-fitter, lamp-cleaner, proof-reader, editor . . ."

After the initial stages, material goods per capita steadily grew, unit costs declined, and Oneida became known as a society in which initiative was encouraged. Far from the absence of private property and the existence of distribution according to need seeming "unnatural," one Oneidan, Pierrepont Noyes, assures us that in his youth it was private possessions and income, as he viewed them in "the world," which seemed "against nature."[9]

As a matter of fact, Oneida was not unusual in its relative economic success when compared with other communities tending in the communist direction. It would seem that when communitarian communist schemes have dissolved, economic considerations have played a relatively small role. As the anthropologists who study primitive societies tell us, emphasis on the personal profit motive, so often deemed essential by twentieth-century Americans, is by no means universal. Oneida demonstrated once more, and within a culture whose ideological basis tends to deny the very possibility, that an economy may be economically successful even though communist.

But however successful a community or culture might be in purely economic arrangements, the purposes of communism look beyond the economic. All communist doctrines have as their goal noneconomic ends; they appeal from man enslaved by the material to man emancipated from domination by economic goods.

While it may be contended that economic success is a necessary condition for the full development of community and personality, in itself it is not a sufficient condition. Community arises out of both the intellectual and the emotional factors of life, which, assuming economic conflicts to have abated, become the center of struggles within the soul and the social organization alike.

One of the major contributions of Oneida to the American cultural heritage bears on this point; for, like Shakers, Mormons, and many others, Oneidans recognized the vital role of sex in the building of community. Oneida differed from many communitarian experiments, however, in its answer to the sexual problem. Its characteristic doctrine was that economic communism must be completed and undergirded by what it called "communism of love."

American culture as a whole has been curiously ambivalent about sex. On the one hand, its alleged Puritanical traditions have discouraged public discussion or even recognition of it as a problem. Laws seek to regulate its every manifestation, particularly its supposedly "unnatural" expressions; the rather naive American confidence in the law's ability to remold man has at no point been better reflected than in the area of sex. Censorship of literature and the cinema has largely centered on sexual themes. On the other hand, and perhaps partly in reaction to the very repressive tendencies themselves, American culture has been peculiarly violent in its rejection of the restraints it imposes.[10]

Oneida sought to eliminate the contradictions of the general culture and to develop an integrated view and practice. The sex doctrine of Oneida, like its economic position, was rooted in the Perfectionists' interpretation of New Testament religion. If love is the central theme and imperative of religion, they argued, then no human institution ought to stand in the way of its expression. The whole community is a family

48

whose adult members should be husbands or wives to all members of the opposite sex.

But what is love? Unfortunately American English is no more subtle in the distinctions it makes between types of love than the original English. Both lack the precision of the ancient Greek. And while imaginative writers like A. T. Wright [11] have sought to remedy this defect, it is to be feared that they have sometimes complicated the issue beyond need.

Oneida discerned two types of love, from which all other varieties are derived. The first, and perhaps the most fundamental, is the amative. The second is the propagative.

It is difficult to convey within brief compass all that was meant by amative love.[12] It was, of course, expressed through physical sex relations and, except for the fact that semen was not emitted, with all the intimacy usually associated with sexual intercourse. But the physical relationship was only the beginning of amative love and of its institutional embodiment, Complex Marriage. The individual aspect was completed at the spiritual level; for amative love was held to be a vehicle through which advanced souls could assist in the development of those who were intellectually and spiritually immature — somewhat as homosexual relations were used in ancient Sparta. Moreover, the individual aspects culminated in social expression: while Christian "charity" may seem to be far removed from the sexual realm, Noyes held that the society in which amative physical relations are present in all their complexity and variety will also be the community in which men and women are most closely knit in cooperative effort. It will, in addition, be an order in which individual creativity flowers most fully.[13]

In all the literature of what twentieth-century Americans call "sexology," one will find no tributes to amative sexual love more glowing than those which Noyes indited. It is not surprising, therefore, that he ranked Complex Marriage next to religion: "Religion is the first subject of interest and sexual morality the second, in the great enterprise of establishing the Kingdom of God on earth."

Just as versatility in economic pursuits was deemed fundamental to full development of the personality and the achievement of community, so variety in sexual partners was held up as a desideratum. "Men and women find universally," observed Noyes, "that their susceptibility to love is not burnt out by one honeymoon, or satisfied by one lover. . . . Variety is, in the nature of things, as beautiful and useful in love as in

49

eating and drinking." After a time together, therefore, lovers in Oneida were not only permitted but encouraged to separate and form other attachments lest their relations become "selfish" and their spiritual growth be stunted through absence of variety.

There are no thorough studies of Complex Marriage as it actually flourished. There is some evidence to show that destructive tensions and conflicts did develop, as in all human relations. But there is also not a little to demonstrate that they were kept within a very narrow range and were probably far fewer than under monogamy; and Noyes may have been partially right when he said: "That we have disclaimed the cast-iron rules and modes by which selfishness regulates the relations of the sexes is true . . . Amativeness, the lion of the tribe of human passions, is conquered and civilized among us."

Whether indeed Oneida did "civilize" amativeness may be an unsettled issue. What is more certain, however, is the attitude which American culture and law have taken toward eccentric positions like that exemplified in Oneida. That the Community should have flourished for a generation under the institution of Complex Marriage speaks well of the tolerance of the New York laws and administrators of the day. American culture since then has curiously enough become much less willing to tolerate overt diversities in the pattern of marriage, however much it may attack covertly, as Kinsey suggests, ostensibly monogamic institutions. Legally, for example, it has long been settled that protection of religious freedom does not include the constitutional right to have more than one wife, even if religious obligations require plural marriages.[14] And in our day, the laws against white slavery have even been applied to cases where plural families were obviously the result of religious conviction.[15] At no point has it been shown in the legal cases that monogamic institutions lead to an ethically superior kind of society — although judges issue much dogma to that effect — and the fact that American marriages are in considerable degree not monogamic is from the viewpoint of the law apparently irrelevant.

Yet it may be asked, as it was at least implicitly asked by Oneida, if America professes belief in the supreme value of freedom, on the one hand, but seeks to imprison sex relations in a monogamic formula, on the other, is it not both denying its own belief and at the same time encouraging a kind of wholesale hypocrisy? Moreover, may not the very conflict between a legally and morally enforced profession and a contradictory social practice contribute measurably to the relatively high incidence of psychoses in twentieth-century American life? It is questions of this kind which Oneidans would be asking today if they could observe the complexities of the general American cultural attitude toward sex.

Of equal significance would be the questions they might raise about future generations and the whole cultural attitude to procreation. Just as amative love gave rise to the institution of Complex Marriage, so the theory of propagative love led to Stirpiculture, or selective breeding. Although flourishing only during the last decade of the Community's existence, Stirpiculture was responsible for some fifty-eight "stirpicults," as the Community-planned children were called.

In initiating the experiment, the Community was, of course, wrestling with as perennial a problem as that, for example, of economy. Why, asked Noyes, should the decision to produce children necessarily have anything to do with the decision of a man and woman to live together? The development of the future generation, he argued, is essentially a communal function, for genetic and economic considerations alike make imperative a collectively planned population. As it is, Oneida implicitly but clearly reminds us, we give as little thought to propagation as we do to the ultimate economic fate of our children. Yet economic fate and population are closely intertwined. A non-planning America, Oneidan doctrine would seem to proclaim, has left to "free enterprise" the stewardship of its natural resources without concern for the coming generation and has felt it could equally trust "free enterprise" to breed qualitatively good children. "Free enterprise," the doctrine would appear to say, has failed on both scores. No critic in American life has been more keenly aware than Noyes of the fortuitous way in which we tend to build the economic and genetic foundations of the future. And no single prophet has endeavored to do more by way of experimentation to overcome the difficulties.

Nor was Oneida unaware of the difficulties involved. There was the issue of "mother love." There was, above all, the question of liberty: men and women should not be compelled to take part in any propagative experiment, least of all in a communitarian communist scheme whose central emphasis was on freedom. Noyes himself emphasized the importance of liberty in the theory of the system: "Man as a race has no visible superior. The fact declares his destiny is self-government . . . The liberty already won must not be diminished, but increased. If there is to be suppression, it must not be by castration and confinement, as in the case of animals, or even by law and public opinion, as men are now controlled, but by the free choice of those who love science well enough to 'make themselves eunuchs for the Kingdom of Heaven's sake.' "

The planning, therefore, depended on volunteers. Some thirty-eight men offered themselves as possible fathers; and fifty-three young women pledged themselves to "put aside all envy, childishness and self-seeking," to "become martyrs to science," if necessary, and to "offer [themselves] 'living sacrifices' to God and true communism." Combinations were to be suggested by a committee with whose activities Noyes himself was prominently identified.

Naturally, the pairing of persons for the experiment was not easy. The Oneidans were aware of their deficiencies in knowledge and the difficulty of defining the precise qualities which they were seeking in the coming generation. Francis Galton had just begun his work;[16] and even in the twentieth century, after three generations of research, we know very little about all the factors involved. Oneida insisted, nevertheless, that some collective forethought was preferable to the carelessness of the worldly society. Laissez faire in propagation, as in economic affairs, was a social wrong.

The exact relationship of Stirpiculture to Complex Marriage sometimes raised difficult psychological and social issues. If, for example, two Stirpiculture volunteers were living under Complex Marriage, should they, simply by virtue of this fact, have a prior claim to become parents? The answer was an emphatic negative.[17]

Oneida's apologists asserted that the whole conventional attitude toward sex relations and toward child bearing had been transformed. Men, women, and children alike had ceased to be "property" and their relations were free, open, frank, and uncontaminated by such emotions as jealousy. Moreover, the clear separation of amative from propagative love relations enabled the community to plan for future generations without injecting the issue of propagation into the essentially unrelated question of free sexual expression.

Negatively, Oneida was somewhat naive in its faith that it could collectively select the pairs which would produce the "best" children in terms of the values deliberately formulated by the committee. While limited studies do show that the stirpicults were unusually healthy and far above average in intelligence and achievement, we must remember the highly select character of the community as a whole: it would have been surprising had the Oneidans *not* given birth to out-of-the-ordinary children. Moreover, the system of communal nurseries and education, together with the extraordinary cultural emphasis placed on intellectual development, undoubtedly played a large role in bringing about the results.

The combination of boldness and naiveté in the Oneidans' faith is dramatized when we recall the limited experience of the United States in planning collectively for the genetic future of America. While there have been no large-scale attempts to develop positive eugenic schemes, there have been many efforts to control births negatively. Indeed, certain American states have been world pioneers in this respect. Thus several — notably California — have sought to prevent some categories of persons from reproducing themselves, sometimes by compulsory process; and the constitutionality [18] of the compulsory features of the programs has been sustained, within limits. Underlying all these attempts has been a faith not unlike Oneida's that it may be possible to elevate the genetic composition of Americans. But our experience is still far too restricted for us to be able to say what the society may have gained or lost by such legislation.

As for the wider applications of positively planned breeding which Oneida attempted with such confidence, it is an understatement to assert that both our experience and our technical knowledge are scanty. Excluding from consideration for the moment religious views which do not countenance such efforts, even the typically American cultural optimism must be considerably strained in the face of the enormous difficulties involved.

Yet the haunting question persists as to whether any culture can make possible the highest degree of moral and intellectual progress if it cannot, to some extent at least, shape collectively and deliberately the genetic future and total numbers of mankind. In posing this question so sharply, Oneida took a position far more revolutionary than any assumed by those who made the Revolution of 1776.

The attitudes of Americans toward government have reflected an ambivalence similar to that embodied in their outlook on sex. On the one hand, they have tended, until recently at least, to view government with a mixture of fear and contempt. On the other, they have — perhaps as the fruit of the Puritan stress on the efficacy of law — conceived legislation to be a kind of philosopher's stone which will resolve all conflicts and settle all issues.

While a small communitarian venture like Oneida may seek to withdraw from the generality of mankind in the name of a higher ethic, within its own confines the fissions in soul and community raise questions not dissimilar to those that plague the general society. This is particularly true since a communitarian communist society will necessarily place under political control a larger segment of life. That is to say, less is left to chance and more questions become subject to collective deliberation. Oneida aptly illustrates both the promise and the problems involved in subjecting larger and larger spheres of life to the process of conscious communal decision-making.

The government of Oneida purported to give due weight both to the need for a private sphere beyond the reach of external controls and to the imperatives implicit in a communist scheme of life. There was, the theory held, no necessary conflict between the two. The living quarters of each member, for example, were deemed to be beyond the reach of the Community authorities and great emphasis was placed on privacy as essential to the growth of the soul. At the same time, there was a system of Community governance for the control of public and economic conduct. Oneida professed to stress personal conscience rather than external government. It is not doing an injustice to its theory if we say that it hoped, in Lenin's well-known words, to become an administration of things rather than a government of persons. And in some respects its political ideal was not unlike that of the well-known American communist anarchist Alexander Berkman.

Decisions of major importance were made by the whole assembly of all men and women, proposals for debate coming from the Business Board composed of the heads of the nearly half-hundred administrative departments. From the Business Board stemmed the agencies which had charge of production and distribution of material goods, supervised the selective breeding plan, and oversaw the conduct of the communal nurseries and schools to which the stirpicults were sent.

The central institution for the implementation of law and decisions was that of Mutual Criticism, which involved exactly what the term implies — formal criticism, under established rules, of a person's conduct by a committee designated for that purpose. All members of the community, including its leaders, were periodically subjected to criticism; and their conduct was scrutinized not only in terms of their adherence to formal law but also by reference to the moral and religious ideals constituting the basis of community life. Aside from this "involuntary" criticism, a member could ask for the appointment of a voluntary criticism committee if he felt the need for scrutiny. Questions in both instances were often rather searching. One might be gently but firmly reminded of one's deficiencies in work; or the committee might ask whether one was not becoming selfishly attached to a given sexual partner. Mutual Criticism as an agency of governance was deemed to be an expression of love and its purpose was not, in fact, primarily negative and inhibitory: it was designed to encourage personal development and, like Complex Marriage, to foster the "ascending fellowship" of spiritual growth. It was even used at times to cure what we should today call psychosomatic illness, a process which the Oneidans termed "krinopathy."

All this represents the formal side of the picture. But the center of the politics of any community lies in the informal relations which develop within the ambit of that framework. Here the central fact in Oneida was the pre-eminent position occupied by John Humphrey Noyes himself. As the "auctor" or founder of the community — the legislator, as the ancient Greeks would have said — he stood above all others and his words in Business Board or Stirpiculture Committee carried a weight not borne by those of any other member. While there is no evidence that Noyes sought to impose his will on the community, the very moral qualities which made him what he was often led others to accept his leadership without question. And in some of the young his status led to antagonism.

Indeed, the position which Noyes occupied in the structure of Oneida raises the larger problem of leadership and particularly leadership in an ostensibly democratic society. On the one hand, the formulator of alternative policies — which is another way to designate the leader in a democratic culture — is essential if the issues are to be defined for decision; on the other hand, the very authority which arises when an individual successfully formulates the issues tends to be self-perpetuating. It has a tendency to survive long after the original basis for its development has passed. When this stage is reached, the leader comes to be valued, not because he has articulated clearly the question and suggested an answer, but rather because of his prestige acquired in the past.

One is reminded, in examining political issues in a small planned community like that of Oneida, that there can be no exact analogy between its politics and those of the great society from which it has sought to withdraw. Each has its own peculiarities and each its own dangers to what Americans call the "democratic way of life." The challenges to democracy in the small community are the invasion of the legitimately private sphere and the rise of a prestige-supported leadership. The great society, particularly in an industrial culture and a society of continental size like that of the United States, must almost always grapple with the problem of bureaucracy.

From another point of view, size of the community would seem to affect the possibility of governance with a minimum of coercion. Because Oneida was closely bound together by a common belief system and was small in size, the institution of Mutual Criticism — a formalization and limitation of the criticism found in most *gemeinschaft* communities — could be relatively successful. In addition, membership in the Community was voluntary, by contrast with the external political society. But when the society becomes complex and is composed inevitably of all human beings within a given territory, how are we to attain the ideal of a social order in which both spiritual and physical coercion will be no more? This becomes a particularly acute question as family ties dissolve and with them the sanctions implicit in the brotherhood of family life. How far could institutions like Mutual Criticism be extended into the great society, as Oneida and many American philosophical anarchists would have us do?

Perhaps it is questions of this order which lie at the root of much of the American ambivalence with respect to government: its denigrating of politics, on the one hand, and, on the other, its implicit and explicit tendency to think that human social destiny can be consciously and deliberately directed. The Jeffersonian vision of small-scale communities and Taoist notions of government have continued to linger and even to animate legislation; yet simultaneously Americans have by and large been unwilling to give up the material fruits of industrialism and large-scale governance in order to implement the vision.

Oneida remains a challenge to American culture. In the first place, its existence and disintegration dramatize both internal and external factors which tend to make eccentric experiments difficult under modern conditions. Secondly, it encourages us to re-examine the validity of the communist ideal as a whole and, of equal importance, of the means by which the ideal — assuming its validity — is to be attained.

Other experiments have been communist in terms of material goods but few have combined, as did Oneida, both economic communism and communism of love. That this combination was tolerated for a generation is almost incredible in light of twentieth-century attitudes toward cultural deviation. Contemporary American culture would probably not tolerate another Oneida.

The destruction of the experiment, indeed, coincided neatly with the beginnings of modern American cultural intolerance. Anthony Comstock began to lay the foundations for contemporary legal control of allegedly obscene literature and Complex Marriage came under the attack of ministers and professors. Oneida tried to make concessions; but its abolition of Complex Marriage led inevitably to the abandonment of economic communism also, so closely were the two associated. And thus the heart was cut out of the great experiment.

Internal fissions, of course, played a vital role in undermining the theory and practice of communism. There was the tension between older and younger generations. The Community had been established by converts and those adults subsequently admitted had been granted a place because of their convictions and agreement with the objectives of Community life. When the children who had entered the Community with their parents grew up, however, many of them lacked the zeal so characteristic of converts. Indeed, the very open-mindedness so often praised at Oneida had encouraged inquiry on the part of the younger generation, and, with inquiry, a skepticism about the ideological foundations of the experiment. Thus what the world thought of as one of the cardinal virtues of Oneida (by contrast with Amish and Hutterite communities, for example) helped to undo it.

Then, too, the administration of Stirpiculture gave rise to certain difficulties, again emphasizing the conflict between old and young generations. It was charged that a disproportionate number of older men were selected to participate in the propagation experiment and that they were allowed to father more children, on the average, than men of the younger group. Thus Noyes himself was responsible for nine of the fifty-eight stirpicults. And there were other miscellaneous conflicts, some of which have been humorously if hyperbolically dealt with in dramatic form by Lawrence Langner and Armina Marshall.[19]

Within the Community no adequate alternative leadership could develop in the shadow of Noyes; and this factor made it more difficult to cope with both internal fissions and external intolerance.

If it is asked whether external or internal factors played the predominant role in bringing Oneidan communism to an end, the probable answer is that the outside pressures of a noncommunist society and culture would have been less effective had the community not already been rent from within by political and psychological differences. As Allan Estlake, himself an Oneidan, once put it: "Pressure from without could have had no power to break up the community so long as the true spirit prevailed within."

But while Oneida ceased to exist in part, then, because of the onset of modern cultural intolerance, it is important, in view of the typical twentieth-century American ideology, to reiterate that the experiment did not come to an end because of economic failure. Indeed, like a large proportion of communitarian communist experiments, it was amazingly successful in this realm. There was no profit motive; yet initiative, self-reliance, and hard work — values so exalted by Americans — have been no better exemplified than in this American communist experiment.

What can we say about the relevance and validity of the communist ideal itself? The fact that Oneida existed should challenge Americans to implement their professions of belief in the value of freedom; to heighten their appreciation of individuality and eccentricity; to resist those tendencies in their culture which would make future Oneidas impossible. The fact that Oneida was communist poses the serious question of whether a communist order is the ideal toward which all cultures should move.

The twentieth century is noted for its hard, "inverse" utopias — constructions like Orwell's *Nineteen Eighty-Four* and Eugene Zamiatin's *We* — which point out the dangers of large-scale "political" reconstruction and cast doubt on the idea of progress to which Oneidans were attached. Anarchists like Marie Louise Berneri[20] have rightly called attention to the rigidity and destruction of freedom characteristic of many utopian schemes, whether literary or experimental. Former Marxists (including not a few Americans), with a bitterness almost peculiar to themselves, have often tended because of their experiences to spurn the very quest for a communist society which originally led them to embrace their revolutionary creed. Despite all this, however, communism as a general ideal is difficult to reject. When its implications are understood, it becomes even more appealing.

It recognizes explicitly the problem of technology — the danger of setting up technical means as ends. It challenges the predominant assumption of general American culture that technological change must be taken as "a given," to which men ought to "adjust," whether they will or not. Thus twentieth-century Americans are told that automation "is coming" and that they must proceed to alter their way of life accordingly. As a community, they are never consulted explicitly about their desires in the matter. Communism assumes, by contrast, that every proposed large-scale technological development should be explicitly adopted by the whole community before it is introduced. Oneida, as we have seen, did not repudiate advanced technology; but it believed, unlike American culture as a whole, that changes in technology should be adjusted to nontechnological values and goals, rather than the reverse. American society is only very dimly beginning to grasp this notion, which consciously planned communities like Oneida take for granted.

Moreover, the communist principle "from each according to his ability, to each according to his need" is an ideal whose ethical validity would seem to be self-evident, particularly in a culture professing "democratic" values. Indeed, it has already been accepted in many sectors of American life — in the educational system, for example, police and fire protection, parks and playgrounds. And it could be vastly extended — into, for instance, the fields of medical and legal service and even the distribution of bread. While the full implementation of the ideal is no doubt remote, it is not at all the fantasy pictured by critics of Oneida-like schemes.

We might suggest, too, that even a system resembling Complex Marriage — coexisting with monogamous, polygynous, and polyandrous patterns — is a not implausible partial answer to certain of the emotional discontents characteristic of twentieth-century American society. Certainly Complex Marriage, or some modification of it, cannot be dismissed out of hand by the imaginative communist, or even by the noncommunist radical critic of American society.

But perhaps a central controversy about communism in our day turns primarily on means rather than ends. While there might be dissent with respect to some aspects of Oneidan communism as an ideal — Complex

59

Marriage, for example, or Stirpiculture — there would be even greater disagreement about methods. Is the goal of communism to be sought through radical and sometimes violent action on a large scale? Or is the end more likely to be attained through many cautious, Oneida-like, small-scale experimental efforts? Martin Buber in his rather careful inquiry into the problem of means has characterized the first method as "political," while he uses the term "social" to designate the second.[21] The social would seem to be, according to him, the fundamental method of true "revolution"; while the political would be at its best superficial, at its worst violent, and always dependent finally on social change.

Even if we assume that basic change must occur at the "social" level, the experience of Oneida would seem to indicate that belief systems and means of communication among men, once attained on a small scale, do not renew themselves automatically. The conflict of generations, the problem of maintaining the convictions associated with "conversion," and the apathy which often foreshadows dissolution — all these factors must be reckoned with. And the alternative method of "political" revolution must grapple with equally persistent issues — the danger of violence, the reduction of human beings to mere tools, and the development of bureaucratic attitudes. Any scheme of organization and any method of revolution will tend to destroy some freedom in the name of an allegedly larger liberty.

Whatever the answer to "social" versus "political" revolution may be — might it not conceivably be a combination of Oneidas *and* the large-scale political action which we have contrasted with communitarianism? — the student of American culture will always remind himself that in its emphasis on experimentalism and in its optimism Oneida was not untypically "American." Its experimental spirit avoided many of the pitfalls inherent in extreme a priori and deductive thinking; while its optimism, persisting even in the face of Community dissolution, sustained its faith in the communist goal.

The factors in American culture which produced Oneida — the evangelical spirit, moral fervor, quest for freedom in community, and revolt against irrational authority — led to a community which still constitutes a challenge to American culture. In its communism, it symbolizes an important criticism of the culture's major tendencies. And in the details of its way of life, it raises basic questions which twentieth-century Americans sometimes consider but more frequently evade.

NOTES

[1] Mark Holloway, *Heavens on Earth: Utopian Communities in America, 1680–1880* (London: Turnstile Press, 1951).

[2] See Paul E. and Blanche R. Alyea, *Fairhope, 1894–1954; the Story of a Single Tax Colony* (University: University of Alabama Press, 1956).

[3] W. A. Hinds, *American Communities* (Chicago: C. H. Kerr, 1902).

[4] Among the classical treatments have been those by Charles Nordhoff (*Communistic Societies of the United States*, New York: Harper and Brothers, 1875); and J. H. Noyes (*History of American Socialisms*, Philadelphia: Lippincott, 1870). And more recently one might mention, for example, the works of Alice F. Tyler and Arthur Bestor.

[5] John W. Draper, *History of the Conflict between Religion and Science* (New York: D. Appleton, 1874).

[6] Andrew D. White, *History of the Warfare of Science with Theology in Christendom* (New York: D. Appleton, 1896).

[7] Hence Oneida sought to establish branches, one of them at Wallingford, Pennsylvania. The belief was not always equally intense, but it persisted. While for the most part it hoped to appeal to men's rational natures and thus make humanity the agent of its own salvation, there seemed to be a minor strain of chiliasm.

[8] Ralph Borsodi, *This Ugly Civilization* (New York: Simon and Schuster, 1929).

[9] Pierrepont Noyes, *My Father's House* (New York: Farrar and Rinehart, 1937).

[10] In the twentieth century, the two tendencies coexist: the repressive laws remain in the statute books and religious groups attempt to provide the necessary moral sanctions; at the same time, no culture has so emphasized sex themes in its literature, commercial advertising, the cinema, and scholarly publications like the several Kinsey reports. European observers have often been amazed by the widespread popular cult of sexual love in the United States. On the latter point, note, for example, Raoul de Roussy de Sales, "Love in America," *Atlantic Monthly*, CLXI (May 1938), 645–651.

[11] In his utopian novel *Islandia* (New York: Farrar and Rinehart, 1942).

[12] The theory and practice of amative love was the subject of much discussion and writing both before the foundation of Oneida in 1848 and during the course of the experiment down to 1878. Noyes' celebrated essay *Male Continence* is only one example of the kind of literature produced.

[13] Here again is a good example of the way in which Oneidan speculations anticipated twentieth-century discussion. The later Freud tended to argue that sexual repression was the price man paid for civilization. But erstwhile disciples of Freud like Wilhelm Reich maintained that free sexual expression promotes creativity. The doctrine of amative love would seem to reflect a middle position.

[14] Reynolds v. United States, 98 U.S. 145 (1878).

[15] Cleveland v. United States, 329 U.S. 14 (1946).

[16] His *Hereditary Genius* was published in 1869, the very year in which the Stirpiculture experiment began.

[17] The complications may be illustrated by an actual case. Charles Jones and Mary Frost were deeply in love — so much so, in fact, that a committee had warned them that their love was in danger of becoming "exclusive." Both, however, had volunteered for the Stirpiculture experiment and the question arose as to whether they should be allowed to become the parents of a child. It was decided in the end that to permit them to do so would only heighten their tendency to exclusiveness. Each was to become a parent through some other combination. Thus Mary gave birth to a child fathered by James Thomas. While at first Charles was beset by anxiety and perhaps jealousy, in the end he grew attached to Thomas, perhaps because their relationship to Mary drew them together. Somewhat later Uriah Hope asked Mary to live with him and she responded favorably. This new relationship, far from dis-

turbing Charles, seemed to evoke sentiments of profound sympathy — he often cared for Mary's infant, for example, in order that the mother and Uriah might pay court to each other without interruption.

[18] Buck v. Bell, 274 U.S. 200 (1927).

[19] Lawrence Langner and Armina Marshall, *Suzanna and the Elders* (New York: Random House, 1940).

[20] Marie Louise Berneri, *Journey through Utopia* (London: Routledge and Paul, 1950).

[21] Martin Buber, *Paths in Utopia* (London: Routledge and Paul, 1949).

⚉ DAVID R. WEIMER

# The Man with the Hoe and the Good Machine

ON THE flat, dry prairie which is American labor historiography, we can still ramble these days seeing little but supply-and-demand curves, safety valves, and scraps of union charters. We are led to believe that books describing these bits and pieces deal with reality — and yet in that desiccated image of the American worker which leans thinly toward us from the pages of American labor history, we hardly recognize the man who must have existed behind the image.

Only yesterday, economics was all. John R. Commons unfortunately stimulated labor historians to nothing so much as imitation. The many volumes produced by Commons and his associates on trade unions and organized workers' movements gave scholars and popularizers not merely facts but a method; their approach was to look upon the American worker as a lower-class version of economic man. The fidelity with which his followers copied this portrait was at once a tribute to Commons and a failure to perceive that other masters might justifiably paint portraits with different colors.

This is not the place to review theories of labor such as Selig Perlman's which, however original and enlightening they may be, are in fact offshoots of an economic view of the world. Let me simply gesture hopefully in the new directions labor historiography today appears to be taking. Even before the first wave of analysts, the economic historians, has fully spent itself, a wave of labor sociologists has arrived. Though not primarily historians, these researchers have studied "labor" in so many more dimensions than their predecessors that historical inquiry in this field will surely be enriched because of their work. C. Wright Mills (*The New Men of Power*) and Arnold M. Rose (*Union Solidarity*), to name only two of the better known sociologists, have analyzed the worker's social background, his attitudes toward class, race, religion, employers,

63

and foremen. While exploiting specifically sociological techniques, they have also turned aside here and there from the usual emphasis on quantity and contemporaneity to construct sociologically oriented histories of labor. In so doing, they have helped reopen the way toward new ideas in this field.[1]

There are of course good and obvious reasons for an economic interpretation of labor. As a rule, the chief impulse toward organizing a trade or industrial union is economic. It has not always been the chief impulse, even in the twentieth century, but it has been the usual one. And this fact has tempted academic analysts into the great reductive fallacy of American labor study to date: the assumption that the simplest explanation of events is necessarily the best. A touching faith in the talismanic value of Occam's razor has everywhere dominated economists' historical thinking about labor. As a result, to others falls the task of reaffirming what life repeatedly tells us, that a complex interpretation of men and events may be best, precisely because it is the most accurate. A century ago, social critics as different as Emerson, Marx, and William Morris were alarmed at the increasing fragmentation of men's lives. Today, most of us have grown unthinkingly accustomed to half-men, and to half-views of men.

To understand how it is that scholars and laymen alike have responded so unreservedly to an economic-determinist explanation of labor history, one would not only have to remember Karl Marx and Charles Beard. It would also be necessary to describe all the cultural energies at work in American society that have fed on power and weakened the ideal of the whole man — the middle-class religious and commercial values inherited from Europe, the settlers' fascination with beating back the woods and the Indians, their early devotion to engineering and warfare, with a consequent lapse of their interest in art.

For the present, I wish only to illustrate what may be done in the reconstruction of labor history by using kinds of materials and of interpretation not ordinarily treated as relevant to this pursuit, and by setting forth the worker's attitudes toward something quite inadequately described in existing studies — the worker, himself, as a human being. Our microcosm will be the American Federation of Labor from its origins in 1881 to World War I, in the green years when trade-union leaders began seriously to challenge the narrow business ideals that had made employers temporarily strong.

64

Two poems by the minor American poet Edwin Markham (1852–1940) can help bring us to the mind and imagination of the AFL leadership.[2] One of the poems, "The Man under the Stone," appeared at the top of the first page in the official AFL monthly magazine, the *American Federationist*,[3] for July 1899. The full text is as follows:

> When I see a workingman with mouths to feed,
> Up, day after day, in the dark, before the dawn,
> And coming home, night after night, through
>     the dusk,
> Swinging forward like some fierce, silent animal,
> I see a man doomed to roll a huge stone up an
>     endless steep.
> He strains it onward inch by stubborn inch,
> Crouched always in the shadow of the rock. . . .
> See where he crouches, twisted, cramped, misshapen!
> He lifts for their life;
> The veins knot and darken —
> Blood surges into his face.
> Now he loses — now he wins —
> Now he loses — loses — (God of my soul!)
> He digs his feet into the earth —
> There's a moment of terrified effort. . . .
> Will the huge stone break his hold,
> And crush him as it plunges to the gulf?
> The silent struggle goes on and on,
> Like two contending in a dream.

The overt conflict is simply enough conceived in this melodrama. The worker — appropriately not a union man but a "workingman" — is described as a beast whose existence is one of perpetual physical labor. His toil and even his appearance call to mind "some fierce, silent animal," not a man. He has a family, but the members exist only as "mouths to feed." Unselfish as he is, slaving "for their life," his progress is nevertheless uncertain. For the AFL unionist, the major conflict in the poem would not have been between the man and the stone (an analogy unlikely to convince anyone); it would have been the one suggested by the imagery, between an animal and a human life.

Markham's more famous poem, "The Man with the Hoe" (also published in 1899), deals with the same theme. Here is the opening stanza, which more than the rest of the poem recalls the Millet painting upon which it was based:

Bowed by the weight of centuries he leans
Upon his hoe and gazes on the ground,
The emptiness of ages in his face,
And on his back the burden of the world.
Who made him dead to rapture and despair,
A thing that grieves not and that never hopes,
Stolid and stunned, a brother to the ox?
Who loosened and let down this brutal jaw?
Whose was the hand that slanted back this brow?
Whose breath blew out the light within this brain?

Both poems depict the same kind of figure — more animal than human, the victim of a lasting struggle for biological survival. In both, the tone is a mingled pity and despair.

Although "The Man with the Hoe" was not reprinted in AFL publications, it had, in the opinion of Henry Nash Smith, a "sensational vogue" around the turn of the century. In his words, the poem "assimilated the American farmer to the downtrodden and brutalized peasant of Europe," but this agrarian reference did not seem to lessen its appeal to urban workers and others engaged in labor-union activity. It was, for example, a favorite poem of Eugene Debs, who was "excited" by the humanitarian implications of its portrayal of the oppressed worker. President Samuel Gompers (1850–1924) of the American Federation of Labor was strongly enough impressed by the dark image of the man with the hoe to comment upon it in his formal report at a national AFL convention. *"Due to the bona fide labor movement of the world,"* Gompers declared to the assembled delegates in 1905, *"we are living in the time when there is disappearing, and soon will be eliminated, the last vestige of that type 'the man with the hoe,' and taking his place is the intelligent worker, standing erect, looking his fellow man in the face, demanding for himself, and according to all, the full rights of disenthralled manhood"* (italics added). The man with the hoe was, in short, a counter-image to that of the trade unionist. A French landscape painter and a popular American poet had provided a name and a concrete focus for this theme which ran through the speeches and writings of AFL spokesmen in the late nineteenth and early twentieth centuries. "There is no shape more terrible than this" — here, in Markham's words, was the union leaders' conception of the exploited worker down the ages. This "thing" symbolized for them the sort of creature that wageworkers, but for the trade union, might have

66

been. Gompers' speech to the convention merely furnishes an explicit statement of this imaginative idea.

Admitting occasionally that the trade unionist had faults, AFL leaders nevertheless believed him to be superior in quality and condition to the nonunionist of past or present. No doubt some awareness of economic and social history helped shape this belief. It was difficult for them to forget the recent past in Europe and the United States, where even skilled craftsmen and industrial workers had led a precarious laissez-faire existence. Many AFL members were familiar with older enslavements through such books as C. Osborne Ward's *The Ancient Lowly* (1888), which also pointed the moral that exploiters must be resisted. In the business decline of 1893, moreover, most union members had had a surer grip on their jobs and self-respect than independent outsiders. In less critical times, the trade unionist's edge over the nonunionist in skill and experience would also have heightened his awareness of the differences between them, just as his shorter workday (commonly eight to ten hours by 1900, compared to about twelve in the nonunion steel mills) strengthened his conviction that to join the union was to have his worth acknowledged. From these sources and others less susceptible of analysis sprang the emotional commitments that could make this epigram self-evidently true to readers of the *American Federationist*: "A workman to be a man must be a union man"!

Embedded in these large sentiments, the AFL faith passed subtly beyond the statement of differences between unionists and nonunionists. It looked upon these differences as evidence of a change within individual workers, and upon the trade union as having *caused* the change. In a widely circulated Federation pamphlet, *Philosophy of Trade Unions* (1892), Dyer D. Lum asserted that the union "has transformed the patient and sodden drudge into a manly and honest worker"; and he noted "the increased hours of leisure it has secured for him . . . the broadening of his mental horizon and . . . sympathies . . ." One whose mental horizon was broadened was Ernest Aldrich, hero of Frank K. Foster's fictionalized autobiography, *The Evolution of a Trade Unionist* (1901). Foster was an AFL member, and while cautious not to make of his novel a partisan tract, his hero inevitably argues for the union. The argument which climaxes his appeal for labor organizations — an argument which except for Foster's lack of dramatic skill might have been impassioned —

is that unions are among "those influences which make the average man physically, mentally and morally stronger."

In this conversion of base metal into gold, Federation spokesmen viewed the trade union as the powerful force that worked the alchemy. I need not dwell upon the fact that they also thought of "the union" as crowded rooms in an old meeting-hall or bitter arguments with employers about working conditions. What should be emphasized is how much fuller their minds were, and hence their lives, than a catalogue of these details or of economic concerns would indicate.

If at times AFL leaders saw the union as an aggregate of single members, at other times it became for them an organic body greater than the sum of its parts. But the feature on which nearly all agreed was that in some dynamic way the trade union found the worker degraded and gave him dignity, cultivated within him the proliferation of interests and capacities that denote the human being. The lurking assumption here of the worker's passivity contradicted the notion of the trade unionist as "demanding for himself," in Gompers' words, "the full rights of disenthralled manhood." This conflict melted, however, in the union leaders' idea of a great crossing over. (An *American Federationist* article describing "the genius of trade unionism, shaking off the depression of centuries," was aptly entitled "The Great Transition.") Before union membership, the worker was inert, powerless; afterward, he became active and strong. The union was thus the catalytic agent effecting the change.

Once metamorphosed into a trade unionist, the worker gained in complexity. Although he favored quick action, physical courage, and simple issues, he also took pride in less primitive responses. One of his virtues lay in steadily resisting anti-union acts or opinions, another in standing up for social and economic rights based on his productive achievements. And the legendary unionist was competent, too, in ways not directly related to his vocation. According to John H. Brinkman, then (1907) secretary-treasurer of the Carriage and Wagon Workers' Union, organized workers were "America's most intelligent and useful citizens." This motif of political awareness and talent, frequent in AFL utterances, was enlarged upon by Herbert N. Casson, whose small book, *Organized Self-Help* (1901), was dedicated formally and in substance to the American Federation of Labor. "The unionist of to-day," Casson wrote, "will be the statesman of to-morrow. A large proportion of trade union secretaries, and thousands of the rank and file, have libraries containing the

68

most thoughtful and profound books on social questions. Their books have not been bought for the sake of the binding, as most Fifth [A]venue libraries are, but for the sake of the contents. They have been read and re-read, and, best of all, verified or corrected by hard experience. When the Great Crisis of the near future comes, the Abe Lincoln who shall guide the nation safely through will be a trade union graduate, at present as inconspicuous as Lincoln was when he split rails, or Grant when he sold potatoes."

During the first thirty-three years of their national organization, AFL leaders spoke of this development of the worker's total capabilities as a principal result of union activity. And this humane effort, in their opinion, was not just a fringe benefit but a legitimate primary aim of the Federation. Of numerous declarations to this effect, the one with the largest audience is to be found in a pamphlet circulated by the AFL from the late 1880's through 1914 and for many years afterward. This pamphlet, *Trade Unions: Their Origins and Objects, Influence and Efficacy*, was condensed from a short book written by an Englishman, William Trant, and originally published in London under the same title in 1884. AFL officials thought highly enough of the work to reissue it often — by 1914 it had gone through seventeen editions — and Gompers later called it the "one important pamphlet" which the Federation had sponsored around 1890. "It was a clear-cut analysis of trade unionism," he wrote in his autobiography (1923), "and made more impression upon my thinking than any other economic dissertation with the exception of Professor Thorold Rogers' *Six Centuries of Work and Wages* . . ."

What Trant had to say about the goals of the trade union was "that although unions may have been founded principally, if not solely, as protective associations, and have developed to some extent into aggressive associations, yet they have long ago embraced other features in their objects. They now aim at every means that will raise workmen to the best position it is possible for them to obtain." That Trant meant much more by "best position" than high wages and short hours he made clear: "The object of a trade union is a wide one, *viz.*, to do all that can be done to better in every respect the condition of its members. The raising of the rate of wages is undoubtedly the principal means to that end, but to say that it is the 'sole aim' is to mistake the one for the other [i.e., the means for the end]. Based upon union, the efforts of these organizations are collective, *and the results general, not special.* Unlike most kinds of individual effort, the object is not to assist men to lift themselves out of their class, as if they were ashamed of it, or as if manual labor were a disgrace, *but to raise the class itself in physical well-being and self-estimation.*" (Italics added.)

Entering the union, the worker grew in "self-estimation" as he increasingly shared the multiple interests of his fellow initiates. We discover in the written records left by these men that they spent many hours searching for proof of their own pedigree in times past: a pedigree presumably attested by historical parallels for the AFL, or by traces of some evolutionary process moving through time to leave as its rich deposit the modern trade union. We discover, further, that in a society whose nominal religious leaders had in the nineteenth century too often failed the lower-class members of their churches, these trade unionists took satisfaction in the para-religious nature of their organization.

To these historical, social, and religious concerns must be added the particular qualities in Samuel Gompers' character upon which the trade unionists placed high value. The AFL president inspired a great deal more than pork-chops agitation among union members. From their many tributes to him over the years there emerges an image whose idealized traits suggest the kind of trade unionist that his associates and followers admired and sometimes patterned themselves after. To them, Gompers' importance was at least double; he was, in Daniel Bell's phrase, their "patristic surrogate," both deputed Leader and Father, labor official and head of the union family.[4] Several of the characteristics which AFL spokesmen ascribed to him were commonplaces of American political eulogy: integrity, sincerity, a spirit of self-sacrifice, devotion to duty, moral courage, a capacity for translating ideas into acts, oratorical prowess, humble birth, and a noble maturity. Less typically American was the praise they sometimes awarded his intellect. And they repeatedly mentioned his feeling for mankind, his role as a sort of religious patriarch, with the moral leadership and close personal interest in the fortunes of his children which that phrase implies, and his being a man whom history would remember.

To identify the worker's humanity with his entry into the union led irresistibly to one conclusion: should the union crumble, the advantages it had bestowed would surely be lost. Glancing into the future, AFL spokesmen were inclined to be optimistic, but their mood was understandably tempered by a knowledge of defeats suffered by the national organization and its scattered affiliates. Because they believed the union cause just, however, and the trade unionists admirable, it was natural for them to attribute failures to hostile forces outside the Federation circle.

These men well understood that if the friendly trade union stimulated the worker in all his various capacities, certain adversaries forever threatened this same growth. Ranged along the periphery of their partly imagined world were the "capitalists" and "scabs" and "Mongolian coolies" menacing the organized labor movement and therefore that measure of humanity which the trade unionist had wrung from history. The capitalist, for instance, was typically represented in AFL speeches and writings not only as avaricious (economic) and powerful (political), but also as inhuman (total).

More directly relevant to our inquiry than these three is a fourth antagonist. This was the efficiency expert, the object of a short-lived but intense AFL animosity. Time-and-motion study came under AFL fire with the publication of F. W. Taylor's ideas on the subject in 1911 (first as periodical essays, then in 1914 as *Principles of Scientific Management*). Writers in the *American Federationist* vehemently attacked the efficiency expert as a "capitalist hireling," but more especially for his mechanistic conception of the worker. The theme of these articles was expressed in one of them by an AFL officer, James Duncan: "We are not mere machines; we are human beings, and protest against being discussed and considered as coequal with machinery." As often happened, President Gompers most completely articulated the unionists' feelings. "Here is the idea," he wrote with unusual bitterness in an editorial of February 1911; "all actual labor consists simply in moving things. See? Just as the work done by a machine is one motion after another, all manipulation of matter by human beings is made up of motions and series of motions. So, there you are, wage-workers in general, mere machines — considered industrially, of course."

It was not a disregard for efficiency itself, he believed, that underlay the workers' objections. "Systematization in getting materials ready for the ultimate workman on the final job is not novel, but scientifically building up the skilled mechanic himself, bodily and mentally, and molding, hammering, filing, and polishing him off in order to fit him for his theoretically best usefulness — that charms us unto the very soul."

"Hitherto," Gompers continued, "the industrial operative has had motives, by some observers deemed sufficiently strong, to qualify himself for his possible tasks. His reputation as a man, his pride in his work, his necessity to make good, his fear of losing employment, his attacks of hunger itself, all these have been deemed rather stirring goads in inducing him to 'get a move on.' But his 'move,' we are now told, guided as it is in the light of his own defective ingenuity and mere workshop instruction, is not the best attainable. He must further be taken in hand and taught the most economical lifts, pushes, jumps, steps, stoops and bends, the quickest looks and thinks, the most dexterous fingering, the most supple wrist-play, the finest elbow work, and the most powerful full-arm swings, throws, blows and jerks. Withal, dangling before him are to be rewards, hanging over him are to be penalties. Then let him go it! He'll do his twentieth century best."

Instead of arrogantly and insensitively trying to convert the craftsman into a "machine-made man-machine," in Gompers' opinion, "Let science, the intellectuals, the employers, and the body politic take hold of the laborer from his earliest years and build him up, clear up to what the original man-maker put into him in the way of physical and mental possibilities. Let the promoters of the proposition study how the laborer may be given his full physical height and breadth, his full mental and moral growth, his full potential worth to society as a good machine. In the end they might find that they had contributed in the construction of a good strong man."[5] This type of "construction," Gompers asserted, was precisely what the workers themselves were embarked upon.

Here is the language of a man to whom the shape and quality of life do matter. Gompers' fundamental considerations in his outcry — which was, of course, not so much an argument as the revelation of a point of view — are most nearly classifiable as aesthetic, although like "economic" or "political" that term is not broad enough to apply in such cases as this one. "Human" would do, or perhaps "civilized"; but the fact is that our society has not yet given us an adequate vocabulary for the purpose at hand, and will do so only when it becomes more conscious of the crucial distinctions to be made between barbarism and civilization.

As a generation attuned to the mythologists and the Freudians, we all know that values are never made wholly explicit; and so what was honored in the young American Federation of Labor must be partly inferred from the alternatives which its spokesmen imaginatively conceived. Behind them, in what they hoped was the past, stood the forsaken brute of

Markham's poem. To these union leaders, the man with the hoe represented a bestiality born of interminable dull labor, a creature whose chief awareness was of servitude and degradation, of never rising above that "emptiness of ages" to which men born into the lower classes had forever fallen victim. Ahead of American workers, on the other hand, was what seemed to them an equally hard fate at the hands of the engineer, who beckoned them always toward the machine. Either way lay dehumanization. The *tertium quid*, the way of the trade unionist, was an alternative that they accepted in order to escape from an existence either too debased or too routinized. But they lived by more than fears — the image of the manly trade unionist gave them a positive and concrete sense of what human life at its best might become.

## NOTES

[1] An important early book apparently not well known to American labor historians is *The Casual Laborer and Other Essays* (New York: Harcourt, Brace and Howe, 1920) by Carleton H. Parker, an economist especially interested in migratory workers, who argued that the roots of labor "problems" and "unrest" were mainly psychological. A recent book which takes a position which is similar to my own is Frank Tannenbaum's *A Philosophy of Labor* (New York: Alfred A. Knopf, 1951). This stimulating history of trade unionism since the Industrial Revolution has rightly challenged conventional, one-sided interpretations of labor history. His thesis, stripped of the complexity and supporting evidence given it in the book, is that "trade unionism is . . . a social and ethical system, not merely an economic one. It is concerned with the whole man. Its ends are the 'good life.'"

[2] The views presented in this essay are necessarily those of the most articulate AFL members, who were for the most part officials — though in some instances merely as delegates to the national conventions — of that organization.

[3] The paid circulation in 1898–1899, according to figures published in the magazine, was approximately 4,000.

[4] Miss Florence Thorne, Gompers' assistant for many years, has told me that she remembers him as having "two sides to his nature — revolutionary and constructive." However one analyzes the specific traits in his character, it seems certain that Gompers appeared in many roles to those around him, not simply as a business type.

[5] For a partial, economic reading of the evidence on this particular AFL animus, see Philip Taft, *The A. F. of L. in the Time of Gompers* (New York: Harper and Brothers, 1957), pp. 299–300.

# The Novel and the "Truth" about America

Sʜᴇʀᴡᴏᴏᴅ Aɴᴅᴇʀsᴏɴ, who is sometimes listed among American "realistic novelists," once wrote some interesting comments on fiction that is said to be true to life: "The life of reality is confused, disorderly, almost always without purpose, whereas in the artist's imaginative life there is purpose. There is determination to give the tale, the song, the painting Form — to make it true and real to the theme, not to life . . . I myself remember with what a shock I heard people say that one of my own books, *Winesburg, Ohio,* was an exact picture of Ohio village life. The book was written in a crowded tenement district of Chicago. The hint for almost every character was taken from my fellow-lodgers in a large rooming house, many of whom had never lived in a village."[1]

Anderson believed there had been some spiritual and emotional failure in modern America, and his sympathies were strongly drawn toward those men and women who were the victims of this failure. He turned them into pathetic grotesques. Presumably a village setting, which ordinarily suggests peaceful simplicity, gave these figures a greater dramatic contrast than Chicago would have provided. It is worth observing that there is no little irony in the fact that a specific town in Ohio is frequently mentioned as the "real" Winesburg, and that visitors sometimes go there, as they go to Oxford, Mississippi, to see with their own eyes what Anderson or William Faulkner had shown them in their respective stories about these towns.

Many of the citizens of Mississippi have felt that they and their state have been misrepresented by Faulkner's novels. And Faulkner himself has acknowledged that his fiction has contributed to misunderstanding. Lynchings, rape, fantastic funeral journeys, idiots in love with cows, Snopesism, and the rest, including the pastoral innocence side, are hardly "typical" of Mississippi.

74

Early in his career as a writer, Faulkner, like Anderson, noted an essential difference between life and literature. The fiction writer, he said, rather frequently meets people who have a fine story to give him — which they present with the invitation to put it down on paper intact. Unfortunately, Faulkner observed, it is not possible to transfer the story directly to paper: "somewhere between the experience and the blank page and the pencil, it dies." [2] The reasons why this is so are probably multiple. Only problems of a certain kind tease a writer's imagination. Again, the "world" (not merely the *mise en scène*) of the novel grows or swarms into being out of the novel's germ, and this is, in considerable part, quite a different, or more specialized, world from the one the novelist himself as citizen inhabits. Two novelists in writing about what would seem to be the same subject can project two quite different worlds. Or, indeed, the same novelist, on different occasions, can project quite different worlds. This latter observation can be illustrated by reference to Faulkner's *Light in August* and *Intruder in the Dust*.

In *Light in August* Faulkner treats the "Negro problem" in relation to the Protestant tradition in the South, and in *Intruder in the Dust* he treats it as a sectional issue. In both novels the setting is the town of Jefferson in Yoknapatawpha County (or Oxford, Lafayette County, Mississippi), but the worlds are not the same. It is true that twenty-odd years separate their respective settings, but this does not account in any major way for the difference. In *Light in August* a Calvinistic gloom pervades the action. Episode after episode touches the central irony that a lynching can grow out of Christian righteousness. There are descriptions of church architecture and services, of life in a seminary, expositions of southern history in relation to the church, speculations about religious and moral conduct, and so on. Collectively such matters make the world of the novel. Presumably Faulkner, at the time he wrote *Light in August*, did not believe that the church alone was responsible for cruel and unsympathetic treatment of the Negro. But it was partially responsible, and Faulkner enlarged upon this partial responsibility until he had created a monstrous irony. The monstrous irony makes a fine novel; it is not, sociologically, a full account of the Negro problem in the town of Oxford, Mississippi.

*Intruder in the Dust* is also concerned with a lynching, or rather the threat of a lynching, but its world is not Calvinistic: this time Faulkner presents a beleaguered South defending itself ideologically against liberal Yankee opinion. The town is peopled, for the most part, by rather easygoing but thoughtless citizens; not intentionally vicious, they are potentially a mob. Either the willfully vicious, like the Gowries from Beat Four, or the intelligent and decent, like Gavin Stevens and Miss Habersham, will win them over, will help them decide how the Negro accused of shooting a white man will be treated. Helping to frame and interpret the action are Gavin Stevens and his young nephew Chick. Gavin Stevens explains that North and South are different countries. And one of the images left in the reader's mind is of the United States as a topographical map, with the North being composed of great cities and the South of small towns. Jefferson itself is seen as poor but genteel. Chick struggles to accept the Negro as a human being. In *Light in August*, the action glowers; in *Intruder in the Dust*, it is essentially bright. Whatever their similarities, they are two distinct worlds. Neither Jefferson is Oxford, Mississippi.

In the article referred to above, Faulkner also said that a novelist is free to put into the mouth of a character better speech than an actual person ordinarily is capable of speaking. He might have added that the milieu which exists inside the covers of a book of fiction is a stylized milieu: each physical presence, each action, and each description serves to dramatize a conception. Faulkner's *Soldiers' Pay*, a world-weary and sophisticated novel, belongs in part to the cut-glass artistry of Oscar Wilde and Aubrey Beardsley, and in part to the languorous gesture common to the "lost generation." *Pylon* symbolizes a waste-land world, and its principal characters suggest the near possibility of creatures "incapable of suffering, wombed and born complete and instantaneous, cunning and intricate and deadly, from out some iron batcave of the earth's prime foundation." *Sanctuary* presents characters either bemused or hypnotized by evil, so that nature herself seems in ripe decay and all modern objects seem metallic, brassy, cheap, and vulgar. And so on. Each novel aspires to live in relation to its own premises, its germ, its initial conception. And, as implied earlier, the degree to which it succeeds is an important clue to its value as a work of art. Conversely, the degree to which it fails to create a self-defining image or symbolic world is an indication of its weakness as a novel.

Three of our nineteenth-century novelists, Hawthorne, Melville, and James, also had something to say about this problem of the fictional representation of life. All of them take positions essentially in accord with Anderson and Faulkner.

Nathaniel Hawthorne in the introduction to *The House of the Seven Gables* made his famous, but probably unnecessary, distinction between the Romance and the Novel:

When a writer calls his work a Romance, it need hardly be observed that he wishes to claim a certain latitude, both as to its fashion and material, which he would not have felt himself entitled to assume had he professed to be writing a Novel. The latter form of composition is presumed to aim at a very minute fidelity, not merely to the possible, but to the probable and ordinary course of man's experience. The former — while as a work of art, it must rigidly subject itself to laws, and while it sins unpardonably so far as it may swerve aside from the truth of the human heart — has fairly a right to present that truth under circumstances, to a great extent, of the writer's own choosing or creation. If he thinks fit, also, he may so manage his atmospherical medium as to bring out or mellow the lights and deepen and enrich the shadows of the picture. He will be wise, no doubt, to make a very moderate use of the privileges here stated, and especially, to mingle the Marvellous rather as a slight, delicate, and evanescent flavor, than as any portion of the actual substance of the dish offered to the public. He can hardly be said, however, to commit a literary crime even if he disregard this caution.

Hawthorne was saying that if he were not free to call what he wrote novels, then he would call them romances. But the "Marvellous" does find its way into most interesting fiction — a setting is meaningful, coincidence and irony move in remarkable ways, language is strangely luminous, and character is singular, living only in relationship to the major impulse of the novel.

At several points in *The Confidence Man* Herman Melville wrote little asides on the problems of fiction, none more interesting than those in Chapter 33:

But ere be given the rather grave story of Charlemont, a reply must in civility be made to a certain voice which methinks I heard, that, in view of past chapters, and more particularly the last, where certain antics appear, he exclaims: How unreal all this is! Who did ever dress or act like your cosmopolitan? And who, it might be returned, did ever dress or act like Harlequin?

Strange, that in a work of amusement, this severe fidelity to real life should be exacted by anyone, who, by taking up such a work, sufficiently shows that he is not unwilling to drop real life, and turn, for a time, to something different. Yes, it is, indeed, strange that anyone should clamor

77

for the thing he is weary of; that anyone, who, for any cause, finds real life dull, should yet demand of him who is to divert his attention from it, that he should be true to that dullness.

There is another class, and with this class we side, who sit down to a work of amusement tolerantly as they sit down at a play, and with much the same expectations and feelings. They look that fancy shall evoke scenes different from those of the same old crowd round the custom-house counter, and the same old dishes on the boarding-house table with characters unlike those of the same old acquaintances they meet in the same old way every day in the same old street. And as, in real life, the properties will not allow people to act out themselves with that unreserve permitted to the stage; so, in books of fiction, they look not only for more entertainment, but, at bottom, even for more reality, than real life itself can show. Thus, though they want novelty, they want nature, too; but nature unfettered, exhilarated, in effect transformed. In this way of thinking, the people in a fiction, like the people in a play, must dress as nobody exactly dresses, talk as nobody exactly talks, act as nobody exactly acts. It is with fiction as with religion: it should present another world, and yet one to which we feel the tie.

Finally, of course, there is the body of criticism written by Henry James, which, along with his fiction, has been so influential in our own time. The prefaces frequently touch on the question of reality, and in "The Real Thing," a fine short story, he has written a parable of the artist in relation to a fixed reality. Here we may quote a few sentences from "The Art of Fiction," his answer to Sir Walter Besant, one of those who feel they know what is real and what is not and how the former is to be put into a work of fiction. Henry James said:

The reality of Don Quixote or of Mr. Micawber is a very delicate shade; it is a reality so coloured by the author's vision that, vivid as it may be, one would hesitate to propose it as a model: one would expose one's self to some very embarrassing questions on the part of a pupil. It goes without saying that you will not write a good novel unless you possess the sense of reality; but it will be difficult to give you a recipe for calling that sense into being. Humanity is immense, and reality has a myriad forms, the most one can affirm is that some of the flowers of fiction have the odour of it, and others have not; as for telling you in advance how your nosegay should be composed, that is another affair.

Should one, for example, read Herman Melville's *Israel Potter* as a trustworthy account of a soldier-hero in the American Revolution? The novel *is* based on a chapbook autobiography, but anyone reading a few chapters into the novel recognizes that this is a picaresque tale.

Israel Potter is a tough-muscled New England Yankee, not very literate but adaptable, witty, and inclined to take the world as he finds it. As the years go by it is clear that he has been defeated: poverty and deaths in his family attend his forty-odd years in London, and upon his return to New England not a single member of his family is remembered by name, and the roads, paths, and house Israel knew have disappeared. Technicalities prevent his obtaining a soldier's pension, and soon he is dead. Who is Israel Potter? He is the wanderer (Israel) and he is the common man (Potter's field) — and, Melville says in his fierce irony, his reward is what the hero can expect. Certainly this is not history; it is Melville's bitter view of things at a stage in his career when the current was running strongly against him, carrying him, like Israel Potter, toward inevitable defeat.

In an early chapter we see Israel Potter as an escaped prisoner meeting George III, finding the king a pleasant man who refuses to have him arrested. We see him meet John Paul Jones, who is presented as a pursuer of pretty wenches and, albeit a fine commander, the most unconscionable of braggarts. Israel himself is reponsible for much of the damage to the *Serapis* — he blows up the ship's magazine. He also is presented as having introduced Jones to Ben Franklin's *Poor Richard's Almanac*, and it is he who names Jones' ship *Bon Homme Richard*. Franklin, who has an important place in the narrative, talks like an American version of Polonius. How much of all this is trustworthy history? Not much of it certainly, which fact, of course, has nothing to do with whether or not we like the story or, privately, agree that Melville has caught the spirit of Jones or Franklin. Anyone reading *Israel Potter* as a good document of the American Revolution would, of course, have an apparitional sense of historical fact.

One might say in reply to this that since *Israel Potter* is a picaresque novel no one would think of reading it for the factual content. But what of a novel written about the problems and facts of our contemporary world?

We have lived, or at least Americans in the last generation or two have lived, in a "scientific" milieu which has invited one to put a premium on facts of a certain kind, the kind that can be measured, weighed, and catalogued. This milieu has encouraged the notion that life-as-it-is-experienced or life-as-it-actually-is can be got inside the covers of a book of fiction. And this milieu has encouraged the notion that certain preoccupations imply coming to terms with, or facing, the actual world and that certain other preoccupations imply a turning away from facts. For example, a novel that tells how to improve race relations is more "real" than a novel showing a young man struggling to decide between a marriage of convenience and a life as a poet. Personal moral struggles are somehow less real than public social questions. This mentality has also helped foster the notion that fiction, at its truest, bears a one-to-one relationship with the society it is treating.

George Santayana says somewhere that exaggeration is an inevitable and necessary part of artistic expression. Stylization involves exaggeration and distortion. The artist who has little or no feeling for stylization usually is not much of an artist. It does not follow, of course, that he does not believe he is telling the truth. But as James said, some fiction has the odor of reality and of truth and some does not. It is up to the reader or the critic to see what conventions, what larger-than-life characters, what bejeweled or suggestive patterns of imagery, what qualities of legend, myth, or fable it does or does not possess.

Rather frequently the fiction writer who has created a vision appropriate to his theme is asked why he did not give a more "realistic" view. Thus we find Nathanael West explaining why, in *The Day of the Locust*, he had not included any sincere or honest Hollywood citizens: "If I put into *The Day of the Locust* any of the sincere, honest people who work here . . . those chapters couldn't be written satirically and the whole fabric of the peculiar half-world which I attempted to create would be badly torn by them." As a matter of fact he was not writing only about Hollywood, he was writing about empty lives, about people who learn too late, if they learn at all, that some forms of easy living and materialistic pursuits are the reverse of what they had seemed. All the characters in *The Day of the Locust* live with a pretense to being something that they are not. Their frustrations increase in intensity until released in cruelty and violence. The characters are grotesques, either pitiful or bizarre dramatizations of artificiality, dishonesty, self-deception, and frustration. The scene being laid in Hollywood makes it relatively easy to introduce other forms of pretense: the movie sets, the eccentric and assorted architecture, the strange religious sects, and the local worship of glamour. West's image of Hollywood, from one point of view, is unfair. From another, it is eminently just.

This is not the occasion for attempting to classify conventions in the

American novel, but a few sentences may suggest the sort of thing that might result from such an attempt. In Nathanael West, Carson McCullers, Truman Capote, Erskine Caldwell, and Eudora Welty, for example, one finds grotesques, the comedy and pathos of the misfit. In William Faulkner, Robert Penn Warren, Katherine Anne Porter, and Caroline Gordon, one finds the ex-member of the regional world suffering from deracination. Consequently there are in their fiction more regional types (hillbillies, evangelical ministers, "rednecks," sectional patriots, and so on) than a visitor might be aware of in the South, and the nineteenth-century character of the South is caught and stressed more vividly (exaggerated, if one will) than it would be, say, by the average southern citizen. A sense of the past informing the present is one of the characteristics of their fiction. These writers are dramatizing man suffering from cosmopolitanism and abstraction — and they choose to stress that which serves their theme.

Another group is suggested by the phrase "the Hemingway world," or, perhaps better, by Edmund Wilson's title *The Boys in the Back Room*. The stories of Ernest Hemingway, John Steinbeck, John O'Hara, James M. Cain, and others suggest common characteristics: the tough, two-fisted hero who believes in little beyond the need to maintain his self-respect, who meets a demanding world on its own terms. Philosophy, rhetoric, even social graces are pointless in such a world. A group related to these latter writers have made a legend of the harshness of the American city: Theodore Dreiser, James Farrell, Nelson Algren, Willard Motley, and Saul Bellow.

Writers discover symbolic situations and settings, a tone and stance appropriate to what they want to say. Certain things go unsaid. And some things, if it may be so put, are more than said.

Some time ago in the magazine *Commentary* there was an article on the types of short stories appearing in American magazines.[3] The author, after reading a dozen or so collections of short stories published in the last few years, decided that there are two current types: first, the sophisticated or "Connecticut" story and, second, the southern or "Yoknapatawpha" story. Connecticut, as a sort of suburb for the upper middle class from New York City (advertising people, successful artists, brokers, etc.), is meant to suggest the urbanite who earns a good salary and is interested in the cultural life: books, theater, music. He also pays a price for his way of life — he pays for it in anxieties and in worry about his job and about his mode of life. In the Connecticut story, everyone is middle-aged, either temperamentally or chronologically; and each day has its crisis, usually a muted or silent crisis — but a crisis nonetheless. In the southern story, the setting is rural; if a city is mentioned it is off in the distance, not in the immediate area. The people tend to vegetate, not to think; they seem akin to the sun and the earth. Money does not complicate their lives; the good earth is there to provide them with potatoes and turnips. (The author does not discuss the convention of violence in southern fiction.)

Perhaps the sociologist studying regions in America would find fewer anxieties in the people south of Washington, D.C. He might find more. Certainly he would find as much industrialization as in New England, and he would find in the village and town life a greater preoccupation with manners and modes of personal relationship. The two regions, that is, would not fit the image one might anticipate merely from reading current American short stories. An astute reader might find out certain things about the American "psyche" from the stories. The foreign reader would not find out very much about American economic and social geography — and what he might think was fact could turn out to be fiction.

There is nothing essentially new in the above argument, except that we are talking about American fiction. Throughout the history of Western literature, indeed beginning with Plato, one finds philosophers and moralists setting certain terms in opposition to each other — real vs. imagined, fact vs. fancy, true vs. beautiful, and other terms as well. The strictest of these categorizers, or perhaps we should say the most literal-minded among them, have not merely favored the first term in each pair but have used "real," "fact," and "true" to berate the poet and the fiction writer because they see them as being preoccupied with the fanciful, the imagined, and the beautiful.

In literary criticism we have had Aristotle, Boccaccio, Sidney, Shelley, or Kenneth Burke attempting to explain to the moralists and the philosophers why the poet or fiction writer finds himself unable and unwilling to accept the dichotomy. Theirs is a statement that apparently has to be made in every generation. Simply, it is that in fiction the "real," the "factual," and the "true" are inevitably caught up in the author's private vision.

It is undoubtedly a tribute to a novelist when a reader believes in the "reality" of his fictional creation, but the reader should not forget what Henry James said, that reality has myriad forms and that the reality of a given piece of fiction is merely one of its guises. Therefore one ought to be wary of finding sociologically valid descriptions of a society in highly imaginative fiction. It would be naive to reconstruct Elizabethan England after reading *The Shoemaker's Holiday* or *As You Like It*. It would be equally naive to reconstruct the Spanish-American War, a small town in Ohio, or middle-class life in Connecticut after having read a novel on each of these subjects. Before attempting any such reconstructions one would have to investigate such aesthetic questions as the literary conventions and the nature of the stylization to be found in the given novel, as well as the author's peculiar or individual way of looking at a subject.

**NOTES**

[1] "On Realism," *Sherwood Anderson's Notebook* (New York: Boni and Liveright, 1926).
[2] "Beyond the Talking," *New Republic*, LVII (May 20, 1931), 23–24.
[3] Steven Marcus, "Terrors of Yoknapatawpha and Fairfield," *Commentary*, XIV (December 1952), 575–585.

✣ BERNARD BOWRON, LEO MARX, AND ARNOLD ROSE

# Literature and Covert Culture

*This essay is an experiment in collaboration between schol-*
*ars associated with literary studies and with sociology. Its*
*authors had the privilege of a year's close association in an*
*American Studies faculty seminar ("Technology and Ameri-*
*can Culture") at the University of Minnesota.*

By COVERT culture we refer to traits of culture rarely acknowledged by those who possess them. In any society men tend to ignore or repress certain commonly learned attitudes and behavior patterns, much as an individual may ignore or repress certain personal experiences or motives. In the case of covert culture, the repressed traits are more or less common to members of a society, and they probably are transmitted in the same informal ways that the basic elements of the overt culture are transmitted. The covert traits are not more "true" or "real" than the overt traits; they are equally representative of people's attitudes and behaviors. The distinction lies in the degree of acknowledgment (to self and to others) and the degree of repression. If one were to suggest to a representative member of a society that his behavior, or that of his community, exhibits a particular characteristic of covert culture, he might be expected to scoff at the idea, even to reject it heatedly. Public responses to the Kinsey report are a case in point. Similarly, Americans might deny the evidence of their disguised hostility toward machine technology which we present in this essay.

How then is covert culture recognized? We may assume we are in the presence of covert culture when we note a recurrent pattern of inconsistent or seemingly illogical behavior.[1] When most people in a given society or subsociety persist in acting inconsistently, when they resist with emotion any attempts to reconcile their actions with their expressed beliefs, and when they persist in this behavior over an extended period of time, then presumably we are dealing with covert culture. For obvious reasons, however, it is difficult to study covert culture. And in a heterogeneous society like our own, where variations in behavior are relatively common, it is unlikely that much of our culture long remains covert. On the other hand, the little that does may be of the greatest importance in certain emotionally charged areas of behavior, such as racial or sexual relations or religion.

At this point it might be well to indicate what covert culture is not. In the first place, it is not a complete culture that exists beneath the surface of the overt culture and "really" directs people's attitudes and behavior. It consists, rather, of parts of culture that happen to be seriously inconsistent with other parts of culture and so get driven underground.

Second, behavior in conformity with covert culture is not the same as alienation from culture (or "anomie," to use Durkheim's term). Covert elements of culture are just as much a part of culture as are overt elements. To be sure, behavior in conformity with an aspect of covert culture will strike an observer as inconsistent with a parallel aspect of overt culture. But we do not mean to imply that every obvious inconsistency in behavior is a result of such a disparity. Many forms of inconsistent behavior have nothing to do with covert culture. They result from the individual's efforts to adhere to elements within the covert culture which are at bottom incompatible. In such cases, where a person acts out more or less commonplace contradictions of his culture, the disharmony is not so great as in cases where the contradiction is repressed or, as we say, covert. In any event, logical incompatibility between two elements of culture is, obviously enough, more likely to occur in a society that embraces heterogeneous traditions, or in a society that is changing rapidly.

Third, covert culture is not a subculture. We are all familiar with the different roles a person plays in the various groups to which he belongs: contrast the behavior of the adolescent in his family and in his peer group. But, while members of each group are, in this case, shocked or scornfully amused by behavior in the other group, they recognize each other's existence and — in a sense — regard the discrepancies as natural and even desirable. The adolescent himself is aware of the disparity in his roles, whether or not it creates a conflict for him. Even the subculture of a minority group (such as, for example, the Mennonites or Jews) is in no way to be equated with covert culture. This is a different culture from the dominant one, practiced by a small section of the society, and while it may be deliberately hidden from the majority, its deviations from the dominant culture are quite well known and apparent to those living in both the minority group and the larger society. Sociologists call those living in two societies "marginal men"; they are understood to be fairly rare in any society. Covert culture traits, on the contrary, are exhibited by the large majority of persons in a society if not by all of them.

But it may be asked how covert culture is learned, if it is unacknowledged and secret. The question, however, implies that the transmission of *overt* culture is deliberate and rational. Actually, only a small part of the education of the young in the overt culture of a society is deliberate. While the child learns through language or other symbols such as gestures, most of the process is very subtle. As Hickman and Kuhn point out: "Few, if any, fathers or mothers take their children aside and say, in effect, 'I will now tell you what I know,' 'I will now tell you what you ought to know and believe,' or 'I will now tell you about our society and our culture.' Any conversations of this general nature could have relatively little over-all influence on the child's attitudes. 'Attitudes are caught, not taught.' " [2] This is true for both overt and covert culture. The difference lies not in manner of learning, but in the degree of the adult's awareness of the cues he is providing, or in the degree of his willingness to acknowledge the cues when they are called to his attention. One characteristic of this learning process is that the child picks up the cues of the covert culture, but at first does not know that they are "secret." He proudly displays the just learned trait openly in behavior or speech, and then the parent is shocked. This negative reaction — coming once or several times — now teaches the child that he must "forget" and "deny" this part of what he has recently learned from the parent. It should be pointed out, however, that the difference between covert and overt culture is a relative matter; some aspects of covert culture are talked over by intimate friends, as it were "over the back fence." Adults "teach" other adults some aspects of covert culture just as they teach children other aspects.

Those who are probably in the best position to study a society's covert traits are observers who come to it with the perspective of an alien culture. Hence anthropologists and perceptive foreign travelers have until now provided much of the evidence of covert culture. The anthropologists have most frequently analyzed the concept itself.[3] This would suggest that the concept is most useful when direct impressions of a living culture are available. The study of covert culture does not at first thought seem possible through the analysis of written documents; hence the concept seems irrelevant to the study of past societies about which we have few other sources of evidence. It is our purpose here to suggest a means of uncovering elements of covert culture through the analysis of written, and particularly literary, evidence.

Now, to be sure, there is nothing new about the idea of studying literature as a source of information about culture. Historians have been doing it for a long time. When allowances are made for shifts in style and taste, the manifest content of literature may be assumed to reflect important characteristics of culture. But what about covert culture? Since we assume, to begin with, that most members of a society do not care to be reminded that they exhibit traits of covert culture, it follows that the writer who seeks a sizable audience will not knowingly portray them. On the other hand, popular literature may be studied for what it betrays as well as what it depicts. In other words, it may be approached as a projection of covert culture. Such an approach to the arts is well established in several areas. Psychologists have for some time been using graphic and lingual expression to get at the unconscious associations of individuals. Of these projective tests, the Rorschach, TAT, and Word Association Test are perhaps the best known. Similarly, literature widely accepted by the public, or a significant segment of the public, may provide an avenue to the unstated ideas of a society. Of course the Freudians and Jungians have studied literature, but not precisely in the way we are suggesting. They have sought recurring popular themes in the classics as projections of what they consider to be universal instincts or complexes. They are concerned with the traits common to virtually all men. What we are concerned with, on the other hand, is a technique for dealing with certain distinctive characteristics of a particular culture located in time and place.[4]

The projective component of written documents is chiefly to be found in imagery and metaphor, using metaphor in the broadest sense to include all the more common figurative modes of expression. When a writer uses such analogizing devices, in which the analogy is either explicit or implicit, he is in effect revealing a pattern of association which can only be partly conscious. That is to say, no matter how many reasons he may acknowledge for selecting a particular figure of speech, the fact remains that he selects it from a virtually infinite range of possibilities. Therefore no degree of deliberate calculation can fully explain his choice. For example, why does an author choose a machine to express menace; why not a storm or an earthquake? We are of course not concerned here with idiosyncratic quirks of personality. Our interest is limited to images and metaphors which recur frequently in the written expression of a particular society. We do not have in mind the mere cliché or faddish expression, but rather the metaphor *repeatedly used in varying language* to describe similar phenomena.[5] We shall provide an example below.

First, however, a word must be said about our apparent tendency to favor the more stereotyped modes of expression. It is true that the more unreflective the creative process, the more useful the work may be as a projection of the psyche, so to speak, of the entire society. But this is not to say that we underestimate the value of less hackneyed literary modes. We assume that written documents are distributed along a spectrum from the most stereotyped or conventional at one end to the most original and perceptive at the other. The great writer is a sensitive observer, and needless to say he does not merely project his culture. On the contrary, often he consciously reveals covert elements that less perceptive artists ignore; moreover, he sometimes reveals them precisely by turning stereotypes inside out. Hence this distinction between overt and covert culture should not seem completely unfamiliar to students of literature. Indeed, it is in some respects akin to a recurrent literary motif, the paradoxical relation between "appearance" and "reality." Not that there is an exact equivalence between the two sets of terms. When a writer indicates the presence of a "reality" hidden beneath "appearances" he usually intends more than we do by covert culture. Nevertheless he often includes an awareness of covert traits. For example, Shakespeare has Lear become aware of covert traits of culture; Cervantes, on the other hand, deliberately makes Don Quixote oblivious of them. In *King Lear* the discrepancy between overt and covert generates a tragic view of life; in *Don Quixote* it is the essence of comedy. In both works, however, the reader's illumination comes at least in part from the author's revelation of the disparity between what we have called overt and covert culture. That disparity is, however, but one aspect of the paradox of appearance and reality.

For an illustration of the use of written documents to reveal covert patterns, consider American culture during the onset of industrialism before the Civil War. Here, as most historians testify, was a society wholeheartedly committed to the idea of progress. This was an era of unprecedented expansion, social mobility, and optimism. In the newspapers, magazines, and orations of the time we find countless celebrations of the new technology as emblematic of man's increasing dominion over nature. Take, as an example, a minister's address to the New York Mechanic's Institute in 1841. In expounding his theme ("Improvement of the Mechanic Arts"), the Reverend Mr. Williamson employed many commonplaces of the hour. The mechanic arts, he said,

. . . change the face of nature itself, and cause the desolate and solitary place to be glad and blossom as the rose — the mountains are levelled — the crooked is made strait [*sic*] and the rough places plain — the ascending vapor is arrested in its upward course and converted into a power that well nigh enables us to laugh at distance and space — the broad Atlantic has become, as it were, a narrow lake. . . . And still the course is onward, and we even threaten to seize upon the forked lightning, and pluck from the faithful magnet a power, that shall render useless the canvass [*sic*] of the mariner and achieve a yet mightier triumph over the obstacles that space has interposed to the intercourse of man with his fellow-man . . . much of human happiness depends upon the cultivation of these arts . . . without them, man is but a helpless child, exposed to ten thousand dangers and difficulties, that he cannot control; but with them, he is strong, and can rule in majesty over that mighty empire which God has given him.[6]

To say that this rhetoric embodies certain dominant values of the culture is not to deny that there also were outspoken critics of technological innovation. There were. But they constituted a relatively small minority. Some spoke for the slavery interest or the emergent labor movement, others for various religious sects or utopian reform groups. By and large, however, Americans at this time enthusiastically endorsed the new machine power, and even more enthusiastically applied it. Many of the respected leaders of society, men like Daniel Webster and Edward Everett, paid homage to technology in language indistinguishable from Mr. Williamson's. On the basis of much written evidence, therefore, one might conclude that American culture, leaving aside a few groups of partially alienated people, exhibited only approval of industrialization.

But that is not quite the whole story. To be sure, it describes the dominant overt response to mechanization, but it fails to account for a certain contrary undertone that any close student of the period recognizes. To be more specific, in examining a large sample of reactions to technological change in this period, we discover some which defy simple classification. Here, for instance, is an article by James H. Lanman on "Railroads in the United States," which appeared in Hunt's *Merchants' Magazine* in 1840.[7] In accordance with the spirit of this journal of commerce, the writer presents an affirmative survey of the advance of steam power in America. He regards "productive enterprise" as the distinguishing feature of American culture, and he praises the new machines as "the triumphs of our own age, the laurels of mechanical philosophy, of untrammelled mind, and a liberal commerce!" He finds railroads particularly inspiring; so far as he is concerned "it is clear that all patriotic and right-minded men have concurred in the propriety of their construction." If we confine attention to Mr. Lanman's manifest opinions, we have no reason to distinguish him from such ebullient devotees of progress as the Reverend Mr. Williamson.

Nevertheless a more searching examination of this article uncovers a curious anomaly. In spite of the writer's evident effort to enlist support for the new power, he repeatedly invokes images which convey less than full confidence in the benign influence of machines. Steamships and railroads are "iron monsters," "dragons of mightier power, with iron muscles that never tire, breathing smoke and flame through their blackened lungs, feeding upon wood and water, outrunning the race horse. . . ." Elsewhere Mr. Lanman is eager to allay fear of railroad accidents. Therefore he carefully evaluates statistics on deaths and injuries. He finds the results clearly favorable to railroads as compared with travel on "common roads." At the same time, however, he describes a train "leaping forward like some black monster, upon its iron path, by the light of the fire and smoke which it vomits forth."

In contrast to the explicit theme of the piece, these images associate machines with the destructive and the repulsive. They communicate an unmistakable sense of anxiety and menace. Without more evidence, of course, we cannot prove that the writer actually was uneasy about the new power. By themselves these images prove nothing. But the fact is that we can produce many other examples of the same kind. Moreover, and this seems to us a most telling point, when we turn to these alienated writers who consciously try to arouse fear of machines, we find them deliberately choosing the same images. Robert Owen, for example, describes the new technology as a power "which neither eats nor drinks, and faints not by over-exertion, brought into direct competition with flesh and blood." "Who is there," he asks, "to check this mighty monster that is now allowed to stalk the earth . . .?"[8] It was in this period that a kind of machine created in a writer's imagination entered the language as the prototype of terror and the demoniacal—Frankenstein's monster. A final example of the simultaneous attraction and fearfulness of the locomotive, with distinct Oedipal overtones, is provided by this doggerel:

> Big iron horse with lifted head,
> Panting beneath the station shed,
> You are my dearest dream come true; —
> I love my Dad; I worship you!
>
> Your noble heart is filled with fire,
> For all your toil you never tire,
> And though you're saddled-up in steel,
> Somewhere, inside, I *know* you feel.
>
> All night in dreams when you pass by,
> You breathe out stars that fill the sky,
> And now, when all my dreams are true,
> I hardly dare come close to you.[9]

To sum up, we conclude that expressions of the overt culture do not provide an adequate conception of the American response to industrialization. From them we get the familiar picture of a confident, optimistic public and a few small dissident groups. But the concept of covert culture makes possible a somewhat different hypothesis. When we analyze the imagery employed even by those who professed approval of technological change, we discover evidence of widespread if largely unacknowledged doubt, fear, and hostility.[10] It is not necessary to our present purpose to account in detail for this phenomenon. Suffice it to suggest that American culture at this time also embraced a set of values and meanings inherently antithetic to the new technological power. This was a time, as everyone knows, when Americans tended to celebrate the "natural" as against the "artificial." At all levels of culture, from the relatively abstruse speculations of Emerson to the popular gift books, from Cooper's novels to the paintings of the Hudson River School, Americans affirmed values and meanings said to reside in nature. Natural process, that is, was conceived as containing the key, barely concealed, to all human problems. Needless to say, this belief was not peculiar to America. But as a consequence of the unique American geography—the actual presence of the wilderness—it did seem particularly relevant to this country. As Perry Miller has pointed out, what the European romantic dreamed the American actually experienced.[11] Now the progress of technology hardly was reconcilable, at least in the long run, with the sanctity of the natural order. For the use of power machines implied that nature was a neutral if not hostile force that men needed to dominate. This view was in obvious contradiction with the idea that man's felicity depended upon the ordering of life in passive accommodation to spontaneous operations of nature.

We are suggesting, though here we can hardly demonstrate, that this conflict of values, when unacknowledged, may have been an important source of the anxiety revealed by the imagery to which we have called attention.[12] This is not to identify approval of technological progress with overt culture, and hostility with covert. What is covert here results from the impulse to adhere (simultaneously) to logically incompatible values. In other words, it is the awareness of the contradiction that is repressed and that gives rise to the covert traits (in this case *unacknowledged* fear and hostility) revealed in imagery. Thus it is worth noting that Lanman, the writer who praised locomotives even as he called them monsters, also praised the "steam screw" which, he said, "should tear up by the roots the present monarchs of the forest, and open the ample bosom of the soil to the genial beams of the fertilizing sun." Recall that the writer speaks for a culture passionately devoted to nature — to Bryant's lyric view that "the groves were God's first temples." Is it surprising that he felt impelled to compare machines to terrible monsters? In any event, the disparity between the feelings latent in his images and the manifest optimism of his theme is highly suggestive. It gives some clue to the correspondence between this writer's strangely mixed feelings and the recurrent, if largely unexpressed, pattern of inconsistency in the culture of nineteenth-century America.

This interpretation, finally, is borne out by the work of the more sensitive and perceptive writers of the age. When we turn, for example, to Cooper, Thoreau, Hawthorne, and Melville we find a reiterated expression of precisely those contradictory meanings the typical magazine writers did not acknowledge. What is more, the great writers in many cases employed the same or similar imagery to get at these conflicts. But with an important difference. When Lanman called a machine a monster he was scarcely aware of what he was doing. We know this because he fails to take into account the negative response to technological change that is the unmistakable burden of his imagery. In other words, his conscious theme expresses one viewpoint and his images another. There is a marked disparity between thought and feeling here. Either the writer is unaware of the contradiction or he is unable to find words capable of expressing it. In either event, this is not what happens in the work of a talented and disciplined artist.

When we look closely at the way Thoreau or Hawthorne handles the same material the difference quickly becomes apparent. In *Walden,* for example, or in Hawthorne's "The Celestial Railroad," we find a deliberate effort to complicate the significance of America's favorite symbol of progress. Here the machine is invested with ambiguous meaning, not because the writers have an inherent passion for ambiguity, but rather because no other interpretation would have seemed adequate.[13] Given the conditions of life in nineteenth-century America, the entire pattern of the culture, the new machine power was bound to represent contrary possibilities. No doubt everyone in some degree sensed the ambiguity. But only a few were able to express it. Among them were the serious writers who made it their business to convey as much of the meaning of experience as possible. Hence it is no accident that they so often employ machine imagery in opposition to various emblems of nature. This device served to express precisely the contradiction that Lanman felt but that he did not fully recognize or express. What we are saying is that the skilled writer confirms the presence of those covert traits of culture which unreflective and untrained writers merely betray. When the two kinds of evidence fit, as they do here, we feel confident that we have uncovered a disparity between covert and overt culture.

Repressed traits and attitudes of former periods need not be a closed book. Dead men answer no poll-takers, but they have left an extensive written record of their underground cultures. This record may be deciphered. One indispensable key is the analysis of systems of imagery and metaphor in diverse popular writings and in works of formal literary art. The sociologist need not regard this method of study as an exclusive possession of the literary scholars who originally developed it. Used with care and discrimination, it is equally available to him.

Such collaboration between literary and sociological scholarship is, fortunately, a two-way street. At least it should be. For the concept of covert culture, in turn, offers a rewarding approach to literary studies. This point cannot be developed here. But it is surely implicit in what has been said about formal literature's significant confirmation of the existence of culture traits that are only revealed inadvertently in popular modes of expression. Critics concerned with the devious ways in which a society nurtures its men of letters cannot afford to neglect the existence of covert culture and the writer's responses to it. Here is a major source of those tensions that give a work of literary art its structure, its irony, and its stylistic signature.

NOTES

[1] This technique for observing covert culture has been presented in Arnold M. Rose, *Theory and Method in the Social Sciences* (Minneapolis: University of Minnesota Press, 1954), Chap. 21, "Popular Logic in the Study of Covert Culture." Some elements of covert culture in the United States are suggested in this chapter.

[2] C. Addison Hickman and Manford H. Kuhn, *Individuals, Groups, and Economic Behavior* (New York: Dryden Press, 1946), p. 30.

[3] The anthropologists have concerned themselves more with the tendency of culture to form patterns or systems covertly rather than with the relationship of covert culture to behavior. See, for example, Edward Sapir, "The Unconscious Patterning of Behavior in Society," in E. S. Dummer, ed., *The Unconscious: A Symposium* (New York: Alfred A. Knopf, 1928); Clyde Kluckhohn, "Patterning as Exemplified in Navaho Culture," in L. Spier, A. I. Hallowell, and S. S. Newman, eds., *Language, Culture and Personality: Essays in Memory of Edward Sapir* (Menasha, Wis.: Sapir Memorial Publication Fund, 1941), pp. 109–128; Laura Thompson, "Attitudes and Acculturation," *American Anthropologist*, L (April–June 1948), 200–215. A few sociologists also have worked with the concept of covert culture: F. Stuart Chapin, "Latent Culture Patterns of the Unseen World of Social Reality," *American Journal of Sociology*, XL (July 1934), 61–68; Robert K. Merton, *Social Theory and Social Structure* (Glencoe, Ill.: The Free Press, 1949), pp. 21–81.

[4] Although the Freudians have characteristically been most concerned with universal rather than particular cultural traits, Freud himself did suggest the possibility of inquiries along the line of this essay. "The analogy between the process of cultural evolution and the path of individual development may be carried further in an important respect. It can be maintained that the community, too, develops a super-ego, under whose influence cultural evolution proceeds. It would be an enticing task for an authority on human systems of culture to work out this analogy in specific cases." *Civilization and Its Discontents*, trans. Joan Riviere, 3rd ed. (London: Hogarth Press, 1946), p. 136.

[5] While popular clichés have some interest for the social scientist, they are to be thought of as habits of speech (e.g., "pretty as a picture") rather than as unconsciously selected projections of covert culture, so that mere recurrence of metaphor is not a sufficient criterion. What is to be sought is a metaphor or image that is expressed recurrently in *varying* language and used to describe the same set of phenomena.

[6] Rev. Bro. I. D. Williamson, *The Covenant and Official Magazine of the Grand Lodge of the United States*, I (June 1842), 275–281. The original lecture was delivered on November 18, 1841. A survey of responses to industrialization was made possible by a grant from the Graduate School, University of Minnesota, and by the research assistance of Dr. Donald Houghton.

[7] James H. Lanman, "Railroads in the United States," *Merchants' Magazine*, III (October 1840), 273–295.

[8] *New Harmony Gazette*, II (August 8, 1927), 347. Owen's words are from an address delivered to the Franklin Institute on June 27, 1827.

## Bernard Bowron, Leo Marx, and Arnold Rose

[9] Benjamin R. C. Low, "The Little Boy to the Locomotive," in David L. Cohn, *The Good Old Days* (New York: Simon and Schuster, 1940), p. 188.

[10] It is possible that people betrayed their fear of the machine in casual conversation. But this source of information usually is not available to sociologists, much less to historians. If the sociologist asks people directly about their attitudes toward machines, he is likely to get "rational" answers about how much labor they save, how they provide products and services previously not available, and so on.

[11] Perry Miller, "The Romantic Dilemma in American Nationalism and the Concept of Nature," *Harvard Theological Review*, XLVIII (October 1955), 239–253.

[12] It is interesting that as early as 1881 Dr. George Miller Beard, an American physician, related the anxiety of Americans to the new technology. His pioneering work, *American Nervousness, Its Causes and Consequences* (New York: G. P. Putnam's, 1881), was taken seriously by Freud. See Philip P. Wiener, "G. M. Beard and Freud on 'American Nervousness,'" *Journal of the History of Ideas*, XVII (April 1956), 269–274.

[13] We agree with Henry G. Fairbanks who, in a recent article, disagrees with scholars who regard Hawthorne as a doctrinaire and romantic opponent of science and technology. But, like the writers he criticizes, Mr. Fairbanks tends to misconstrue Hawthorne's aim in mentioning machines at all. Hawthorne was not concerned to convey his opinions about the new technology, but rather to express its meaning, often ambiguous, within the larger pattern of human experience. In doing so, as we have tried to indicate, he revealed contradictions characteristic of American culture generally. See "Hawthorne and the Machine Age," *American Literature*, XXVIII (May 1956), 155–164. For a somewhat different method of interpreting the response of American writers to the onset of industrialism see, for example, Leo Marx, "The Machine in the Garden," *New England Quarterly*, XXIX (March 1956), 27–42; "The Pilot and the Passenger: Landscape Conventions and the Style of *Huckleberry Finn*," *American Literature*, XXVIII (May 1956), 129–146.

# A Southern Mode of the Imagination

W H A T I am about to say will be composed of obscure speculation, mere opinion, and reminiscence verging upon autobiography. But having issued this warning, and given notice to the scholars of American literature that the entire affair will be somewhat unreliable, I must allude to some of the things that I shall not try to discuss. I shall not analyze or "place" any of the southern writers of the period now somewhat misleadingly called the Southern Renaissance. It was more precisely a birth, not a rebirth. The eyes of the world are on William Faulkner; for that reason I shall not talk about him. I take it to be a commonplace of literary history that no writer of Mr. Faulkner's power could emerge from a literary and social vacuum. It is a part of Mr. Faulkner's legend about himself that he did appear, like the warriors of Cadmus, full-grown, out of the unlettered soil of his native state, Mississippi. But we are under no obligation to take his word for it. Two other modern writers of prose fiction, Stark Young and Eudora Welty, quite as gifted as Mr. Faulkner, if somewhat below him in magnitude and power, are also natives of that backward state, where fewer people can read than in any other state in the Union. I shall not pause to explain my paradoxical conviction, shared I believe by Donald Davidson, that the very backwardness of Mississippi, and of the South as a whole, might partially explain the rise of a new literature which has won the attention not only of Americans but of the Western world.

If the Elizabethan age would still be the glory of English literature without Shakespeare, the new literature of the southern states would still be formidable without Faulkner. I have promised not to discuss any one writer in detail, but I shall evoke certain names: Elizabeth Madox Roberts, Robert Penn Warren, Eudora Welty, Stark Young, Du Bose Heyward, Ellen Glasgow, James Branch Cabell, Katherine Anne Porter,

Carson McCullers, Tennessee Williams, Thomas Wolfe, Paul Green, Caroline Gordon, Flannery O'Connor, Truman Capote, Ralph Ellison, John Crowe Ransom, Donald Davidson, Peter Taylor, Andrew Lytle. It is scarcely chauvinism on my part to point out that, with the exception of Fitzgerald and Hemingway, the region north of the Potomac and Ohio rivers has become the stepsister of American fiction. And it has been said so often that I almost believe it, that the American branch of the New Criticism is of southern origin — a distinction about which my own feelings are neutral.

Before I turn to the more speculative part of this discussion, I should like to quote a paragraph written in the Reconstruction period — that is, around 1870 — by a New England novelist who had come to the South as a benign carpetbagger to observe and to improve what he observed. He was John William De Forest, of Connecticut, whose works were almost completely forgotten until about ten years ago. He was not only one of the best American novelists of his time, but a shrewd social commentator, whose dislike of southerners did not prevent him from seeing them more objectively than any other northerner of his time: "Not until Southerners get rid of some of their social vanity, not until they cease talking of themselves in a spirit of self-adulation, not until they drop the idea that they are Romans and must write in the style of Cicero, will they be able to so paint life that the world shall crowd to see the picture. Meanwhile let us pray that a true Southern novelist will soon arise, for he will be able to furnish us vast amusement and some instruction. His day is passing; in another generation his material will be gone; the chivalrous Southron will be as dead as the slavery that created him." It was not until fifty years later that De Forest's demands upon the southern novelist were fulfilled, when the writers whose names I have listed began to appear. My own contemporaries called the nineteenth-century Ciceronian southern style "Confederate prose," and we avoided it more assiduously than sin. Of a southern woman novelist of the 1860's, it was said that her heroines had swallowed an unabridged dictionary.

My reason for adopting here the causerie instead of the formal discourse is quite simple. I have no talent for research; or at any rate I am like the man who, upon being asked whether he could play the violin, answered that he didn't know because he had never tried. Apart from inadequate scholarship, it would be improper of me to pretend to an objectivity, which I do not feel, in the recital of certain events, in which

I have been told that I played a small part. Thirty-five years ago, none of us — and by us I mean not only the group of poets who with unintentional prophecy styled themselves the "Fugitives," but also our contemporaries in other southern states — was conscious of playing any part at all. But I ought not to speak for my contemporaries, most of whom are still living and able to talk. The essays and books about us that have begun to appear give me a little less than the shock of recognition. If one does not recognize oneself, one may not unreasonably expect to recognize one's friends. One writer, John Bradbury, in a formidable book of some three hundred pages entitled *The Fugitives*, says that John Crowe Ransom taught his students, of whom I had the honor to be one, the knowledge of good and evil. I don't recognize in this role my old friend and early master; I surmise that he has found it no less disconcerting than I do. Our initiation into the knowledge of good and evil, like everybody else's, must have been at birth; our later improvement in this field of knowledge, haphazard and extracurricular. John Ransom taught us — Robert Penn Warren, Cleanth Brooks, Andrew Lytle, and myself — Kantian aesthetics and a philosophical dualism, tinged with Christian theology, but ultimately derived from the *Nicomachean Ethics*. I allude to my own education not because it was unique, but because it was the education of my generation in the South. But we said at that time very little about the South, an anomalous reticence in a group of men who later became notoriously sectional in point of view.

We knew we were southerners, but this was a matter of plain denotation: just as we knew that some people were Yankees; or we knew that there were people whom —if we saw them — we would think of as Yankees; we might even have said, but only among ourselves, you understand: "He's a Yankee." Brainard Cheney told me years ago that when he was a small boy in southern Georgia, down near the Okefenokee Swamp, the rumor spread that some Yankees were coming to town. All the little boys gathered in the courthouse square to see what Yankees looked like. This was about 1910. My boyhood, in the border state of Kentucky, was evidently more cosmopolitan. There were a few northerners, no doubt; there were a few elderly gentlemen who had been southern Unionists, or homemade Yankees, as they were discourteously described, who had fought in the Federal Army. One of these, old Mr. Crabb, white-haired, beak-nosed, and distinguished, frequently passed our house on his morning walk. He had an empty sleeve, and my mother said he had got his arm shot off at the Battle of Gettysburg. I knew that my grandfather had been in Pickett's charge, and I wondered idly whether he had shot it off. I do not remember whether I wished that he had.

This was our long moment of innocence, which I tried to recover in a poem many years later. And for men of my age, who missed World War I by a few months, it was a new Era of Good Feeling between the sections. Some time before 1914 the North had temporarily stopped trying to improve us, or had at least paused to think about something else. Having just missed being sent to France in the A.E.F., I came to Vanderbilt University from a rural-smalltown society that had only a superficial Victorian veneer pasted over what was still an eighteenth-century way of living. It has been said that Kentucky seceded in 1865. In my boyhood, and even much later, Kentucky was more backward and southern, socially and economically, than Tennessee or North Carolina. This preindustrial society meant, for people living in it, that one's identity had everything to do with land and material property, at a definite place, and very little to do with money. It was better for a person, however impoverished, of my name, to be identified with Tate's Creek Pike, in Fayette County, than to be the richest man in town without the identification of place. This was simple and innocent; it had little to do with what the English call *class*. Yet from whatever point of view one may look at it, it will in the end lead us towards the secret of what was rather grandiosely called, by the late W. J. Cash, the Southern Mind.

If I may bring to bear upon it an up-to-date and un-southern adjective, it was an extroverted mind not much given to introspection. (I do not say meditation, which is something quite different.) Such irony as this mind was capable of was distinctly romantic; it came out of the sense of dislocated external relations: because people were not *where* they ought to be they could not be *who* they ought to be, for men had missed their proper role, which was to be attached to a place. Mr. Faulkner's lawyer Benbow and the Compson family, in *The Sound and the Fury*, are people of this sort; I know of no better examples than Andrew Lytle's Jack Cropleigh, in his novel *The Velvet Horn*, and the narrator of his powerful short story "Mister McGregor." It is the irony of time and place out of joint. It was provincial or, if you will, ignorant of the world. It was the irony of social discrepancies, not the tragic irony of the peripety, or of interior change. It is premodern; it can be found in the early books of Ellen Glasgow and James Branch Cabell, as different at the surface as their books may appear to be.

But with the end of World War I a change came about that literary historians have not yet explained; whether we shall ever understand it one cannot say. Southern literature in the second half of this century may cease to engage the scholarly imagination; the subject may eventually become academic, and buried with the last dissertation. Back in the 1930's I wrote for the tenth anniversary issue of the *Virginia Quarterly Review* an essay entitled "The Profession of Letters in the South," which glanced at a possible explanation by analogy to another literary period. If I refer to it here I hope I shall not seem to be taking advantage of an opportunity to call attention to myself. So far as that old essay is concerned, other persons have already done this for me. When I look at the index of a work of contemporary criticism (I always look there first), and see my name, I get a little nervous because the following passage has a two-to-one chance over anything else I have written to be quoted: "The considerable achievement of Southerners in modern American letters must not beguile us into too much hope for the future. The Southern novelist has left his mark upon the age; but it is of the age. From the peculiarly historical consciousness of the Southern writer has come good work of a special order; but the focus of this consciousness is quite temporary. It has made possible the curious burst of intelligence that we get at a crossing of the ways, not unlike, on an infinitesimal scale, the outburst of poetic genius at the end of the sixteenth century when commercial England had already begun to crush feudal England. The Histories and Tragedies of Shakespeare record the death of the old regime, and Doctor Faustus gives up feudal order for world power."

My purpose in quoting the passage — I marvel that prose so badly written could have been quoted so much — is not to approve of the approbation it has received, but to point out that whatever rightness it may have is not right enough. It says nothing about the particular quality of the southern writers of our time.

The quality that I have in mind, none too clearly, makes its direct impact upon the reader, even if he be the foreign reader: he knows that he is reading a southern book. But this explains nothing, for a quality can only be pointed to or shared, not defined. Let me substitute for the word "quality" the phrase "mode of discourse."

The traditional southern mode of discourse presupposes somebody at the other end silently listening: it is the rhetorical mode. Its historical rival is the dialectical mode, or the give and take between two minds, even if one mind, like the mind of Socrates, prevail at the end. The southerner has never been a dialectician. The antebellum southerner quoted Aristotle in defense of slavery, but Plato, the dialectician, was not opposed to the "peculiar institution," and he could have been cited with equal effect in support of the South Carolinian daydream of a Greek democracy. Aristotle was chosen by the South for good reason: although the Stagirite (as the southerners called him) was a metaphysician, the South liked the deductive method, if its application were not too abstruse, and nobody could quarrel with the arrangement, in the order of importance, of the three great Aristotelian treatises on man in society: the *Nicomachean Ethics*, the *Politics*, and the *Rhetoric*. Aristotle assumed first principles from which he — and the old southerners after him — could make appropriate deductions about the inequalities of men. Plato reached first principles by means of dialogue which can easily become subjective: the mind talking to itself. The southerner always talks to somebody else, and this somebody else, after varying intervals, is given his turn; but the conversation is always among rhetoricians; that is to say, the typical southern conversation is not going anywhere, it is not about anything. *It is about the people who are talking*, even if they never refer to themselves, which they usually do not, since conversation is only an expression of manners, the purpose of which is to make everybody happy. This may be the reason why northerners and other uninitiated persons find the alternating, or contrapuntal, conversation of southerners fatiguing. Educated northerners like their conversation to be about ideas.

The foregoing, rather too broad distinction between dialectic and rhetoric is not meant to convey the impression that no southerner of the past or the present was ever given to thought; nor do I wish to imply that New Englanders were so busy thinking that they wholly neglected that form of rhetoric which may be described as the manners of men talking in society. Emerson said that the "scholar is man thinking." Had southerners of that era taken seriously the famous lecture entitled "The American Scholar," they might have replied by saying that the gentleman is man talking. The accomplished Christian gentleman of the old South was the shadow, attenuated by evangelical Calvinism, of his Renaissance spiritual ancestor, who had been the creation of the rhetorical tradition, out of Aristotle through Cicero, distilled finally by Castiglione. By contrast, the New England sage, embodied in Ralph Waldo Emerson, took seriously what has come to be known since the Industrial Revolution as the life of the mind: an activity a little apart from life, and perhaps leading to the fashionable alienation of the "intellectual" of our time. The protective withdrawal of the New England sage into dialectical truth lurks back of Emerson's famous definition of manners as the "invention of a wise man to keep a fool at a distance." (There is little doubt of the part Emerson conceived himself as playing.) The notorious lack of self-consciousness of the antebellum southerner made it almost impossible for him to define anything; least of all could he imagine the impropriety of a definition of manners. Yet had a southern contemporary of Emerson decided to argue the question, he might have retorted that manners are not *in*ventions, but *con*ventions tacitly agreed upon to protect the fool from consciousness of his folly. I do not wholly subscribe to this southern view; there is to be brought against it Henry Adams' unkind portrait of Rooney Lee, a son of Robert E. Lee, who soon became a Confederate officer. The younger Lee, said Adams, when they were fellow students at Harvard, seemed to have only the habit of command, and no brains. (Adams didn't say it quite so rudely, but that is what it came to.) Rooney Lee, like his famous father, was a man of action, action through the habit of command being a form of rhetoric: he acted upon the assumptions of identification by place. The Lee identification, the whole Virginian myth of the rooted man, was the model of the more homely mystique of Tate's Creek Pike in the frontier state of Kentucky, whose citizens the Virginians thought were all Davy Crocketts — a frontiersman who described himself as "half-horse and half-alligator." Virginia was the model for the entire upper South.

Northern historians were for years puzzled that Lee and the southern yeoman farmer fought for the South, since neither had any interest in slavery. The question was usually put in this form: Why did Lee, who never owned a slave and detested slavery, become the leader of the slavocracy? Because he was a rhetorician who would have flunked Henry Adams' examination as miserably as his son. A southern dialectician, could he be imagined in Lee's predicament, would have tossed his loyalties back and forth and come out with an abstraction called Justice, and he would have fought in the Federal Army or not at all. The record seems to indicate that the one dialectical abstraction that Lee entertained came to him after the war: the idea of constitutional government, for which in retrospect he considered that he had fought. Perhaps he did fight for it; yet I have the temerity to doubt his word. He fought for the local community which he could not abstract into fragments. He was in the position of a man who is urged by an outsider to repudiate his family because a cousin is an embezzler, or of the man who is tempted to justify his own ill-use of his brother by pretending that his entire family is a bad lot. I trust that in this analogy it is clear that the brother is the Negro slave.

What Robert E. Lee has to do with southern literature is a question that might at this point quite properly be asked, as I can assure you it has already confronted me. Lee has a good deal to do with it, if we are going to look at southern literature as the rhetorical expression of a Southern Mind. But even to be conscious of the possibility of a Southern Mind could lead us into a mode of discourse radically different from that of the rhetorician. We are well on the way toward dialectics. If we say that the old southern mind was rhetorical we must add that our access to it must be through its public phase, which was almost exclusively political. I do not believe that the antebellum southerners, being wholly committed to the rhetorical mode, were capable of the elementary detachment that has permitted modern southerners to discern the significance of that commitment, and to relate it to other modes of discourse. For the rhetorical mode is related to the myth-making faculty, and the mythopoeic mind assumes that certain great typical actions embody human truth. The critical detachment which permits me to apply this commonplace to the Southern Mind would not, I believe, have been within the grasp of better intellects than mine in the South up to World War I.

It has been said that the failure of the old southern leaders to understand the northern mind (which was then almost entirely the New England mind) was a failure of intelligence. In view of the task which the South had set for itself — that is, the preservation of local self-government within a framework of republican federalism — the charge is no doubt true. The old southerners, being wholly committed to the rhetoric of politics, could not come to grips with the dynamic forces in the North that were rapidly making the exclusively political solution of their problem obsolete: they did not understand economics. The dramatis persona was supported by what W. J. Cash called, in a neo-Spenglerian phrase, the "proto-Dorian" myth. This persona was that of the agrarian patriot, a composite image of Cincinnatus dropping the plough for the sword, and of Cicero leaving his rhetorical studies to apply them patriotically to the prosecution of Catiline. The center round which the southern political imagination gravitated was perhaps even smaller than the communities of which the South was an aggregate. In the first place, that aggregate was not a whole; and in the second, it would follow that the community itself was not a whole. The South was an aggregate of farms and plantations, presided over by our composite agrarian hero, Cicero Cincinnatus. I can think of no better image for what the South was before 1860, and for what it largely still was until about 1914, than that of the old gentleman in Kentucky who sat every afternoon in his front yard under an old sugar tree, reading Cicero's Letters to Atticus. When the hands suckering the tobacco in the adjoining field needed orders, he kept his place in the book with his forefinger, walked out into the field, gave the orders, and then returned to his reading under the shade of the tree. He was also a lawyer, and occasionally he went to his office, which was over the feed-store in the county seat, a village with a population of about 400 people.

The center of the South, then, was the family, no less for Robert E. Lee than for the people on Tate's Creek Pike; for Virginia was a great aggregate of families that through almost infinite ramifications of relationship was almost one family. Such a society could not be anything but political. The virtues cherished under such a regime were almost exclusively social and moral, with none of the intensively cultivated divisions of intellectual labor which are necessary to a flowering of the arts, whether literary or plastic. It is thus significant that the one original art of the South was domestic architecture, as befitted a family-centered society. It has been frequently noted that the reason why the South did not produce a great antebellum literature was the lack of cities as cultural centers. This was indeed a lack; but it is more important to understand why the cultural center was missing. The South did not want cultural centers; it preferred the plantation center. William Gilmore Simms argued repeatedly in the 1850's that no exclusively agrarian society had produced a great literature. Was this a failure of intelligence? I think not, if we look at the scene from the inside. After Archimedes had observed that, had he a fulcrum big enough, he could move the world, was it a failure of the Greek intelligence that it did not at once construct such a fulcrum? Were the Greek philosophers less intelligent than Albert Einstein and Professor Teller, who found a way not only to move the world but perhaps to destroy it? But the plantation myth — and I use the word "myth" not to indicate a fantasy, but a reality — if Greek at all, was the limited Spartan myth. It was actually nearer to Republican Rome, a society which, like the South, was short in metaphysicians and great poets, and long in moralists and rhetoricians.

Lionel Trilling has said somewhere that the great writer, the spokesman of a culture, carries in himself the fundamental dialectic of that culture: the deeper conflicts of which his contemporaries are perhaps only dimly aware. There is a valuable truth in this observation. The inner strains, stresses, tensions, the shocked self-consciousness of a highly differentiated and complex society, issue in the dialectic of the high arts. The Old South, I take it, was remarkably free of this self-consciousness; the strains that it felt were external. And I surmise that had our southern persona, our friend Cicero Cincinnatus, been much less simple than he was, the distractions of the sectional agitation nevertheless were so engrossing that they would have postponed almost indefinitely that self-examination which is the beginning, if not of wisdom, then at least of the arts of literature. When one is under attack, it is inevitable that he should put not only his best foot forward, but both feet, even if one of them rests upon the neck of a Negro slave. One then attributes to "those people over there" (the phrase that General Lee used to designate the Federal Army) all the evil of his own world. The defensive southerner said that *if only* "those people over there" would let us alone, the vast Sabine Farm of the South (where men read Horace but did not think it necessary to be Horace) would perpetuate itself forever.

The complicated reasons for this southern isolationism were, as I have tried to indicate, partly internal and partly external; but whatever the causes, the pertinent fact for any approach to the modern literary renaissance is that the South was more isolated from 1865 to about 1920 than it had been before 1865. It was the isolationism of economic prostration, defeat, and inverted pride. And the New South of Henry W. Grady's rhetoric was just as isolated and provincial as the Old South of Thomas Nelson Page. For Grady's New South, the complete answer was the factory, and it was put into the less than distinguished verse of "The Song of the Chattahoochee," by Sidney Lanier. I venture to think that there was more to be said for Page's Old South, even if we agree that, like Grady's New South, it was unreal: I take it that a pleasant dream is to be preferred to an actuality which imitates a nightmare. Neither the unreal dream nor the actual nightmare could lead to the conception of a complete society. If we want proof of this, we need only to look at the South today.

I should like now to return to the inadequacy of my speculations, a quarter-century ago, on the reasons for the sudden rise of the new southern literature — a literature which, I have been told often enough to authorize the presumption, is now the center of American literature. (I do not insist upon this.) Social change must have had something to do with it, but this does not explain it. I do not hope to explain it now. I wish only to add a consideration which I have already adumbrated. If it seems narrow, technical, and even academically tenuous, it is probably not less satisfactory than the conventional attribution of literary causation to what is called the historical factor. No doubt, without this factor, without the social change, the new literature could not have appeared. One can nevertheless imagine the same consciousness of the same change around 1920, without the appearance of any literature whatever. Social change may produce a great social scientist, like the late Howard W. Odum, of North Carolina. Social upheaval will not in itself produce a poet like John Crowe Ransom or a novelist like William Faulkner.

There was another kind of change taking place at the same time, and it was decisive. The old southern rhetor, the speaker who was eloquent before the audience but silent in himself, had always had at his disposal a less formal version of the rhetorical mode of discourse than the political oration. Was it not said that southerners were the best storytellers in America? Perhaps they still are. The tall tale was the staple of southern conversation. Augustus Baldwin Longstreet's *Georgia Scenes* is a collection of tall tales written by an accomplished gentleman for other accomplished gentlemen; this famous book is in no sense folk literature, or an expression of V. L. Parrington's democratic spirit. It is the art of the rhetorician applied to the anecdote, to the small typical action resembling the medieval *exemplum*, and it verges upon myth — the minor secular myth which just succeeds in skirting round the superhuman myth of religion.

We have got something like this myth in *Huckleberry Finn*, which I take to be the first modern novel by a southerner. We are now prepared by depth psychology to describe the action of *Huckleberry Finn* as not only typical, but as archetypal. What concerns me about it, for my purposes, is not whether it is a great novel (perhaps the *scale* of the action and the *range* of consciousness are too small for a great novel); what concerns me is the mode of its progression, for this mode is no longer the mode of rhetoric, the mode of the speaker reporting in person an argument or an action in which he is not dramatically involved. The action is generated inside the characters: there is internal dialogue, a conflict within the self. Mark Twain seems not to have been wholly conscious of what he had done, for he never did it again.

Ernest Hemingway has said that the modern American novel comes out of *Huckleberry Finn*, and William Faulkner has paid a similar tribute. But this is not quite to the point.

Mark Twain was a forerunner who set an example which was not necessarily an influence. The feature of *Huckleberry Finn* which I have tried to discern, the shift from the rhetorical mode to the dialectical mode, had to be rediscovered by the twentieth-century novelists of the South. The example of Mark Twain was not quite fully developed and clean in outline. None of the recent essays on *Huckleberry Finn* — by Lionel Trilling and T. S. Eliot, for example — has been able to approach the end of the novel without embarrassment. Huck himself is a dramatic dialectician; Tom Sawyer, who reappears at the end and resolves the action externally with the preposterous "liberation" of Nigger Jim, who is already free, is a ham southern rhetorician of the old school. He imposes his "style" upon a reality which has no relation to it, without perception of the ironic "other possible case" which is essential to the dramatic dialectic of the arts of fiction.

Here, as I come to the end of these speculations, I must go off again into surmises and guesses. What brought about the shift from rhetoric to dialectic? The southern fictional dialectic of our time is still close to the traditional subject matter of the old rhetoric — the tall tale, the anecdote, the archetypal story. The New England dialectic of the Transcendentalists, from which Hawthorne had to protect himself by remaining aloof, tended to take flight into the synthesis of pure abstraction, in which the inner struggle is resolved in an idea. The southern dramatic dialectic of our time is being resolved, as in the novels of William Faulkner, in action. The short answer to our question How did this change come about? is that the South not only re-entered the world with World War I; it looked round and saw for the first time since about 1830 that the Yankees were not to blame for everything. It looks like a simple discovery, and it was; that is why it was difficult to make. The southern legend, as Malcolm Cowley has called it, of defeat and heroic frustration was taken over by a dozen or more first-rate writers and converted into a universal myth of the human condition. W. B. Yeats' great epigram points to the nature of the shift from melodramatic rhetoric to the dialectic of tragedy: "Out of the quarrel with others we make rhetoric; out of the quarrel with ourselves, poetry."

# The Vernacular Tradition in American Literature

From the beginning writers have had much less trouble finding an American subject than a mode appropriate to its expression. In 1620 William Bradford recognized an inevitable subject even before he stepped off the *Mayflower*. Gazing toward the forbidding shore he asked, in effect, "What is to be the fate of civilized man in this prehistoric landscape?" Later the question was reformulated. Writers like James Fenimore Cooper, Nathaniel Hawthorne, and Henry James asked, "What does it mean to be an American?" Around this theme they elaborated an infinitely complex art. To get at the meaning of American experience they submitted the native character to the test of Europe. They created a drama of cultural contrast. What gave their work its American stamp was their vivid awareness of certain cultural differences.

And yet, having said all that, we are not satisfied that we have settled the old problem: what *is* different, after all, about American literature? Granted that the "international theme" is American, can a particular subject ever make for a lasting distinction between one national literature and another? If we ask what is different about German writing, we know very well the first answer to expect: it is written in German. But the language of Cooper is not all that different from the language of Scott, and with Cooper's generation the boundary between British and American literature remains uncertain. When we come to "Song of Myself" or *Huckleberry Finn*, however, the line is much more distinct. That may explain why Walt Whitman and Mark Twain are so widely respected, nowadays, as the two great seminal figures of modern American writing. They establish, once and for all, the literary usefulness of the native idiom. With it they fashioned a vernacular mode or, if you will, a national style. This style marks a major difference between English and American literature, and it is the one I propose to consider here.

However, I do not mean to suggest, as many contemporary critics do, a violent opposition between two strains in American writing. In *The Complex Fate*, for example, Marius Bewley deplores the influence of Whitman and Twain, seeing in it a narrow chauvinism, a kind of literary isolationism in marked contrast to the scope and subtlety of Hawthorne and James. My own view is quite different. The style of Whitman and Twain seems to me to serve as a measure, even an embodiment, of the very cultural differences that preoccupy Hawthorne and James. The image of America that we find in the work of Hawthorne and James, though depicted from another angle, is really the same image we find in Whitman and Twain. All these writers were concerned with what it means to be an American; all felt — though in different degrees to be sure — the tension between the possibilities and the dangers of the new society. And not one was a narrow chauvinist. Much of Mr. Bewley's contempt for the work of Whitman and Twain derives, I believe, from a mistaken conception of the vernacular tradition.

To see what is contained in that tradition — if the word can be used to describe so rebellious a state of mind — let us first consider Walt Whitman.

When Whitman's first poems were taking shape, America was preoccupied with the slavery problem — another rather special American subject. Whitman's contemporaries turned out a large volume of poetry about slavery. Here is a fair sample by the most popular poet of the age, Henry Wadsworth Longfellow:

THE SLAVE IN THE DISMAL SWAMP

In dark fens of the Dismal Swamp
    The hunted Negro lay;
He saw the fire of the midnight camp,
And heard at times a horse's tramp
    And a bloodhound's distant bay.

Where will-o'-the-wisps and glow-worms shine,
    In bulrush and in brake;
Where waving mosses shroud the pine,
And the cedar grows, and the poisonous vine
    Is spotted like the snake;

Where hardly a human foot could pass,
    Or a human heart would dare,
On the quaking turf of the green morass
He crouched in the rank and tangled grass,
    Like a wild beast in his lair.

A poor old slave, infirm and lame;
    Great scars deformed his face;
On his forehead he bore the brand of shame,
And the rags, that hid his mangled frame,
    Were the livery of disgrace.

All things above were bright and fair,
    All things were glad and free;
Lithe squirrels darted here and there,
And wild birds filled the echoing air
    With songs of Liberty!

On him alone was the doom of pain,
    From the morning of his birth;
On him alone the curse of Cain
Fell, like a flail on the garnered grain,
    And struck him to the earth!

Now let us set beside Longfellow's poem these lines from Section 10 of "Song of Myself":

The runaway slave came to my house and stopt outside,
I heard his motions crackling the twigs of the woodpile,
Through the swung half-door of the kitchen I saw him limpsy
    and weak,
And went where he sat on a log and led him in and assured him,
And brought water and fill'd a tub for his sweated body
    and bruis'd feet,
And gave him a room that enter'd from my own, and gave
    him some coarse clean clothes,
And remember perfectly well his revolving eyes and
    his awkwardness,
And remember putting plasters on the galls of his neck and ankles;
He staid with me a week before he was recuperated and
    pass'd north,
I had him sit next me at table, my fire-lock lean'd in the corner.

One might easily use this comparison to demonstrate the difference between good and bad poetry. But that is not my purpose. The point is that Longfellow's poem was written in a shopworn literary language then still thought to be poetic in America. To get near his subject Whitman felt it necessary to dispense with the entire apparatus of such poetry: not only the diction, but the meter and rhyme as well. Indeed, he went further than that; he dispensed with the poet. By this I mean that in Longfellow's poem the traditional calling of the man of letters is obtrusive. The words carry our thoughts not to a slave in a swamp, but to a man using the special equipment reserved for men of letters when they write poems. In Whitman's lines, on the contrary, the poet disappears. Like Huckleberry Finn, the "I" of Whitman's poem is at once the hero and the poet. That is to say, both Whitman and Twain resorted to the old device of the persona — the first-person narrator; and the result was a new sort of immediacy. The American subject was brought up closer than it ever had been before. If the device was old, the particular persona was new. Whitman's hero is the product of a new sort of culture, and appropriately enough, he speaks a new language.

There is no need to insist that Whitman's language literally was the spoken language of his time. Indeed, we can be sure that it was not. What matters is that at his best he succeeds in creating the illusion that a certain kind of man is speaking. In his case the illusion probably stems from the cadence, and the absence of traditional meter and rhyme, rather than from the diction. In any event, his poetry is nearer to the spoken language of Americans than our poetry had ever got before. I do not mean to imply that there is any absolute value in using the spoken language in poetry. That depends upon the particular aims of the writer. But given Whitman's problem, his desire to convey ideas and emotions for which the standard manner of poetry was inappropriate, the vernacular was a source of immense vitality. To see this one only has to compare Whitman with Longfellow:

> In dark fens of the Dismal Swamp
> The hunted Negro lay;

> I heard his motions crackling the twigs of the woodpile,
> Through the swung half-door of the kitchen I saw him limpsy
>     and weak.

What is most striking here is the extraordinary sense of immediacy that the vernacular mode conveys. We see Longfellow's subject through a murk of tired images: "like a wild beast in his lair"; to Whitman he is a man with "sweated body and bruis'd feet." Everyone knows that the more specific image is likely to be the more evocative. But why does one writer seize it while another avoids it? Longfellow says of the slave, "great scars deformed his face." Whitman says, "And remember putting plasters on the galls of his neck and ankles." The fact is that Whitman imagines a completely different relation to the Negro, and it takes us back of language to something more fundamental, to the kind of persona Whitman felt impelled to employ. He is a man "hankering, gross, mystical, nude." He is aggressively ungenteel, and he thinks about the slave in a very different way than Longfellow does.

> In all people I see myself, none more and not one a barley-corn less,
> And the good or bad I say of myself I say of them.

Given this sort of hero, Whitman can introduce details once thought to lie outside the bounds of respectable poetry. Among other things, the vernacular made possible a long step forward in the candor of modern writing, as in Whitman's daring treatment of physical love.

There is another kind of immediacy that results from the use of the vernacular narrator. That is the way meaning comes to us here by what Whitman called "indirection" rather than by use of personification, abstraction, or, for that matter, direct statement. Longfellow finds it necessary to tell us of the slave, "on him alone the curse of Cain / Fell . . ." Whitman avoids comment. He describes the relations between his mythic hero and the slave, and then at the end he casually mentions the gun in the corner. The image *is* the meaning; it is a perfect expression of the democratic hero's relaxed but militant egalitarianism. Right here, incidentally, Whitman anticipates that mode of ironic understatement that was to become a dominant accent of twentieth-century American poetry.

But it must not be thought that a mere technical device enables Whitman to convey so much in so little. If he does not need to proclaim the solidarity between the two men, it is because he can describe it so vividly. That is, the style has been called forth as a fitting expression of something else, an ideal human situation, indeed a kind of model society. The slave and the hero exemplify the egalitarian community of Whitman's imagination. It is a society that stands in relation to the actual society as the vernacular language to the stock elevated language of poetry. All of Whitman's poetry exalts this conception. It is the same sort of community, as a matter of fact, that Mark Twain later sets up aboard a Mississippi raft. Here is the core of the American vernacular. It is not simply a style, but a style with a politics in view. The style is a vehicle for the affirmation of an egalitarian faith so radical that we can scarcely credit it today. It sweeps aside received notions of class and status — and literature. In Whitman's mind all of these inherited forms are identified with Europe.

This is where the problem of chauvinism arises. There can be no question that Whitman celebrates America at the expense of Europe and the past. Of course the notion that stylistic elegance was the literary counterpart of European political oppression arose in America long before Whitman. In 1787, for example, Royall Tyler had expressed this prejudice in his play *The Contrast*; speaking of aristocratic titles, ornaments, and manners, Tyler said:

> Our free-born ancestors such arts despis'd;
> Genuine sincerity alone they priz'd;
> Their minds, with honest emulation fir'd,
> To solid good — not ornament —aspir'd . . .

Constance Rourke has shown how this "contrast theme" runs through our tradition of native humor. By Whitman's time the animus against a European style of life had been strengthened by the repeated European sneer against the crudities of American culture. To establish his identity the American is impelled to defy tradition:

> I too am not a bit tamed, I too am untranslatable,
> I sound my barbaric yawp over the roofs of the world.

Now granted that as a view of human experience there are serious limitations to this Whitmanian yawp, it does not seem to me that chauvinism is one of them. Whitman does not celebrate the vernacular hero because he is an American, but the other way around. It is because he is "untranslatable" that the American must be allowed to have his say in his own idiom. He is a new kind of man, and the social conditions which brought him into being may (at least theoretically) be reproduced anywhere. In reality the vernacular character is of an international cast. Hence Whitman's attitude is not to be confused with what Mr. Bewley calls "literary isolationism." To see that, one has only to read what Whitman had to say later when he thought that America was betraying the egalitarian ideal. Like Hawthorne and James, he put his country to a severe test. It was not the same test they used, but it was exacting nevertheless. In point of fact it proved finally to be too exacting.

Curiously enough, Whitman represents that side of the vernacular tradition which drew its inspiration from Europe in the first place. We know that he was inspired by Emerson, who recognized what American poets needed to do, even if he was not the man to do it. And behind Emerson, of course, we are led directly to England, and the revolution in poetry Wordsworth had announced fifty-five years before *Leaves of Grass*, in the Preface to the second edition of *Lyrical Ballads* in 1800. I do not mean to imply that in Whitman we have a simple case of delayed literary influence, of what is sometimes called "cultural lag." Whitman went much further than Wordsworth, and he did so largely because American conditions imparted a special intensity to Wordsworthian doctrine. Was it a good thing for poets to escape the refinements of civilization, to catch impulses from the vernal wood? Then how lucky to be an American poet! Was it true that Wordsworth's country neighbors spoke a language more vivid and precise, hence more poetic than the language of cultivated men? Again, this idea touched an American in ways unimaginable to an English poet. In America the exaltation of what Wordsworth called "humble and rustic life" could not be received as a mere program for poetry. By Whitman's time it had already become something like a national ethos. In the defiant accent of Whitman's hero we recognize how far we have come from Wordsworth's simple peasants.

> Who goes there? hankering, gross, mystical, nude;
> How is it I extract strength from the beef I eat?
> What is a man anyhow? what am I? what are you?
>
> . . . . . . . . . . . . . . .
>
> I wear my hat as I please indoors or out.
> Why should I pray? why should I venerate and be ceremonious?
> Having pried through the strata, analyzed to a hair, counsel'd
>     with doctors and calculated close,
> I find no sweeter fat than sticks to my own bones.

This boast is a self-portrait of Whitman's democratic man. It is a revealing and ironic fact that the average American reader preferred Longfellow's poetry. Whether this had anything to do with Whitman's style, his success or failure in catching the popular tone of voice, is a question that is probably unanswerable. But in any event Whitman was never persuaded that he was speaking the truly distinctive native idiom, and what is more, he had a good idea where that idiom was likely to arise. "Today," he wrote in 1871, "doubtless, the infant genius of American poetic expression . . . lies sleeping far away, happily unrecognized and uninjur'd by the coteries, the art-writers, the talkers and critics of the saloons, or the lecturers in the colleges — lies sleeping, aside, unrecking itself, in some western idiom . . ."

This brings me to Mark Twain and the other or frontier side of the vernacular tradition. His mature style, the very essence of his humor, is grounded in a sensitivity to language as an index of cultural difference. He felt that the distinguishing trait of the American story was its emphasis upon *manner* rather than matter. That also explains why Mark Twain was so exasperated by the work of James Fenimore Cooper. For him reading Cooper was like listening to a tone-deaf man trying to sing. "He keeps near the tune," said Twain, "but it is *not* the tune. . . . you perceive what he is intending to say, but you also perceive that he doesn't *say* it." In other words Cooper, like Longfellow, had spoiled a fine subject by encasing it in a foreign idiom. As it happens it was Twain's chosen subject, so he had a special reason for wanting to dispose of Cooper. Fitness of language to subject was a cardinal point in the literary ethic of Mark Twain. He felt that Cooper achieved his blurred effect by virtue of his unfailing instinct for the *approximate* word. As his best work suggests, the *precise* word for Twain was the word spoken by his native hero himself.

Twain's feeling for language was in large measure derived from the oral tradition of the West. The frontiersman was a celebrated boaster. He screamed his barbaric yawp to call attention to his strength, and his many triumphs over nature. The vocabulary of the boast was itself a form of triumph. He used it to display his dexterity and ingenuity with language: "Mister . . . I can whip my weight in wild cats, and ride straight thro' a crab apple orchard on a flash of lightening — clear meat axe disposition — the best man, if I an't, I wish I may be tetotaciously exfluncated." The western man's idiom made him conspicuous, and sometimes it made him feel a fool. Actually, he was sensitive about it, and his tall tale was in part an effort to get his own back from those who mocked his barbaric speech. We see this clearly in T. B. Thorpe's classic, "The Big Bear of Arkansas" (1841) — a story which belongs to the long line of American hunting fantasies which include Melville's *Moby Dick*, Faulkner's "The Bear," and Hemingway's *Old Man and the Sea*. Here the western narrator introduces his tale with a brief account of his visit to the big city, from which he is returning. There he had met some gentlemen who interrogated him about his home state, Arkansas. But they did not speak his language, and when they asked him about "game" in Arkansas he mistook them and told about "poker, and high-low-jack." They laughed at him, and called him green. "Strangers," he says he told them, "if you'd asked me *how we got our meat* in Arkansaw, I'd a told you at once . . . Game, indeed, that's what city folks call it . . ." With this prelude, he launches his boastful story. Of course he tells it in the same vernacular idiom that had marked him for a rustic dolt in the eyes of gentlemen. But he has learned that his speech is his identity, and now he will use it to glorify himself at the expense of those who patronize him. Here again is the hostility, the defiance of what pretends to be a superior culture that so often animates the vernacular style.

In *Huckleberry Finn* Mark Twain exploits similar misunderstandings on the part of his western hero for similar purposes. For example, in reporting the king's funeral oration, Huck says that he "slobbers out a speech, all full of tears and flapdoodle, about its being a sore trial for him and his poor brother to lose the *diseased*, and to miss seeing *diseased* alive." Clearly, this joke has two edges. We are intended to laugh at Huck's ignorance, to be sure; the real butt, however, is the pompous euphemism, the respectable burial rhetoric which he does not recognize for what it is. This is a minor example of the satiric device that Mark Twain uses throughout. In the magnificent description of the Grangerford house he turns it against all the pretensions of refinement associated with the sort of people Huck calls the "quality." He has never been in such a nice house before, and he is impressed. He admires everything from the brass door knob to Emmeline Grangerford's poetry. But at the same time his keen eye makes it possible for us to see how spurious it all is: "On the table in the middle of the room was a kind of a lovely crockery basket that had apples and oranges and peaches and grapes piled up in it, which was much redder and yellower and prettier than real ones is, but they warn't real because you could see where pieces had got chipped off and showed the white chalk, or whatever it was, underneath."

Huck is less certain about the pictures on the walls: "They was different from any pictures I ever see before — blacker, mostly, than is common. One was a woman in a slim black dress, belted small under the armpits, with bulges like a cabbage in the middle of the sleeves, and a large black scoop-shovel bonnet with a black veil, and white slim ankles crossed about with black tape, and very wee black slippers, like a chisel, and she was leaning pensive on a tombstone on her right elbow, under a weeping willow, and her other hand hanging down her side holding a white hand-kerchief and a reticule, and underneath the picture it said 'Shall I Never See Thee More Alas.' " In conclusion, Huck says: "These was all nice pictures, I reckon, but I didn't somehow seem to take to them, because if ever I was down a little they always give me the fan-tods." (When reading these words to a European audience one feels the need to provide a gloss on "fan-tods." Not that Americans necessarily can define the word with precision. It is not even to be found in the *Dictionary of Americanisms*. But a native audience can be relied on to get the point.) The passage contains the recurrent pattern of the book: Huck knows how he is supposed to feel about many things, but he cannot always feel that way.

Much the same thing happens to his feelings about Jim and obedience to the laws enforcing the slave system. He knows that he should pray for divine help to return Jim to his "rightful owner," and occasionally this knowledge takes possession of his will, as in the moral crisis of the book — when he writes to Miss Watson to tell her of Jim's presence. But having written the letter, Huck says: "[I] got to thinking over our trip down the river; and I see Jim before me all the time: in the day and in the night-time, sometimes moonlight, sometimes storms, and we a-floating along, talking and singing and laughing. But somehow I couldn't seem to strike no places to harden me against him, but only the other kind. I'd see him standing my watch on top of his'n, 'stead of calling me, so I could go on sleeping; and see him how glad he was when I come back out of the fog . . . and at last I struck the time I saved him by telling the men we had smallpox aboard, and he was so grateful, and said I was the best friend old Jim ever had in the world, and the *only* one he's got now; and then I happened to look around and see that paper. It was a close place. I took it up and held it in my hand. I was a-trembling, be-cause I'd got to decide, forever, betwixt two things, and I knowed it." Here, at the level of social morality, is the same distinction Huck had felt in the Grangerford house. Indeed, the respectable values of society prove to be like the lovely crockery basket of fruit that "warn't real because you could see where pieces had got chipped off and showed the white chalk, or whatever it was, underneath." In the crisis Huck finally is forced to choose between two things: the demands of the crockery culture and those of the egalitarian community he and Jim have established aboard the raft.

In the background we can still discern the contrast theme in slightly modified form. Here the young barbarian is compared to a spurious local culture. But in the moral geography of America, this sentimental elegance is associated with the culture of the eastern seaboard, which in turn is but an American extension of European civilization. Here the vernacular humor also is used against the old European targets. The two rogues, the Duke and the Dauphin, are the crockery royalty that serves to expose the real thing:

"Don't it s'prise you [Jim asks] de way dem kings carries on, Huck?"
"No," I says, "it don't."
"Why don't it, Huck?"
"Well, it don't, because it's in the breed. I reckon they're all alike."
"But, Huck, dese kings o' ourn is reglar rapscallions; dat's jist what dey is; dey's reglar rapscallions."
"Well, that's what I'm a-saying; all kings is mostly rapscallions, as fur as I can make out."
"Is dat so?"

Mark Twain pushes this republican piety right back to the genesis of the contrast theme, the American Revolution itself: "You don't know kings, Jim, but I know them; and this old rip of ourn is one of the cleanest I've struck in history. Well, Henry he takes a notion he wants to get up some trouble with this country. How does he go at it — give notice? — give the country a show? No. All of a sudden he heaves all the tea in Boston Harbor overboard, and whacks out a declaration of independence, and dares them to come on. That was *his* style — he never give anybody a chance."

So far I have talked about the vernacular mode of *Huckleberry Finn* in its negative aspect, that is, the aggressive use of the style. But in this book we also find an affirmation, the hero's self-exaltation: "Well," says Huck, "the days went along, and the river went down between its banks again; and about the first thing we done was to bait one of the big hooks with a skinned rabbit and set it and catch a catfish that was as big as a man, being six foot two inches long, and weighed over two hundred pounds." Actually, there is not much of this sort of thing in *Huckleberry Finn*. The reason is that the entire book, in its total conception, is a westerner's boast. He is telling the story in his own idiom, hence the tale is a celebration of his point of view from beginning to end. Like Whitman's hero, Huck is a rebellious, democratic barbarian. He lies, he steals, he prefers magic to religion, he identifies his interests with those of escaped slaves, and above all he speaks the vernacular. The largest boast of *Huckleberry Finn* is reserved for the language itself — its capacity to take on the dignity of art, to replace the elevated style of Longfellow or Cooper.

The vernacular style bears many marks of its plebeian origin. For example, it has been peculiarly useful in expressing a preoccupation with process, with the way things are done. By its very nature a genteel style implies an invidious distinction between intellectual and manual work. But the vernacular hero does not honor the distinction, and moreover his very language seems to deny its significance: "Well, last I *pulled* out some of my hair, *and blooded* the ax good, *and stuck* it on the back side, *and slung* the ax in the corner. Then I *took* up the pig *and held* him to my breast with my jacket (so he couldn't drip) till I got a good piece below the house *and then dumped* him into the river. Now I thought of something else. So *I went and got* the bag of meal and my old saw out of the canoe, *and fetched* them to the house. *I took* the bag to where it used to stand, *and ripped* a hole in the bottom of it with the saw . . ." What we have here is a meticulous rendering, one by one, of physical actions or manipulations. A series of verbs (here italicized) is strung together, largely by the word "and," and the total effect is an immediate impression of a process. The writer takes it for granted that we are as interested in *how* he does things as *what* he does. From this passage one can make a direct link to the style of many of our modern writers, say Ernest Hemingway describing in the same way how he baits a fishhook.

Vernacular narration is the key to Mark Twain's style just as it is the key to Whitman's. Twain uses a naive character and his naive language to convey a highly complicated state of mind. But the point of view and the idiom finally are inseparable: together they form a style. And it is this style that lends immediacy to the affirmation without which the book would be morally empty. Huck compresses his whole conception of felicity into one sentence: "It's lovely," he says, "to live on a raft." Actually there are two separate but analogous ideals implied in Huck's pastoral emotion here. The first is a relation between men (it is in a sense political), while the other is a relation between man and nature (it is religious or, if you will, metaphysical).

The political ideal is freedom, freedom *from* the oppression of society, and freedom *to* establish the egalitarian community. The escaped slave and the son of the village drunkard set up their model society on the raft. "What you want," says Huck, "above all things, on a raft, is for everybody to be satisfied, and feel right and kind toward the others." This sort of community only can exist on the river, insulated from the surrounding culture, and even there it is terribly vulnerable. Rogues take over the raft, a steamboat smashes into it, and the river's current carries it steadily toward the slave society its occupants want to escape. But vulnerability, after all, is appropriate to what is essentially a utopian conception. The anarchic impulse that leads the vernacular hero to renounce the existing society is much stronger, needless to say, than the impulse to create a new one.

Although the vernacular ideal of the raft turns upon human solidarity, it derives its ultimate support from another sort of solidarity — one which is given to us only indirectly, by way of the lyrical strain in the book: "Sometimes we'd have that whole river all to ourselves for the longest time. Yonder was the banks and the islands, across the water; and maybe a spark — which was a candle in a cabin window; and sometimes on the water you could see a spark or two — on a raft or a scow, you know; and maybe you could hear a fiddle or a song coming over from one of them crafts. It's lovely to live on a raft. We had the sky up there, all speckled with stars, and we used to lay on our backs and look up at them, and discuss about whether they was made or only just happened." In such passages Mark Twain manages to convey a feeling of belonging to the physical universe comparable to the feeling of community aboard the raft. That is, he suggests a grand analogy between the political and metaphysical relations within the novel. The vernacular thereby receives its final sanction from nature itself. It is a fitting sanction for a literary style developed in a new society in a prehistoric landscape.

The vernacular style is a distinctive achievement of American culture. But this is not to say that it has served to convey anything like an adequate view of experience, or that it has yet given America a great literature. Its creativity came from the radical program of freedom it affirmed, but like any such program, it demands an exceptional discipline. The writer who works in the vernacular takes great risks. To see this we have only to recall those excesses of uncontrolled improvisation that mar the work of Whitman and Twain. This literary barbarism follows from the rejection of inherited forms and theories. It is of course a symptom of primitivism, and along with it we get what is perhaps the chief defect of the vernacular mode — its unremitting anti-intellectualism. This seems to me a more valid point of attack than chauvinism. In defying the constraints and oppression identified with the European past, our writers also have tended to ignore the achievements of the trained intellect. This familiar primitivist bias has retained its affinity to the mode in our time. It seems to have followed the style from Walt Whitman to Carl Sandburg, from Mark Twain to Ernest Hemingway.

But it is one thing to charge the vernacular with an anti-intellectual bias, and quite another to think it (as Mr. Bewley does) "uncritically acceptant" of America. In Hawthorne and James criticism arose from a comparison of America to tradition, to the past. In Whitman and Twain, on the other hand, the criticism was based on utopian standards. It came from a comparison of an actual America with an ideal vision of the nation's destiny. That is what led to the writing of such uncompromising works as *Democratic Vistas*, *A Connecticut Yankee*, and "The Man That Corrupted Hadleyburg." My point has been that from the beginning the vernacular was more than a literary technique — it was a view of experience. When the style first emerged it was nourished by an egalitarian faith that we can scarcely imagine nowadays. Since that time the history of the vernacular has been a history of its fragmentation. The technique has been separated from the belief it originally was designed to affirm. But that is another story.

◣ J. C. LEVENSON

# Henry Adams and the Culture of Science

Sᴄɪᴇɴᴄᴇ, in the view of Henry Adams, was far too important to leave it to the scientists. In his time as in ours, the arts and sciences constantly drifted apart. The whole world might know that modern man lives in a scientific culture and yet the traditional carriers of culture, and the technicians as well, act as if the skills of understanding and control were irrelevant to the techniques of power. Adams saw this "drift" as the failure of intelligent responsibility, a prelude to disaster. His own way of taking action was to ask, more cogently than any of his countrymen then or since, the leading questions about science – in what spirit to cultivate it, in what ways to use it, how to relate it to other kinds of knowledge. But it is not his questions alone that we need: taken by themselves, they might serve posterity little better than mere pat answers. The process of inquiry is what counts as vital culture, the difficult and probably endless struggle to make science an integral part of one's intellectual, social, and personal apprehension of life. This is Adams' special value: he arrived at his questions by the arduous process of which *The Education of Henry Adams* is both testimony and result. What is more, in both the process and the product, he showed us how to affirm a cultural heritage which included science by creatively repossessing it. Adapting the American Enlightenment to twentieth-century conditions, he pointed the way to a culture of science that might redress a technological civilization.

Adams' first qualification for his prophetic role was that he saw the modernity of modern science so acutely. One reason for this is simply that he lived during what Percy W. Bridgman has called the great crisis of scientific history, when our present century began confronting the physicist with "experimental facts of a sort which he had not previously envisaged, and which he would not even have thought possible." [1] Being there at the right time partly explains the intensity of Adams' eyewitness account, but as he himself continually stressed, most people who lived through the revolution of the age were unconscious of it. His own awareness had not just intensity but depth. The luck which furnished the right moment would have been wasted if he had not himself provided the intellectual dimension of history. Few had the wit to see, much less to say as he did, that Roentgen and Mme. Curie had introduced new forces "before which the man of science stood at first as bewildered and helpless, as in the fourth century, a priest of Isis before the Cross of Christ." [2] Even so, this well-known sample of Adams' historical comment is somewhat deceptive: it reminds us that he looked to Lucretius, St. Thomas, and Montaigne for a philosophy of science as well as to Ernst Mach, Karl Pearson, and Judge Stallo, but it partly conceals the fact that his basic attitudes were circumscribed by a more limited era. Yet the hint is there to be taken that in an age of radiation and electrons, "he greatly preferred his eighteenth-century education when God was a father and nature a mother, and all was for the best in a scientific universe." [3] In his approach to science, he confirmed the truth that he was a child of the eighteenth century who made a life and career in the nineteenth and lived long enough into the twentieth to be one of its most dedicated observers. From this historical baseline we can measure his responses to the scientific revolution which still dominates our age.

Adams' three-century biography includes of course that of a family whose distinction, for three generations before his, helps illustrate the citizen's changing relation to science. John Adams, the friend of Jefferson and Rush and the unimpressed acquaintance of Franklin, provides the starting point. He discussed natural philosophy almost as readily as politics, for the two were sciences of virtually equal status in the mind of the Enlightenment. In the lifetime of John Quincy Adams, these two realms were not so easily interchangeable, but by the Adamses' theory they should have been and in practice the sixth President proved more versatile than the second. His *Report on Weights and Measures* showed that an orderly, well-disciplined mind could still, without professional training, make an original contribution to science — and could do so in the course of an active public career. The line seemed to continue straight when Henry Adams' father was elected to the American Academy of Arts and Sciences in the year before the boy graduated from Harvard. The son in his turn, an enthusiastic student of Louis Agassiz during an undergraduate career hardly notable for zeal, surely looked forward to similar honors. His hopes are suggested by the title of one of the earliest surviving volumes in his library, Oliver Wendell Holmes' *Border Lines of Knowledge in Some Provinces of Medical Science*.[4] The little book testified that while for his father's contemporaries science had become a profession, it was not yet so demanding as to cut a man off from literary, civic, and social life. Even for the younger generation, the border lines of most sciences were within easy reach and the spirit of the old scientific culture seemed renewable at will. Thus, when Sir Charles Lyell brought out the tenth edition of his *Principles of Geology*, young Adams, on the basis of his undergraduate course and his intellectual earnestness, did a long critical notice for the *North American Review* of October 1868, and thereby made himself an apostle of Darwinism in America. The next decades kept up the illusion of brightness. Adams was as actively engaged in the advancement of science with his friends at the Cosmos Club as in plans for political reform with his friends on the *Nation*. But science and politics ran curiously parallel in the dwindling prospects they offered a child of the old order, and though Henry Adams resisted both kinds of change, he ended the century in unanticipated straits. Just as in politics he came to speak as a citizen rather than a statesman-*manqué*, in science he finally spoke as a mere layman who knew what had happened to his qualifications as a part-time scientist. Writing at the age of seventy, he saw the difference as simple and absolute: "The average man, in 1850, could understand what Davy or Darwin had to say; he could not understand what Clerk Maxwell meant."[5] After a century of scarcely visible change, the revolution of modern science had become all too clear.

Science had outreached common sense. By its very advancement, it had brought about the failure of mind at just the point where intelligence was most needed. A child of the Enlightenment might well behold and despair, but to Adams' credit he responded in a more lively way. In order to make responsible judgments of his situation in nature and society, he set himself a formidable course of reading in the new sciences. Even when he let himself be tempted, as he occasionally did, to cut short his study and indulge in careless speculation, he shaped his comments to stimulate younger men and make them seek better answers than his own. He did not intend to unnerve his readers, but he did mean to alarm them. His thesis was that the twentieth century presented not only physical and moral but intellectual terrors. Though he foresaw intercontinental wars and ceaseless human ferocity, he considered worse than either the breakdown of intelligence, for mind was the one last means of running order through chaos. For his part he committed himself, without undue hope or despair, to help refashion common sense and the social imagination. By his reading and his tireless inquiries of the experts, by amateur ventures of his own and discreet patronage for professionals, most of all by the labors of his imagination, he kept up the quest. The border lines of knowledge had receded out of sight, but he stubbornly refused to give himself up as lost.

External facts may sketch the three centuries' change in the relation of the citizen to science, but only a history of beliefs and assumptions can suggest the full meaning. Once again the story begins with John Adams in eighteenth-century New England. For him as for so many of his contemporaries, the great scene of intellectual drama had shifted from theology and metaphysics to science and politics. To use the phrase of John Dewey, nature was for him the only authentic revelation. Besides the unbelief we notice when we see his views against those of a more remote past, we had better make out the equally important signs of belief. Nature was still, to him, a *revelation*. Some of its laws were veiled in obscurity, but all the more necessary truths were self-evident and could guide mankind through the course of human events. His faith was strong enough to transcend the paradox of determinism and free will, and his creed was straightforward: "Animal life is a chemical process, and is carried on by unceasing motion. Our bodies and minds, like the heavens, the earth, and the sea, like all animal, vegetable, and mineral nature, like the elements of earth, air, fire, and water are continually changing. The mutability and mutations of matter, and much more of the intellectual and moral world, are the consequence of laws of nature, not less without our power than beyond our comprehension. While we are thus assured that, in one sense, nothing in human affairs will be perpetual or at rest, we ought to remember, at the same time, that the duration of our lives, the security of our property, the existence of our conveniences, comforts, and pleasures, the repose of private life, and the tranquillity of society, are placed in very great degree in human power. Equal laws may be ordained and executed. . . ."[6]

The faith of the Enlightenment, formulated thus, became the heritage of the Adamses. It is especially worth a close look because, seen in the perspective of four generations, it shows at once its eighteenth-century origin and the Adams family stamp. On this particular statement, John Adams and Thomas Jefferson, who was even more the representative of the age, would have agreed almost to the letter, just as they had agreed earlier on Jefferson's formulation in the Declaration of Independence. But the assumptions of the two men were not precisely the same. They might set the boundaries of knowledge in exactly the same place, but Jefferson's abiding belief in the progress of the human mind made an important difference: he was sure that nature's operations would be better and better known. His confidence that an American mammoth would be found as big as any European specimen — or bigger — was typical. While Jefferson faced the unknown with sanguine tolerance, however, John Adams enjoyed no such speculative calm. He revealed his temperament when he spoke awesomely of "laws of nature, not less without our power than beyond our comprehension," and temperamental difference amounted to difference of idea. If the universe of his conception was utterly rational up to the limit of the known and a magnificent dark mystery beyond, he felt no difficulty in that. He was renewing in his way the tough-minded and fervent Puritan culture of an earlier time, and when Henry Adams renewed the spirit of the Enlightenment in a still later age, traces of the same pattern would emerge again.

John Adams' secularized and transformed Puritanism, like the actual religious culture of the early settlers, went through stages of subsiding fervor until its cool orthodoxy invited a reaction. John Quincy Adams, seen, as the *Education* presents him, straight and formidable in his pew in the Old Stone Church in Quincy, supplies a sharp image of New England Unitarianism after it had become the established order, but it should perhaps be balanced by the softer picture of Oliver Wendell Holmes regaling his breakfast table with "The Wonderful 'One-Hoss Shay.'" To a young Transcendentalist, the sternness of President Adams was no doubt less provoking than the complacency of Doctor Holmes, since sternness is akin to fervor, but the variation between them was not very great and together they defined a historical norm. Natural theology, rational morality, and careful science, ornamented by sound scholarship and decorous semi-literature — these were the principal cultural attributes of the society which Emerson tried to revolutionize. And the new call for an "awakening" differed from that of Jonathan Edwards' time in being consciously revolutionary: even in the preliminary theological skirmishing, everyone knew that a total renovation of culture was at issue. When New England divided into opposing parties of the spirit, the conflict extended to science as well as to religion, politics, and art. In this context, old beliefs took on changed meanings. Though John Adams was less completely a rationalist than Jefferson, the differences between them had after all been reconcilable. Later Adamses showed how essentially rationalistic they were as their scientific "orthodoxy" took its definition in part from the Emersonian heterodoxy they withstood.

What the Adamses opposed seems innocent enough, especially when we pass over the effect on church, state, business, and slavery which the intellectual debate entailed. Emerson's dangerous question which he put to his fellow citizens was simply whether their prudent practical prosperous regularity allowed enough scope to life. Yankee as well as seer, he had a shrewd respect for science, commerce, and good works, but he felt bound to condemn a culture which made these the sum of existence. His path of escape is well known. Taking the distinction from Coleridge and ultimately from Kant, he declared a radical difference between the Understanding which functions objectively in the practical world and the Reason which operates subjectively in the realm of spirit. With this distinction in hand, he was able to render unto science what was proper thereto and then gently shift his point of view to the world of spirit. He saw the two orders as existing quite discretely, and when spirit called, he seemed not so much to transcend science as to drop it from consideration. He might seem to be talking about science when he suggested that generalizing made all data beautiful, but he regarded generalizing as something utterly remote from the murdering to dissect which constituted most scientific labor. When his mind was on Beauty, he saw things from the empyrean, and in the empyrean there were no laboratories. There he could sublimely pronounce: "The naturalist is led *from* the road by the whole distance of his fancied advance. . . . Astrology interested us, for it tied man to the system. Instead of an isolated beggar, the farthest star felt him and he felt the star. . . . Chemistry takes to pieces, but it does not construct. Alchemy, which sought to transmute one element into another, to prolong life, to arm with power, — that was in the right direction." [7] When Emerson said that modern botany, astronomy, and chemistry were uninspired and uninspiring, he was being antirationalistic and he meant to be. His excesses at the literal level were obviously rhetorical, but his logical postulate was clear: he was saying that the rational elements of experience (matter for the empirical sciences) do not determine the irrational (immediate perceptions of things or unconditional feelings about them). In his rejection of the unexalted life, he considered himself justified by the mysterious occasions of perception and feeling when all things seem to depend on spirit. His sanction was his own experience, and to the teacher of self-reliance this was unquestionable.

Emerson was the most eloquent voice of his generation, but he did not win the intellectual victories for which he set out. For one thing, the ruling minority to which his contemporaries Doctor Holmes and Charles Francis Adams belonged remained unaffected by him until the prophet of Young America had devolved into the older and tamer gentleman of letters. More important, events in politics and science, if once they had been dully practical, began after mid-century to take on new qualities of magnitude and wonder.

A letter which Henry Adams wrote in his early twenties bears witness to the excitement and fearfulness that the classic areas of intellectual interest once again provoked. In London as private secretary to his father the American Minister, he received his first word of the *Merrimac* and rightly guessed that Britain's wooden navy, the greatest in the world, had been rendered obsolete in a single stroke. His prompt reaction was that "our good country the United States is left to a career that is positively unlimited except by the powers of the imagination." He went on: "I tell you these are great times. Man has mounted science, and is now run away with. I firmly believe that before many centuries more, science will be the master of man. The engines he will have invented will be beyond his strength to control. Some day science may have the existence of mankind in its power, and the human race commit suicide by blowing up the world. Not only shall we be able to cruize [*sic*] in space, but I see no reason why some future generation shouldn't walk off like a beetle with the world on its back, or give it another rotary motion so that every zone should receive its due portion of heat and light." [8]

The letter jumps back and forth between the delusions of science-fiction and the delusions of atomic nightmare, but by its very immaturity it shows how completely the mind of youth was captured. A somewhat older Henry Adams, when he undertook in 1868 to review the foremost geologist in the world, confirmed the point. And when he questioned Lyell's uniformitarianism because it left the glacial period unexplained, he was showing off not only his knowledge and his logic but the intellectual daring of his generation. Those who had cultivated science while Emerson was saying to cultivate *men*, lived to see the young swing round to their view.

New men maturing in the new age had the chance to restate old ideas in their own way. By 1877, the onetime critic of Lyell for the *North American* had become editor of that review, served with distinction until he had enough, and then quit. Indeed, Professor Adams was about to conclude his term at Harvard, disenchanted with politics but still loyal to science. In his final academic year, he interspersed his professional reading with *Don Quixote* on the one hand and Huxley, Wallace, and Darwin on the other.[9] Both excursions from history could be connected with his friend Clarence King, who was almost as widely known a raconteur and lover of Cervantes as he was a geologist. The representative equally of science and culture, King seemed the man to whom the future belonged. Indeed he was publicly honored as the spokesman for the generation just coming into its own, being invited to give the 1877 anniversary address at the Sheffield Scientific School of Yale. He was evidently Henry Adams' spokesman, too, for when Adams received his printed copy of "Catastrophism and the Evolution of Environment," he underscored without comment several passages which gave, as it were, official scientific approval to his own thoughts and attitudes. One such instance was King's flat statement that, with the acceptance of glacial theory, "uniformitarianism pure and simple received a fatal blow." King's scorn for the uniformitarians happened to coincide with that of the theistic objectors to Lyell, but his verbal pieties rang hollow: mention of the bringer of "that mysterious energy we call life" glorified the bringer but little, while the last phrase, which Adams marked, did express a naturalistic awe before the unknown. The longest passage which Adams noted was a challenge to both religious and Transcendentalist opponents of science: "Let us hope that as a means of clearing away the endless rubbish of false ideas from the human intellect, for the lifting of man out of the dominion of ignorance, scientific method and scientific education are acknowledged to be adequate, if not supreme. We may congratulate ourselves: for that victory is won. At last modern society admits that a knowledge of the laws which govern the cognizable universe and the possession of the only methods which can advance that knowledge, presupposes, indeed even develops, an intellect both vital and broad." [10]

While Henry Adams might readily affirm King's view that scientific education could produce "an intellect both vital and broad," he had reason to qualify his assent to the blandly stated nineteenth-century shibboleths about progress. One use of the historian's, as against the geologist's, past was to extend experience and reduce naiveté. When John Adams, contemplating history, had written three generations earlier, "The world grows more enlightened," he had gone on to ask, "Has the progress of science, arts, and letters yet discovered that there are no passions in human nature? no ambition, avarice, or desire of fame?" [11] Now the same question rang through the work of Henry Adams' maturity, his *History of the United States during the Administrations of Thomas Jefferson and James Madison.* Early in that work, setting the problems with which he was going to concern himself, he did not forget to ask of his subject — the American democracy — "What will you do for moral progress?" [12] And on the last page of the last volume, by a whole series of further questions he made it clear that no answer had yet been found. While many of his countrymen were assuming that the development of science, technology, and morals was one and indivisible, he looked for and could find no necessary connection between the progress of power and the advance of human good. In fact, his alertness to the one and his skepticism of the other create the central ironic tension of the *History*.

Adams' partial acceptance of the doctrines of progress was no less important than his reservations. The historian argued that the American democracy of 1800, in order to survive as the widest-extended republic in history, had to abandon conservatism and become "a speculating and a scientific nation." [13] Only thus could the natural obstacles to unity be overcome and the threat of foreign aggression be turned aside. The thesis was simple, but the story of science and progress was not. One complication was that in the epical struggle with nature, there were apparently no heroes — at least not among those who were acclaimed at the time. The *History* did bear the names of Jefferson and Madison on its covers, but it rather notoriously found them wanting in their statecraft; as for science, it recounted the historic western crossing of Lewis and Clark, yet called their exploring expedition "a great feat, but nothing more." Neither irony was frivolous. Adams carefully gave their due to statesmen and explorers, but he gave credit to the nearly anonymous labors of Robert Fulton and other "visionaries" for solving the essential problem, that of "bringing the headwaters of the western rivers within reach of private enterprise and industry." [14] The steamboat, rather than intelligent direction given to the American democracy by its leaders, seems to be the most effective historical agent in the *History*. Thus, even though intelligent direction failed, the work still recorded the popular, scientific triumph which established, against all the odds of historical experience, a democratic and technologically innovating nation.

In the irony of his *History*, which related at once the decline and fall of eighteenth-century statesmanship and the rise of a popular, industrializing society, Henry Adams hit upon the dilemma of his later reflections. The more successfully he proved that events followed the course of a necessary progress, the less likely he was to find that intelligent direction was responsible for social advance. Reason, in constructing a historical order, seemed to jostle reason from the seat of political power where once it had conscientiously tried to ordain and execute equal laws. If history was a science, politics could not be. The nineteenth-century concern for a science of history seemed logically to exclude an eighteenth-century concern for a science of politics, but for Henry Adams the dilemma was not a matter of logic only. In his deepest being, the forces were almost balanced, whether to rationalize his own career as a historian rather than a statesman or to search out a continuance for the tradition handed down from John Adams. Early in his career, he had been forthright in his eighteenth-century reactions and had shown how deeply ingrained they were. For example, when as a professor of American history he studied the historical positivism of Calhoun's *Disquisition on Government*, he underlined the statement "Power can only be resisted by power, and tendency by tendency"; in the margin he put his dry rebuttal: "*Reason* has no place in Calhoun's conception of human society." [15] But Calhoun was an opponent outside himself, and so natural an opponent as to make answering almost a matter of simple reflex. In the prolonged inward discussion which was to follow, all kinds of answers and all kinds of doubts presented themselves.

Adams in his letters often expressed the notion that man might have "as fixed and necessary development as that of a tree; and almost as unconscious."[16] Nevertheless, that must be taken as interim opinion or private doubt, for the ultimate considered judgment of the *Education* was neither so simple nor so unqualified. By that time, he was prepared to mock the religion of progress which had swept his age, and he did so by using the familiar argument of catastrophism to thwack the historical uinformitarians: Rome was to history as glaciation had been to geology, for "Rome could not be fitted into an orderly, middle-class, Bostonian, systematic scheme of evolution."[17] When, at the end of the book, he offered his own "Dynamic Theory of History," he tried to account for Rome as well as for modern "progress," but at least as important as the theory was the warning that went with it. He explicitly cautioned that he was offering only a "chart of relations" and that "any serious student would have to invent another, to compare or correct its errors."[18] The chart was not a paradigm of necessity but, as he went on to say, a means of navigating the future, a convenience for making an experiment. In short, while he might overwhelm the timid reader with his grand theoretical effort, he was inviting the studious and strong to use his scheme as a help to intelligent, purposive action. Reason, if it should be vigorous and capable enough, could once again have a constructive role.

The inventing by Adams of a catastrophist rebuttal to the idea of necessary and uniform historical development can be traced to his own youthful questioning of Sir Charles Lyell and to Gibbon's questions on the fall of Rome, but there were other causes more immediate and more personal. His wife's death by suicide, the great disaster of his personal life, first drove his mind from the comforts of system-making. It was a shattering blow to the expectable order of things. When he eventually returned to his old lines of thought he had a heightened consciousness of other values than those by which progress is conventionally measured. The poignancy of *Mont-Saint-Michel and Chartres* gives evidence of this in one way, the cold taciturnity of the *Education*, with the theme of death running through the text and yet no mention of Adams' wife, does so in another. The snapped continuity which was the central fact of his private life led Adams to think he could tell his own story and expound his theories at the same time. If he omitted to specify the crucial episode, he nevertheless rendered its effect as completely as if he had given every detail. Indeed, his capacity to fuse his most intimate suffering and his most abstract deliberations is the mark of Adams' genius. He made the story of his scientific education, another instance of catastrophism as we have seen, as personal as it was abstruse.

The catastrophe of Adams' intellectual biography was the scientific revolution of which he was to become the reporter. Canvassing the new science at the turn of the century, he found that there was no refuge from the irrationalities of politics or life in the supposed rationality of science. The old border line between the known and the unknown, as sketched by John Adams, had evoked both awe and human confidence, but if the intervening generations had erred on the side of confidence, Henry Adams found his contemporaries and juniors to be thrusting the pendulum in the opposite side. Reading Karl Pearson, in *The Grammar of Science*, he marked what was for him a key passage: "*In the chaos behind sensations*, in the 'beyond' of sense-impressions, *we cannot infer necessity, order or routine, for these are concepts* formed by the mind of man on this side of sense-impressions." [19] The idea had not greatly changed from John Adams' time, but Pearson's emphasis on the epistemological predicament made the human being seem a prisoner where before he had felt himself a lawmaker and replaced the God-like mystery of the beyond with the terrible dark of "chaos." If a man held to the eighteenth-century assumption that science described what was metaphysically real, then chaos was come again in the outer world; on the other hand, if he gave up the assumption, his ceasing to know where he was would be like having his intellect suddenly blinded. Furthermore, very much within the range of sense-impression, Henry Adams saw what science was doing on its practical side. He watched technological advances increase human destructiveness while in politics he noted the signs that the human impulse to destruction was stronger than ever. Practically as well as metaphysically, so-called progress seemed catastrophic. Writing to his brother Brooks in 1902, Adams commented: "I apprehend for the next hundred years an ultimate, colossal, cosmic collapse; but not on any of our old lines. My belief is that science is to wreck us, and that we are like monkeys monkeying with a loaded shell; we don't in the least know or care where our practically infinite energies come from or will bring us to." [20] The great catastrophe of history turned out to be not in the past, but in the future — and not far away. The vision of an apocalypse came more and more into focus, and the problem for Adams was much like that which he was to set for readers of the *Education* — whether to give himself up to his vision or to try thinking his way past it.

Adams held out against the threat of chaos by using the rational instruments which were his by tradition and by training. Reading the new science, he exploited the methods of logical analysis he had learned with his philosophical friends like Chauncey Wright and the verbal scrutiny he had practiced in the criticism of historical documents. By such means he could detect confusions in the theory of the ether even though his own conception of what was being said was often shaky. Invoking his non-scientific canons of judgment, he could protest against Sir Oliver Lodge's text on electrical theory, "Nonsense as English, and not sense as science. Muddled to despair." [21] Even with Karl Pearson, whose positivist views he accepted with docility, he was quick to spy the touches of optimistic glibness. He questioned with his pencil whether, as Pearson claimed, science "aims at, and results in, unity," he wondered what the *more* could be in the claim that through cultivating pure science "more will be achieved," and he ridiculed Pearson's offhand evaluations of the scientist's work above that of the poet. [22] He derived a sense of keeping his bearings from not being so lost as he might have been. And as he got used to his intellectual situation, he found that his imagination could deal with the new world of science without having to be assured that its picture was realistically exact. If the old realism was outmoded, the mind could learn to be at ease with symbols. Intellectual vitality would not be downed: before long Adams could report to a friend that he found the world "vastly more exciting and entertaining than it was sixty years ago as I first remember it." While his predictions remained in substance what they had been before, he now set them forth in a language that no ancestor of his would have understood nor even himself in the earlier stages of his study, for he went on about the twentieth-century world:

It interests me almost too much, but its logic is startling. It is the logic of a bicycle; an equilibrium maintained only by violating gravitation. One force annihilates another for the time, and man does nothing but upset what little equilibrium the forces had reached by habit. The fabric of human society we have long seen to be upset, but we can remodel that, on lines of force sufficiently safe. What excites me is that we have upset the equilibrium of nature, and that nature has got to turn on us, as it does in every explosion, combustion, or disease. Logically the planet should at last explode or burn up.

I should think my mind affected by it, if it were not that much scientific writing now takes the same form. [23]

The difficulties of remodeling society seemed much less great, once

Adams had learned to live with the difficulties of understanding modern science. As his critics have for a long time pointed out, he had not mastered the latest physics in the sense of technical comprehension, and he had even less become a philosopher of science as the term is now professionally used. But learning to live with what he knew to exist and what he saw to be shaping his world was, nonetheless, a philosophical act.

The drama of Adams' struggle against intellectual chaos did not take place merely in the library of his Washington home, but one of its most personal and crucial scenes was enacted there in the pencil-versus-book dialogue which occurred when the historian read his old friend William James' *Principles of Psychology*. James seemed to remove the last stay of the old assurance that when politics, or even the physical world, outran comprehension, rationality still prevailed in the more limited area "this side of sense-impressions." The fact that Adams re-used his figure of a bicycle-rider in the *Education* as an image for the psyche teetering over a "subconscious chaos" [24] helps us measure the import of his climactic discovery: the forces of chaos worked in the knowing mind as well as in the world known to it. It was James who apprised Adams of the treason within, and no amount of resistance could make the news less fateful. Resistance there was, and Adams seemed to avoid the subject matter of James' text by attacking the presentation. About the chapter on "The Perception of Things" he wrote caustically: "Surely all this chapter is as chaotic as a dream! it wants cohesion, relation of parts, clearness of purpose, and coordination of facts in any defined field." But the phrase "chaotic as a dream" gave away the resistance. As his comments went on, he revealed that James was forcing him to question the ultimate basis of his rationalism. "Is the chaotic mind the healthy state," Adams asked, "and is the ordered intelligence the abnormal?" [25] This problem stayed in his mind while he read until, a good while later, he set down an answer that would work at least for himself: "Instincts ought to be habits founded on appetites incident to self-preservation. Other habits would be mere tricks or incidental vices. But is my habit of mind — reasoning by analysis or synthesis — an instinct incident to self-preservation? Reason is an instinct." [26]

In those ruminative sentences, we can follow step by step Adams' victory over ultimate doubt. The logic by which he retrieved reason from chaos was similar to that of James' solution to the problem of freedom of the will: "Freedom's first deed should be to affirm itself." But the difference is more interesting than the similarity. For Adams the solution to his ultimate problem lay in the assertion of mind, while for James it lay in the assertion of will. When Adams underscored that all-important sentence of James', he added a comment that made still clearer his affirmation, not of his own will, but of his eighteenth-century heritage: "Freedom seems rather to consist in keeping one's mind free to choose." [27]

Henry Adams' ideas on the function and duties of the mind underlie the argument of the *Education* and are more important to that work than his tentative chart of historical development or his narrative of the revolution in science as he witnessed it. His belief that reason could solve its problems in science, politics, and morals did not mean he thought he had himself solved those problems. On the contrary, he wrote just because the problems were unsolved. His job, as he conceived it, was not to provide answers except as illustrative examples; the task of the educator was to point to questions and suggest methods. One of the unities of the book comes from his suggesting that the same intellectual virtues ought to be cultivated by the statesman, the artist, and the man of science, namely, "self-restraint, obedience, sensitiveness to impulse from without." [28] He brought together the several realms of intelligent discourse when he developed his political thesis artistically with a scientific figure, that of Newton's comet which would have suffered annihilation had it not defied common sense in motion and made a sharp parabolic turn.

He put his moral still more explicitly by describing the movement of thought in terms of Newton's formula for gravitation — and Gibbs' rule of phases as well: "The movement from unity into multiplicity, between 1200 and 1900, was unbroken in sequence, and rapid in acceleration. Prolonged one generation longer, it would require a new social mind. As though thought were common salt in indefinite solution it must enter a new phase subject to new laws. Thus far, since five or ten thousand years, the mind had successfully reacted, and nothing yet proved that it would fail to react — but it would need to jump." [29] The joining, in this sample of Adams' exposition, of the old science and the new is the clue to his final achievement: by means of learning, thought, and imagination, he established a link between the Enlightenment of the eighteenth century and that which the twentieth is still required to formulate.

### NOTES

[1] Percy W. Bridgman, "Philosophical Implications of Physics," in American Academy of Arts and Sciences, *Bulletin*, Vol. III, No. 5 (February 1950), quoted by

James B. Conant, *Modern Science and Modern Man* (New York: Doubleday Anchor Books, 1953), pp. 65–66.

[2] *The Education of Henry Adams* (Boston: Houghton Mifflin, 1918), pp. 486–487.

[3] *Ibid.*, p. 458

[4] Oliver Wendell Holmes, *Border Lines of Knowledge in Some Provinces of Medical Science* (Boston: Ticknor and Fields, 1862). This, and other books from Adams' library cited below, are in the Adams Collection of the Massachusetts Historical Society. My references to Adams' underscorings and my quotations from his marginal notes are made with the kind permission of the Society.

[5] "The Rule of Phase Applied to History," in Brooks Adams, ed., *The Degradation of the Democratic Dogma* (New York: Macmillan, 1919), p. 303.

[6] John Adams, *Discourses on Davila*, in *Works*, ed. C. F. Adams, 10 vols. (Boston: Little, Brown, 1850–1856), VI, 395.

[7] Ralph Waldo Emerson, "Beauty," in *The Conduct of Life* (Boston: Ticknor and Fields, 1860), p. 268.

[8] Henry Adams to Charles Francis Adams, Jr., London, April 11, 1862. Worthington C. Ford, ed., *A Cycle of Adams Letters, 1861–1865*, 2 vols. (Boston and New York: Houghton Mifflin, 1920), I, 135.

[9] Harvard Library Records, 1876–1877 (Harvard Archives, Harvard University Library).

[10] Clarence King, *Catastrophism and the Evolution of Environment* (New Haven, Conn., 1877), pp. 21, 4.

[11] *Discourses on Davila*, in *Works*, VI, 274–275.

[12] Henry Adams, *History of the United States during the Administration of Thomas Jefferson and James Madison*, 9 vols. (New York: C. Scribner's Sons, 1889–1891), I, 179.

[13] *History*, I, 73.

[14] *Ibid.*, III, 216.

[15] John C. Calhoun, *A Disquisition on Government and A Discourse on the Constitution and Government of the United States*, ed. Richard K. Cralle (Columbia, S.C.: Printed by A. S. Johnston, 1851), p. 12.

[16] Henry Adams to Francis Parkman, Washington, December 21, 1884. *Henry Adams and His Friends, A Collection of His Unpublished Letters*, compiled with a biographical introduction by Harold Dean Cater (Boston: Houghton Mifflin, 1947), p. 134.

[17] *Education*, p. 91.

[18] *Ibid.*, p. 488.

[19] Karl Pearson, *The Grammar of Science*, 2nd ed., revised and enlarged (London: A. and C. Black, 1900), p. 137. Adams' underscoring is indicated by italics.

[20] Henry Adams to Brooks Adams, Fort William, Scotland, August 10, 1902. *Henry Adams and His Friends*, p. 529.

[21] Oliver J. Lodge, *Modern Views of Electricity* (London and New York: Macmillan, 1889), p. 24.

[22] *The Grammar of Science*, pp. 7, 12, 17.

[23] Henry Adams to Charles Milnes Gaskell, Paris, June 26, 1904. Manuscript in the Library of the Massachusetts Historical Society. Quoted by permission of the Society.

[24] *Education*, p. 433.

[25] William James, *The Principles of Psychology* (Adams Collection), 2 vols. (New York: Henry Holt, 1890), II, 133.

[26] *Ibid.*, II, 441.

[27] *Ibid.*, II, 573.

[28] *Education*, pp. 485–486.

[29] *Ibid.*, p. 498.

❦ DAVID W. NOBLE

# Dreiser and Veblen and the Literature
## of Cultural Change

ONE of the major traditional disciplines which influences students of American culture is history and no aspect of history is more pertinent to their investigations than intellectual history. And yet, while many rely on intellectual history to enlarge the vision of other disciplines, few have been concerned with attempts to refine its concepts. True, this has the advantage that the large purpose of such study — the clarification of the whole culture — is not lost in a morass of overspecialization and technical jargon. But, if kept in perspective, conceptual schemes can contribute importantly to the understanding of the whole culture. One of these is surely "climate of opinion," the concept used by Carl Becker so effectively a quarter of a century ago in his study of the Enlightenment,[1] but unaccountably avoided since then by so many of those concerned with intellectual history.

As Becker used the term, borrowed from Whitehead, it merely means looking at ideas within the context of a specific historically defined society. For Becker, ideas operate on two levels. There are technical ideas, consciously held and elaborated into logical patterns. And then there are ideas that have the quality of faiths. They are the instinctively, unconsciously held ideas about nature and God and society. They are the real philosophical structure of an age, because they give final meaning to the world. It is within the framework of these preconceptions that men do their conscious and so-called rational thinking.

Becker's book was written to demonstrate this thesis. Taking the Enlightenment, he distinguished between the avowed ideas of the *philosophes* and the faiths that were the foundations of their world. The eighteenth-century intellectual had verbally accepted a positivistic tradition of science as a guide for understanding the world. Nothing was true or good if it did not coincide with empirical fact. And Becker suggested what a magnificent weapon science was for destroying the established historical position of the *ancien régime* and its historically defined political, social, and religious values. But then, Becker declared, when the *philosophes* turned to offering alternative values to society, they built them around the same inherited medieval Christian tradition and view of the world. The Heavenly City of the philosophers was merely a secularized version of that synthesized by St. Thomas.

The philosophical implication for intellectual history in Becker's analysis, therefore, is that one must consider man's preconceptions, emotionally held, as basic, and that one should not accept explicit ideas as the key to the man or the times. Almost inevitably, technical ideas will be bent to fit inherited attitudes. A further implication then follows that if there are to be major changes in ideas, whereby one society will be distinguished from another in time, such changes will be in the area of preconceptions, which are the real climate of opinion of an age. And, finally, Becker's study implies that such changes cannot be instituted by dependent technical ideas, but will come as fundamental changes in social structure force a change in the climate of opinion.

This is in the realm of hypothesis, and the present essay is not written to defend the total philosophical validity of Becker's speculations; it is, rather, a case of special pleading, asking that those interested in American culture make greater use of the hypothesis. There is nothing to lose but our preconceptions.

One period to which the hypothesis may be usefully applied is the transition of American society from the nineteenth to the twentieth century. Historians have written of the massive social change which followed the industrialization of the economy during the 1870's and 1880's. But this tremendous material transformation was not accompanied by a comparable spiritual change. Seemingly, the American mind was insulated from the world of change by a traditional separation of intellectual life and everyday experience. It was insulated by what Santayana called the Genteel Tradition. But the inclination of the American thinker to ignore the external environment was based on more than habit. Running through the smug complacency of the Gilded Age, giving it form and substance, was a faith in progress. If the industrial revolution was the most important social and economic fact of late nineteenth-century America, a belief in progress was the most important intellectual fact.

For most Americans between 1870 and 1900, this belief in progress found sanction and expression in the evolutionary theories of Herbert Spencer, who was truly, for that generation, America's philosopher. It was Spencer who took the uneasiness, the uncertainty, out of the doctrines associated with Darwin's name. For those who wanted to know that there was a place for the deity in a world controlled by natural law, he gave reassurance by asserting the fact of an unknowable first cause; for the more numerous persons who wanted the assurance of continued material progress, he affirmed that evolution means progress, that natural law is carrying men irresistibly onward and upward; and for conservatives who wished to preserve the status quo of American institutional life, he provided the quietist argument that man has no free will or ability to change the present social structure, which represents the forces of natural law. In effect he underwrote the conservative social philosophy of extreme individualism that postulated society as the mechanical aggregation of self-contained atomistic individuals. Complacent America, without changing its institutions or traditions, could await the fruits of unending progress.

We know that this smug philosophy had been seriously challenged by 1920. But most historians of ideas have explained this challenge as the product of the writings of a new generation of social scientists who came of age around 1900. Basically ignoring the manner in which fundamental changes in the social structure may have undermined the faith in progress, the historians have written about the discovery of more incisive intellectual implications in Darwin's theories by the young academic writers. These were implications which allowed the sociologist, the economist, the political scientist, and the historian to destroy not only Spencer but the whole philosophy of the inevitability of progress. By 1920 these men had so revised the American intellectual world that it was impossible for the literate American to create a logical defense of inexorable progress.

Wielding a knife sharpened with biting irony, this new generation demonstrated that Spencer had tried to use the Darwinian concept of evolution to defend the older romantic and metaphysical beliefs of Western life; his had been merely a nominal, a verbal, acceptance of new ideas. Boldly, the young men announced their verdict that Spencer belonged to the pre-Darwinian era of history. Brashly, they declared that a philosophy of inevitable progress was equally outdated and impossible in an age that took evolution seriously. In the post-Darwinian climate of opinion, men could be interested only in the fact of consecutive change, in unending, meaningless process. This was the true meaning of Darwin, and this was the heart of the intellectual revolution that was now taking place.

Perhaps the man who is best known as a symbol of this movement in the social sciences is Thorstein Veblen. Dividing the thinkers of his day into the pre-Darwinians and the post-Darwinians, he attacked the theories of the pre-Darwinians, such as Spencer, because their science had been based on definition and classification and because it assumed that first cause and final consummation could be found and that the purpose of science was to discover "the body of natural law, governing phenomena under the rule of causation." Although pre-Darwinian science, continued Veblen, had emphasized the importance of facts and the placing of facts within the sequence of process, it had not been truly evolutionary because it did not share the spiritual attitude of post-Darwinian science. The modern scientist is concerned only with the colorless impersonal sequence, but the classical economists, posing as scientists, now placed their study of process within the framework of natural law. "To meet the high classical requirement, a sequence — and a developmental process especially — must be apprehended in terms of a consistent propensity tending to some spiritually legitimate end." This use of static natural laws was the basis of Spencer's position; it was, indeed, the basis for a belief in progress. And this belief, therefore, was not tenable in the light of modern scientific theory. The ultimate implication of Darwinism, Veblen insisted, was an unending, formless flux. Modern scientific theory was based on the acceptance of flux. And the Spencerian metaphysical doctrine of absolutes was therefore destroyed by modern science.

A total philosophy of evolutionary change logically implied a historical approach to society and the individual. Spencer and the classical thinkers had postulated man as a creature of fixed qualities, controlled always by his calculation of the amount of pleasure or pain to be gained from an activity. For this school, man "has neither antecedent nor consequent. He is an isolated definitive human datum, in stable equilibrium except for the buffets of the impinging forces that displace him in one direction or another."

This doctrine, declared Veblen, is unacceptable because its philosophical base is fallacious and because modern psychology has proved it erroneous in detail. Scientifically, it can be proved that man is created by society, which is itself part of the changing stream of history. Scientifically, it can be proved that "In all the flux, there is no definitive adequate method of life and no definitive or absolutely worthy end of action." There are no universal values and there is no universal human nature.

Then, taking up these theoretical weapons of evolution, historicism, and relativism, Veblen proceeded to use them to attack the social values of the status quo which the conservative Spencerians had claimed were an expression of a necessary stage of social progress. With precision, he revealed that the mores of middle-class America were the antithesis of progressive evolution.

The decorum of the Gilded Age, he proclaimed in *The Theory of the Leisure Class*, far from being evidence of civilization, was in truth the symbol of barbarian triumph. The manners of the leisure class, he insisted, could be traced to the age of barbarism, where it was the function of men to kill and destroy all competitors. It was a sign of the overwhelming success of the aristocracy over the common man that it could now put away the means of direct physical coercion, although slaughter and its instruments were still honorific badges of the upper class. With the poorer classes in disciplined bondage, however, the upper class could satisfy its barbaric urge to superiority in peaceful invidious distinction, in conspicuous waste and leisure, in special insignia of honor such as useless clothes and manners. For all that, Veblen reminded his readers, these were evidences of superior strength, and the lives of the upper classes were still marked by a callous disregard of the feelings and wishes of others.

There now arises an interesting problem. Unavoidably, Americans of 1900 were being educated by writers like Veblen to understand that there was a growing division between the world of ideas and the new industrial environment. Veblen, for instance, is best known for the distinction he made between the attitudes of the business class and the demands of the industrial system. He related the business code of America to the historical tradition of barbarism which he had so viciously attacked in his *Theory of the Leisure Class*; it was a code based on the motive of immediate profits, which was hopelessly outdated in a complex age whose dominant theme was efficiency. Surely here is undeniable evidence that the social sciences, led by men like Veblen, had emancipated themselves from the Genteel Tradition and were providing the knowledge of the new environment necessary for a reordering of social principles and social values to coincide with this new order of things.

But had this really happened? Had the Veblens broken from the old hierarchy of social values which had rested on a belief in progress? Had they made possible a reformulation of the normative world in which men lived? Were they really engaged in a creative process that would replace inevitable progress with another value system?

Certainly, the theories of evolution, historicism, and relativism were directed against those who believed in an unchangeable human nature as the basis of universal values. But is it not possible that the social scientists, who had been taught to believe passionately in inevitable progress, could not easily break from this faith? Is it not possible that in the face of the forces of industrialism which suddenly challenged this faith, these men reacted to defend their belief by redefining its supporting principles? Given the strong element of Enlightenment philosophy which was part of their heritage, they may have found this the logical course. For after all industrialism was only destroying society, society which for the *philosophes* had kept the natural man from being free to express his innate qualities of goodness and rationality. There is a great deal of evidence that the men of Veblen's generation were not freed from their climate of opinion by a close reading of Darwin. There is much to indicate that they criticized what they considered the ephemeral details of social life and philosophy in order to clear the way for the most extensive period of progress the world had ever known. Destructive industrialism became creative as men were stripped of the nonessentials of social institutions and traditions and were allowed to achieve and represent the truth of the Enlightenment, the truth of the natural man.

Follow Veblen, therefore, into the core of one of his critical scientific essays, "The Place of Science in Modern Civilisation." Listen while he relates that the nature of our culture is "peculiarly matter-of-fact," and that men have now accepted the idea that there are no ultimate values. But listen even more attentively when he asks an innocent question fraught with inconsistency: "How far is the scientific quest of matter-of-fact knowledge consonant with the inherited intellectual aptitudes and propensities of the normal man?" And then it is indeed time to follow Veblen to a place which he vehemently denied existence — to his hidden belief in a normal man, a man above and outside historical change. Once this fundamental presupposition of the existence of a normal man is accepted as part of Veblen's climate of opinion, an entire philosophy of primitivism emerges from what have always been described by Veblen scholars as incongruous elements in his writings.

Yes, Veblen talked in terms of fixed social stages of savagery, barbarism, and civilization; and, yes, he associated the present flowering of civilization with the innate qualities of the primitive man. "It may seem a curious paradox," he wrote, "that the latest and most perfect flowering of western civilization is more nearly akin to the spiritual life of the serfs and villeins than it is to that of the Grange or the Abbey." It was no paradox, however, as Veblen made clear: because his anthropology postulated a natural man in the era of savagery who was motivated by certain social instincts that led him into purposeful, constructive cooperation with his fellows; because his history postulated that this savage, altruistic nature had been submerged in the next stage of social evolution, barbarism, by the aristocrats who, living by a historically acquired set of psychological habits, were not normal men; because his faith in progress postulated that throughout history the common man had retained his original, primitive nature, which was much stronger than the barbarian traits that represented merely a passing historical era.

In *The Theory of Business Enterprise* Veblen made clear the manner in which modern industrial conditions were destroying these barbarian qualities. The machine, he believed, was dissolving the institutional heritage of his society; it was undermining, therefore, the very legal sanction upon which the business community had rested; it was creating a new intellectual atmosphere of standardized conduct and quantitative precision; it was allowing the mechanically trained to live without traditional myths or conventions. But then the modern man did not need new myths or conventions, because, stripped of the weight of barbarian culture, his savage nature with an innate set of values was reappearing. This, in turn, is the message of Veblen's key book, *The Instinct of Workmanship*. Savage man had the instinct of workmanship, which leads to high economic productivity and pride of work; the instinct of parental bent, which is broader than family solidarity and leads to broad humanitarianism and concern for the welfare of the whole community; and idle curiosity, which is the basis of all true, scientific knowledge. When the primitive social group became confused in the complexity of civilization, these instincts contaminated one another, and this allowed their perversions, the barbarian qualities that mark our business culture, to take control. The discipline of the machine, however, is reviving these instincts, by re-establishing on a worldwide scale the solidarity of the smaller social groups of savagery. The matter-of-factness of the machine is strengthening idle curiosity and the instinct of workmanship; the destruction of class divisions and the establishment of group solidarity is reinforcing the parental bent.

The coming of industrialism to America had meant initial confusion as business culture disintegrated, but it meant an increasing and, finally, a culminating society of perfect order, based on the natural altruism and social solidarity of the primitive man. Once before, when the collapse of the Roman Empire had brought complete social disintegration, "The pride of caste and all the principles of differential dignity and honor fell away, and left mankind naked and unashamed and free to follow the promptings of hereditary savage human nature which make for fellowship and Christian charity." Now this was happening again, with the added assurance that the machine discipline would restrain the contamination of man's instincts.

Veblen modified, at times even denied, this extreme optimism, but the central theme of his writings, the logical arguments he used, all pointed directly to the paradox that the increasing complexity of American life was really an increasing simplicity, that industrial progress meant a return to primitive solidarity. It is also arguable that the majority of the social scientists of Veblen's generation followed him in this paradox of progress and primitivism, in spite of their acceptance of evolution and historical relativism.[2]

It is clear that the American social philosophers, drawn from the ranks of the social sciences and technical philosophy, retained their fundamental allegiance to a faith in an irresistible progress up to the catastrophe of World War I. They did this by forcing their technical ideas into strange patterns, and by ignoring the actual behavior of men in the new urban-industrial communities. They are, indeed, a perfect example of the Genteel Tradition, as they blandly coerced experience into the mold of abstract thought. The inescapable fact of World War I, a war that had not been included in the vision of utopia, succeeded in finally undermining this castle in the air. It did so at the price of a debilitating confusion on the part of those who had held the true faith.

The new technical, scientific, and philosophical ideas had not been used as means to understand the emergence of a new environment which contradicted in so many ways the old social patterns and values which had provided the standards for the American definition of progress. Instead they were taken as the foundations of the homogeneous cooperative commonwealth itself; the word was to become the fact. And so Americans were not informed by their technical social philosophers of the possibility of the distintegration of their controlling myth, until 1917 transformed possibility into actuality.

The present attitude of historiography is to discount the intellectual importance of the literary men at the turn of the century. Emphasizing explicit philosophy rather than underlying attitudes, the historian of ideas has found a curious gap between the novelist and the social scientist. A symbolic figure here might be Theodore Dreiser. It has been asserted that Dreiser, though he attacked the smug and stilted hypocrisies of the middle class in the same general way as Veblen did, had none of the precision of his academic contemporary, none of the razor-sharp intellectual weapons, none of the penetrating and informed understanding of the situation's historical background. Worst of all, he had no grasp of the intellectual revolution through which he was living; he was striking out blindly and blunderingly, handicapped by the formal philosophy he retained, a philosophy borrowed from Spencerian sources. The temptation is to accept Dreiser's avowed debt to both Spencer and Haeckel. Dreiser related that their ideas, when he read them in his youth, "blew him to bits"; this was a lasting impression, he claimed, providing the philosophy of determinism that would inform his books almost throughout his career.

Dreiser, then, was almost a generation behind the sweep of American intellectual life. The unsophisticated Dreiser took up Spencerian philosophy when the country's best minds had moved beyond it. His specific errors in the light of the advances made by men like Veblen are legion. He accepted the notion that man is controlled by physical law when his philosophic contemporaries had moved on to the position that human nature is largely outside the influence of the physical environment and is, rather, shaped by social forces. He accepted the sensationalism of the pleasure-pain calculus when social psychologists were emphasizing that human nature is extremely complex and that its motives to action change with the values learned from its social environment. He accepted the position of atomic individualism, that society is a mechanical aggregation of isolated, self-contained individuals, when sociologists were proclaiming the unity of social life and the impossibility of an atomic individual, since human nature is itself a social product. In short, if the historian of ideas is searching for a manifestation of some philosophic or scientific theory in Dreiser's literature, he will be confronted with what the scholars of a generation ago called cultural lag, the delayed filtering down of advanced ideas from their first exponents to the rest of the community.

This is one way of interpreting Dreiser's place in the history of ideas. It is one level of criticism which can be used when he is compared to those contemporaries like Veblen who had rejected Spencer. But is it really Dreiser rather than Veblen who continued to express the traditions of Spencer's generation?

Veblen, beneath all the sound and fury that he directed at Spencer's specific concepts on man and nature, clung to the heart of Spencer's position — a determined process of progress. And because of this continued faith, he could not provide his readers with a real working knowledge of the revolutionary implications of industrialism; he could not direct attention to the latent consequences of the new material order; he did little to focus attention on the problem men would have of keeping order in a world in which the individual had lost his sense of belonging to a firm and supporting social framework. It is Dreiser, then, rather than Veblen who speaks for a new generation and a new appraisal of the world. It is Dreiser who has rejected the heart if not the details of Spencer's philosophy — his belief in an inevitable and controlled progress. It is Dreiser who interprets the coming of industrialism as a truly autonomous and unpredictable force, not controlled and channeled by an all-pervasive progress, as it had been for Spencer and Veblen.

Almost without exception the academic social philosophers of the progressive period came from smalltown or rural backgrounds. They were not directly influenced in the formative years of their youth by the new forces of industrialism or urbanism. Dreiser, on the other hand, developed emotionally within the most extreme conditions of the new order that was supposed to precipitate the forces of progress into more complete expression. Child of an immigrant family that seemed to belong nowhere in the post-Civil War world, he watched his isolated father disintegrate spiritually under the pressure of the unsettled urban industrial economy of the 1870's and 1880's. Dreiser saw him break up, crushed by the impact of impersonal forces that continued to threaten the only unity Dreiser knew, his family, until it too dissolved into formlessness and emptiness as its members drifted apart, lost from contact in the anonymity of cities that were everywhere so much the same.

The machine process, a Veblen would say, was obliterating the institutional framework of the past; it was grinding down the old world of values, including the family. But beyond destruction and despair Veblen saw emancipation, because man, freed from his commitments to the partial and narrow and incomplete loyalties of the past, would now merge with all the members of the community in mutual affection and solidarity. Dreiser did not, could not, believe that this social dissolution preceded social consolidation. The collapse of society had to be accepted at face value, resulting in loneliness and insecurity and fierce competition for the individual. And experience in the newspaper world of the midwestern cities of Chicago and St. Louis, and in the eastern cities of Pittsburgh and New York, did nothing to alter this feeling in Dreiser.

Man was essentially a solitary animal struggling for survival in a world governed by a cold impersonality. Believing this and aspiring to artistic expression, Dreiser could not readily have understood or appreciated the revolutionary academic ideas of the 1890's that proclaimed man's freedom from physical law: man's social nature and social freedom. Rather, it was from the tradition of Huxley and Spencer that Dreiser found technical theories to express his experience. But he accepted these on emotional, not on logical grounds. He was selective: he ignored Spencer's promise of unending progress and chose to think that man was a prisoner of natural forces that had no direction and no culmination. Now he had philosophic justification for his belief that "of one's ideals, struggles, deprivation, sorrows and joys, it could only be said that they were chemic compulsions, something which for some inexplicable but unimportant reason responded to and resulted from the hope of pleasure and the fear of pain. Man was a mechanism, undevised and uncreated, and a badly and carelessly driven one at that."

With justification but also ironically, it is Dreiser, then, who is criticized for making his characters unhistorical, for catching them up in the control of natural laws, for explaining their actions in terms of their "chemisms." Supposedly, Dreiser had no sense of the social conditioning of his individuals, of the historical complexities that make understandable the uniqueness of each individual's experience. And yet, just as Veblen consciously supported a philosophy of historicism and unconsciously expressed a historical position, it is possible that Dreiser, in spite of his predilection for natural law, expressed a world of historical individuals. Indeed, the America described by Dreiser in *Sister Carrie* is an entirely different world from that of Thorstein Veblen.

Veblen wrote that life is without ultimate meaning, but he ordered it with a rigid discipline. Middle-class mores were not desperately held badges of status, clutched at to provide security in a truly fathomless cosmos; they were the solid facts of barbarian behavior. And the members of the lower class, who in the future would be equated with society itself, carried the instincts of workmanship, of idle curiosity, of parental bent, which would provide the ultimate criteria for the meaning of existence.

Opposed to this, Dreiser presented two characters who can dramatically serve as symbols for Veblen's class traits. *Sister Carrie* is concerned with the decline of Hurstwood, a middle-class man, and the rise of Carrie, a lower-class girl. Somehow it was Dreiser, who had no theory of the social nature of man, who provided a much more compelling portrait of the condition of man in the new world of the city; somehow it was Dreiser who provided, in a moving manner, the histories of individuals caught up in a society that had lost its capacity to believe in the values that gave it order and continuity.

Carrie, on her arrival in Chicago, has none of the socially inculcated morality of the middle class. But, free from this grip, she reveals none of the social instincts Veblen attributed to the lower class. Indeed, if she has an instinct, it is only that of self-preservation. Essentially lonely and incapable of close human associations, she is nevertheless fascinated by the life and possibilities of the city. And she reaches out for the obvious middle-class symbols of prestige, such as clothes, not in the spirit of conspicuous waste, but for the strength they might add to her solitary position. Capable of a limited personality development, endowed with a certain circumscribed strength of character, she is motivated neither by extreme selfishness nor by loyalty. Her rise in the world in financial terms is made possible because of her natural gifts, but is brought about, in the final analysis, by chance acquaintances and occurrences. Throughout her upward progress she makes no lasting human contacts, and fails to reach the security of a final social equilibrium. When left at last at the pinnacle of her small success, she is surrounded by the same circle of meaninglessness as when we first met her, because, in Veblen's terms, she has the support of neither lower-class instincts nor middle-class mores. Success in a world that is crumbling is necessarily solitary and momentary.

In Hurstwood, the second protagonist of the story, Dreiser was capable of creating a still more moving symbol of the ever-present possibility of individual disintegration resulting from the impersonality that marked the new cities. He and Carrie demonstrated Dreiser's attitude that there was no static equilibrium in the new environment, that there was a constant flux of individuals going up or down. Symbolically, Hurstwood must go down. Here is Dreiser's fullest sense of the truly fragile nature of security in a world undergoing dissolution. Once Hurstwood exposes himself to the completely cold and heartless anonymity that forms the endless sea around the small island of middle-class meaning, he is hopelessly lost. There is not enough middle-class solidarity, not enough class consciousness, to motivate other middle-class men to try to save him.

Here too is personal tragedy, because Hurstwood, having lost the dignity and respectability of his middle-class position, has lost the qualities that had given his personality strength. In Veblen's terms, such a loss should have brought about his salvation because, for the first time, his innate, universal human nature of social service and social solidarity would have the opportunity to flower; or he would find support from an altruistic lower class that would sympathize with a new-found comrade. Instead, without the supporting elements of his previous environment, Hurstwood ceases to have personality or character and steadily disintegrates as a person until his death ends his intolerable isolation.[3]

It is arguable that *Sister Carrie* would have been a greater work of art if Dreiser had not been handicapped by many of the specific technical concepts of the Spencerian world. More important for the argument under review here, however, is the fact that, as an artist, Dreiser transcended these technicalities and wrote a novel with living individuals, whose personalities express with sensitivity their historical environment and do not reflect merely the abstract motivations of "chemisms." One can learn much from the pages of *Sister Carrie* about the nature and structure of American society in the years before the turn of the twentieth century In emphasizing the disintegrating social effects of the new industrial order, Dreiser taught his contemporaries what they had not yet come to see in their environment.

Here is the possibility of literature performing a creative role in changing the basic values of society when it has become an absolute necessity for such a change to take place. Dreiser did not give us a picture of the world as it actually existed. Most Americans were not so divorced from society as were Carrie and Hurstwood. What was important about Dreiser's exaggeration, however, was its possible ultimate relation to the value structure of his society. Dreiser's destructive theme was a direct challenge to the idea of progress, which was the major value or myth of his culture. In giving a one-sided knowledge of the new industrial world, by destroying the myths of the current culture, he was also creating the basis for a new value structure to accompany this environmental change.

It was the overwhelming experience of World War I, and not the writings of the academic social philosophers or the literary men, which brought the American intellectual to question the fact of progress at the basic level of emotion. But this experience merely emphasized the message of writers like Dreiser, who had already suggested in emotional terms the destructive possibilities of the new environment in negating human relationships.

One may hope, therefore, that historians of ideas will in the future focus their attention less exclusively on the concepts of technical philosophy and science, and increasingly appreciate the dynamic importance of literary and, indeed, all artistic expression in illuminating the mainstream of intellectual history — an illumination that is fundamental to understanding, because it not so much reflects as creates history. And one way in which they may approach this goal is through a reappraisal of Becker's suggestive use of the concept of climate of opinion.

### NOTES

[1] Carl Becker, *The Heavenly City of the Eighteenth Century Philosophers* (New Haven, Conn.: Yale University Press, 1932).

[2] See David W. Noble, *The Paradox of Progressive Thought* (Minneapolis: University of Minnesota Press, 1958).

[3] Much of this analysis of *Sister Carrie* depends on the essays by James T. Farrell, Eliseo Vivas, and Charles C. Walcutt, contained in *The Stature of Theodore Dreiser*, ed. Alfred Kazin and Charles Shapiro (Bloomington: Indiana University Press, 1955).

⚓ JOSEPH J. KWIAT

# Robert Henri and the Emerson-Whitman Tradition

THROUGHOUT his life as teacher and lecturer and author of numerous articles, as well as in his letters and journal, Robert Henri gave vigorous expression to attitudes and ideas which exerted a pervasive and significant influence upon his contemporaries.[1] The patterns of these ideas were ultimately linked with the great intellectual tradition of American Transcendentalism whose leading exponents — Emerson, Thoreau, Melville, and Whitman — explored, among other problems, the persisting cultural dependence of America on Europe and the individual, social, political, and artistic implications of the new democracy. David Bowers has commented that the movement's "vitalizing effect upon American art and literature, and, indeed, upon the development of American democracy as a whole, remains unrivaled."

The two voices of nineteenth-century American Transcendentalism that spoke most powerfully for Henri were Emerson and Whitman. They were the major sources for his ideas. If we look at these ideas in the context of their relation to the Emerson-Whitman tradition, we may see in broadened perspective Henri's role as a leading spokesman for the continuing tendency toward revolt in American thought in the crucial years after the turn of the century.

In 1886 Henri entered the Pennsylvania Academy as a student when Thomas Eakins, distinguished American painter and friend of Walt Whitman, had already been dismissed as a teacher. Although Eakins went on to form the Art Students' League of Philadelphia, Henri, nevertheless, elected to continue at the Academy under Thomas Anschutz. The young art student insisted upon expressing his own individuality in his work, and he found Anschutz's method of teaching congenial. For

153

one thing, Anschutz did not strive for a sterile perfection; and, further-more, he did not force his personal tastes upon his students. Thomas Hovenden, another of Henri's teachers at the Pennsylvania Academy, was molded by the academic tradition of France and was himself a mem-ber of the National Academy. His appeal for Henri was negative in the sense that he spurred on the student's early revolt against the tradition-alist's approach to art. From the numerous comments in his journal dur-ing this period, it appears that Henri did not wish to develop his artistic theories at the expense of artistic accomplishment while he was studying at the Pennsylvania Academy.

Henri's European period, from 1888 until 1891, included study at the Julian Academy under Bouguereau and others as well as at the École des Beaux-arts, a brief stay in Concarneau, where he attempted to de-velop his own style, and travel in Italy. During these years Henri formu-lated his conceptions of the American artist's proper relation to foreign influences, of the American artist as a free and independent exhibitor of his paintings, and of the artist as a practitioner of "good artistic theory." In a sense, these ideas triggered the movement toward revolt in twen-tieth-century American painting.

The young art student's journal, at the time of his European experi-ence, reveals the effect of his readings in Emerson upon his mind and attitude. He writes: "Emerson does not try to bring people to reason by disproving the Bible, but looks clear of everything straight at truth and lets facts speak for themselves." [2] Henri explicitly states his indebtedness to Emerson's teaching: "Reading Emerson has taught me two great les-sons. The first, to believe implicitly that it is worth while to do our best, though what we strive for may not be ours immediately; second, to have self-confidence, to trust our own convictions and gifts such as they are or may become, without echoing the opinions of others or desiring their more brilliant attainments. Emerson has taught me much besides, but these two doctrines of respectful self-reliance on one's own individual-ity have had the most invigorating influence on me. He knew that each one of us can receive only that for which he has an affinity, can give forth effectively only what is his birthright or else has become his own." [3] Henri's respect while in Europe for Emerson's two leading doctrines, self-reliance and reverence for one's individuality, anticipated the con-sistent intellectual direction that the painter was to take in later years.

Fresh from the stimulation of his recent readings in Emerson, Henri began to develop a conception of the relationship between the work of art and the artist: "One must work in the manner his own mind and nature dictates if he wants to last. What a man says and does in his paintings should be an expression of his reaction to the life about him. Ancient, modern, and new schools may teach him but to 'last' he must belong to none of them." In his own creative work, he expressed his antipathy toward the academic ideal of mere "finish" in a painting and he implied that he preferred to emphasize insight and intuition. "I am working on another picture of the road. . . . Today I finished the picture a little too literally for I lost the vagueness of blowing dust and with it truth. I started another keeping the overstatement of the morning in mind." Dissatisfaction with mere technical facility as an end in itself is evident in his criticism of one of his street scenes: "I think I am nearing the stopping place. . . . The cold facts of careful execution — if that is art I shall never be an artist. Strong impression should lift things above the plane of visual facts." [4]

What, then, was "good artistic theory" for Henri during this period of apprenticeship? Negatively, it was opposition to the academic ideal of mere technical facility, workmanship, and "finish." Positively, an intellectual attitude within the artist, the honest expression of his emotions, the communication of his individuality, and the effort to achieve the effect of the vitality of life in the work itself — these Emersonian ideas constituted "good artistic theory" for Henri.

Henri's later years revealed the importance of Walt Whitman, who supplemented Emerson as a significant personal force. The painter was ready to acknowledge his appreciation for Whitman's role in strengthening the idea of individuality: "It seems to me that before a man tries to express anything to the world he must recognize in himself an individual, a new one, very distinct from others. Walt Whitman did this, and that is why I think his name so often comes to me. The one great cry of Whitman was for a man to find himself, to understand the fine thing he really is if liberated." [5]

Of the American painters who most deeply impressed Henri two held a particularly high place. These were Thomas Eakins and John Twachtman and, significantly, Henri's admiration for both painters was associated with his admiration for Whitman. It was the essential integrity of Eakins' work that so greatly impressed Henri. He pointed out that Eakins, like Whitman, "cared nothing for prettiness or cleverness in life or in art. He struggled to apprehend the constructive force in nature and to employ in his works the principles found. His quality was honesty. 'Integrity' is the word which seems best to fit him." [6] Twachtman was ranked by Henri as "one of the giants in America" who, along with Whitman and others, illustrated the younger painter's conception of the American artist who finds meaning in American life, gets at the essential beauty of his environment, develops a technique to express his ideas, and, being American, reflects an American point of view.[7]

We are reminded of Henri's assertion that Whitman's name "so often comes to me" when, for example, the painter followed the writer in rejecting the inference that since the American heritage is younger it is therefore inferior to the European heritage. In fact, Henri suggested, the reverse is true: "It is a very interesting idea to me that we are as old as any European people, that we are, in fact, the same people vastly strengthened by the fate that made us pioneers in successive generations." [8] Similarly, Whitman wrote in "Nationality (and Yet)": "We need this conviction of nationality as a faith, to be absorb'd in the flood and belief of the people everywhere, south, north, west, east, to emanate in their life, and in native literature and art. We want the germinal idea that America, inheritor of the past, is the custodian of the future of humanity." But Henri is neither chauvinistic nor provincial in his cultural outlook. The American of whom his country will be most proud, he thinks, will be a world citizen, one who "will be heir to the world instead of a part of it." [9]

As a corollary to his profound reverence for the individual's freedom, Henri subscribed to Emerson's and Whitman's belief that man's most noble expression results from following his intuition. This theory compelled Henri, like his two intellectual ancestors, to be skeptical of institutionalized religion and to rest his faith upon humanity: "It is better that every thought should be uttered freely, fearlessly, than that any great thought should be denied utterance for fear of evil. It is only through complete independence that all goodness can be spoken, that all purity can be found. . . . When we think honestly, we never desire individuals bound hand and foot, and the ethical side of man's nature we cannot picture as overwhelmed and smothered with regulations if we are to have a permanent human goodness; for restrictions hide vice, and freedom alone bears morality." [10]

Although the dancer Isadora Duncan had shocked the sensibilities of her contemporaries when she attempted to apply her theory of artistic freedom to her personal life as well as to her art, she earned the devotion and admiration of Henri. He regarded her method of rearing her adopted children along "free lines" as one of the hopeful manifestations of the age. "It is but an expression of our present groping toward the freedom of the individual. . . . The great men of our time, Walt Whitman, and Ibsen and Tolstoy were working toward the same ideal." [11] Henri was, in effect, recognizing an inevitable connection between a "free art" and a "free life."

In attempting to formulate a theory of art, Henri insisted, first of all, that it is impossible to divorce a work of art from the character of its creator. Such words as "independence," "sincerity," "truthfulness," and "honesty" appear again and again in the painter's speculations on the nature of the creative artist. Two letters suggest the impact of Emerson's and Whitman's ideas upon this aspect of Henri's thought.

In the first letter (August 21, 1916), Emersonian echoes are heard: "The vision and expression of one day will not do for the next. Today must not be a souvenir of yesterday. And so, the struggle is everlasting. Who am I today? What do I see today? How shall today's expression be invented? How shall I *use* what I know and how shall I avoid being victim of what I know? Life is not repetition." Over against this, we are reminded of the familiar passage in "Self-Reliance": "A foolish consistency is the hobgoblin of little minds . . . With consistency a great soul has simply nothing to do. He may as well concern himself with his shadow on the wall. Speak what you think now in hard words, and to-morrow speak what to-morrow thinks in hard words again, though it contradict every thing you said to-day." An illuminating passage in Henri's second letter (April 1, 1917) explicitly reveals the thrust of Whitman's thought upon the painter:

There is little use in painting — in living in fact — unless you let yourself grow your natural course. . . . The big men have been rare simply because most men heed the dictators. Nobody wanted Walt Whitman, but Walt Whitman wanted himself — and now we have Walt Whitman. Of course it isn't easy to go one's road — because of our education we continually get off our track — but the fight is a good one and there is joy in it if there is any success at all. After all the goal is not making art — it's living a life — those who live their lives will leave the stuff that's really art. Art is a result. It is the trace of those who have lead [*sic*] their lives.

. . . The great revolution in the world which is to equalize opportunity, bring peace and freedom must be a spiritual revolution. A new *will* must come. . . . Our education has lead [*sic*] away from the realization that the mystery of nature is in each man. When we are wiser we will not assume to mould ourselves, but will make our ignorance stand aside — hands off — and we will watch our development, we will learn from ourselves. . . . Of course for us — for our generation — it must be a great struggle.

The relative importance of the emotions over against the intelligence was a matter of serious concern to Henri, and he would have agreed to Emerson's thought that "the fine arts have nothing casual but spring from the deepest instincts of the people who created them." A good artist, Henri suggested, "must have been capable of intense feeling, and capable of profound contemplation." The mind should be the tool and servant of the heart. "Walt Whitman," Henri noted, "was such as I have proposed the real art student should be. His work is an autobiography — not of haps and mishaps, but of his deepest thought, his life indeed." Henri then indicated his spiritual kinship to the poet, whose words on his own poetry suggest what Henri proposes the "real art student" should be. He referred approvingly to the following passage from "A Backward Glance o'er Travel'd Roads": " 'Leaves of Grass,' indeed . . . has mainly been the outcropping of my own emotional and other personal nature." [12] For Henri, like Whitman, strongly believed that every aspect of the artist, his emotions as well as his intelligence, is necessary for the creation of significant work.

Henri's indebtedness to the thought of Emerson and Whitman is, furthermore, reflected in his observations on the general relationship between art and "life." He theorized during the revolutionary "Eight" Show in 1908: "Always art must deal with *life*, and it becomes important as the ideas of the artist are significant. Art to every man must be his personal confession of life as he feels it and knows it. The lack of human quality in painting or sculpture means the lack of that vitality which makes for permanence." [13] Two years later, at the time of the Independent Exhibition in New York, he wrote: "Art cannot be separated from life. It is the expression of the greatest need of which life is capable, and we value art not because of the skilled product, but because of its revelation of a life's experience. The artists who produce the most satisfactory art are in my mind those who are absorbed in the civilization in which they are living." [14] Henri's portrait paintings represented a similar artistic intention: "I am looking at each individual with the eager hope of finding there something of the dignity of life, the humor, the humanity, the kindness, something of the order that will rescue the race and the nation."[15] When he was asked whether it was more important for an artist to paint or to illustrate, Henri answered: "The only important thing is that a man should have a distinct vision, a new and fresh insight into life, into nature, into human character, that he should see the life about him so clearly that he sees past the local and the national expression into the universal . . ."[16] And again: "I am not interested in any one school or movement, nor do I care for art as art. I am interested in life." [17]

Between 1891 and 1894, when he was an instructor at the Philadelphia School of Design for Women and held informal gatherings at his studio, Henri preached his "advanced" views. Here he taught his friends and pupils to record the life of the street, cafés, theaters, tenements, and prize fights directly and spontaneously; and he discussed books, music, politics, and ethics.[18] When he settled in New York in 1901, he established his reputation as a leader of a new movement in art. "At present," commented a contemporary critic, "he is the patriarch of the Café Francis crowd, a number of young painters, illustrators and *literati* who believe in the poetical and pictorial significance of the 'Elevated' and the skyscraper, of city crowds and rows of flat houses. To these men Henri expounds his theories of art." [19] These men included that group of painters known as the New York Realists or, less respectfully and more colorfully, the "Ash-Can School," "Revolutionary Black Gang," and "Apostles of Ugliness"—John Sloan, William J. Glackens, George Luks, and Everett Shinn. Henri's leadership culminated in the formation of the "Eight" Show in 1908 and the Independent Exhibition idea several years later; these, in turn, challenged the dictatorial policies of the entrenched academicians and assisted in the liberation of American artistic taste.

Writing for a magazine in the early years of the century, Henri stated: "Although our artists must be individual, they must also be students, men who think a great deal about life, who read, study, men of the widest possible attainment, and who are constantly engaged in finding the special means of expression best suited to the thing they have to say."[20] One of Henri's students, Guy Pène du Bois, picturesquely described the manner in which the painter led his American colleagues toward a keener and fresher understanding of what was vital in their environment for their art: "He [Henri] taught these men to grin at the historical novelists of the day and to side with Theodore Dreiser when he came along. They soon had no patience with escapists. Here, before their eyes, was the untouched panorama of life, an unlimited field, an art bonanza. Here in the Alligator Cafe on the Bowery, the Haymarket on Sixth Avenue, the ferry-boats, the lower East Side, in any number of cheap red-ink restaurants, one found subjects as undefiled by good taste or etiquette or behavior — that national hypocrisy — as a new-born babe." The "seat of sedition among the young," du Bois points out, was the Henri class at the New York School of Art, where his preaching of art for life's sake ("It isn't the subject but what you feel about it") clashed with the art for art's sake doctrines of William Merritt Chase, academic painter-teacher.[21]

Whitman would have derived satisfaction from the quickened sense of social responsibility which characterized American political and economic life from about 1890 to World War I. Industrial unrest in the early years culminated in trust-busting, muckraking, the municipal reform movement, the popular primary, the Australian ballot, the initiative, referendum, and recall, the woman's suffrage movement, the conservation movement, and social legislation guaranteeing factory inspection, limitation of hours, and improvements in labor conditions. All these represented a new emphasis upon the welfare of the common man and practical attempts to realize the long-promised "American dream" of social justice, opportunities for economic equality, and renewed respect for the dignity of the individual.

The artistic effects of these powerful currents in the life of the nation are evident in many of Henri's utterances, since any recognition of the artist's social responsibility will generate such problems as the relationship between art and nationalism, and art and humanitarian feelings. "To have an art in America," Henri stated, "will not be to sit like a pack rat on a pile of collected art of the past. It will be rather to build our own projection on the art of the past, wherever it may be, and for this constructiveness, the artist, the man of means, and the man on the street should go hand in hand. And to have art in America like this will mean greater living, a greater humanity, a finer sense of relation through all things." [22] Similarly, Whitman noted in *Democratic Vistas*: "America, betaking herself to formative action . . . must sternly promulgate her own new standard, yet old enough, and accepting the old, the perennial elements, and combining them into groups, unities, appropriate to the modern, the democratic, the west, and to the practical occasions and needs of our own cities, and of the agricultural regions. Ever the most precious in the common."

Henri expressed some of his maturing views on the relationship between art and nationalism in an article for the *Craftsman*. A genuinely American art, he noted, should not be limited to mere problems of subject or of technique. What is necessary for art in America is "an appreciation of the great ideas native to the country and then the achievement of a masterly freedom in expressing them." Obviously, then, it is impossible to create an American art from the outside in, since "for successful flowering it demands deep roots, stretching far down into the soil of the nation, gathering sustenance from the conditions in the soil of the nation, and in its growth showing, with whatever variation, inevitably the result of these conditions." He then presupposed certain conditions for art to flourish: "The men who become the artists must feel within themselves the need of expressing the virile ideas of their country; they must demand of themselves the most perfect means of so doing, and then, what they paint or compose or write will belong to their own land." [23]

America's "art spirit" was associated by Henri with a popular idea, the idea of progress. He stated the proposition, which both Emerson and Whitman had affirmed, that a major justification for the development of an American art is that the people might learn to express themselves in their own time and in their own land. Henri dismissed the notion that America needs art merely for its cultural value. What we do need, he asserted, "is art that expresses the *spirit* of the people today." And this would be voiced by the young people who represent the forces of "advancement" and "progress." [24]

Shocked by the social, intellectual, and artistic reactions accompanying World War I, Henri shifted his emphasis from nationalism to the vision of a universal brotherhood of man bound together by the universality of art. Unlike Whitman, however, he found it difficult to reconcile completely nationalism with a larger world-view. Henri now stated that art has nothing to do with nations: "The great masters of art, and of the sciences, the free creative spirits — belong to no boundried [*sic*] country. They do belong to a great free Brotherhood, a brotherhood which exists all the world over and the members of this brotherhood, unlike those of the state, never die. . . . It is this brotherhood alone than can stop warfare. Great men like Whitman, Poe, Ibsen, Wagner and such knew each other well and that they belonged to each other — the countrys [*sic*] where they were born have no right to claim them." [25]

In the following years, Henri was preoccupied with the idea of transforming America by impregnating the art spirit into the life of the country. He believed that "greatness can only come by the art spirit entering the very life of the people not as a thing apart but as the greatest essential of life to each one," and that "when America is an art country there will not be three or five or seven arts, but there will be the thousands of arts — or the one art, the art of life manifesting itself in every work of man." [26] Emerson, it will be recalled, made this point in his first essay on "Art" when he refused to make a distinction between the useful and the fine arts: "Beauty must come back to the useful arts, and the distinction between the fine and the useful arts be forgotten. If history were truly told, if life were nobly spent, it would be no longer easy or possible to distinguish the one from the other. In nature, all is useful, all is beautiful. . . . Beauty will not come at the call of a legislature. . . . It will come, as always, unannounced, and spring up between the feet of brave and earnest men." And in his *Democratic Vistas*, Whitman argued persuasively and comprehensively for "a literature underlying life, religious, consistent with science, handling the elements and forces with competent power, teaching and training men . . ."

Henri made a strong plea for the idea of the open forum which permits the unrecognized artist, as well as the established one, to exhibit his pictures. He firmly believed that the public must fulfill its responsibilities if America is to develop from an art-owning into an art-living country. He suggested the "democratic" function of art for individuals and for nations, and he insisted that the artist, through his attempt to make art pervade people's lives, contributed not only to good taste but also to "the means of freedom in the world." [27]

The true artist who recognizes his social responsibilities regards his work, Henri thought, as "a means of talking with men, of saying his say to himself and to others." The artist is one who gives "evidence." But the artist also produces a reaction. He creates "a stir in the world" when his motives are profound and when he believes in the importance of what he is doing; the stir may shower the artist either with abuse or with praise. The artist, then, is a person who "disturbs, upsets, enlightens, and . . . opens ways for a better understanding." For through the democratic nature of art, bonds of understanding and of knowledge are established

162

among men; and these, Henri wrote, "are the bonds of a great Brotherhood." [28]

In discussing the idea of the organic principle in American thought, F. O. Matthiessen described Emerson's repeated affirmation of the correspondence between art and nature and pointed out the indebtedness of the American architect Louis Sullivan to Whitman for "his most compelling suggestion of how art could grow organically from the forces of American life." [29] Similarly, Henri expressed various ideas which are consistent with the doctrine of the organic principle.

The idea of the intrinsic correspondence between art and nature was essential for Henri. Emerson wrote in his second essay on "Art": "Hence it follows that a study of admirable works of art sharpens our perceptions of the beauty of Nature; that a certain analogy reigns throughout the wonders of both; that the contemplation of a work of great art draws us into a state of mind which may be called religious." And Whitman, in the preface to the first issue of *Leaves of Grass*, 1855, made this observation: "The rhyme and uniformity of perfect poems show the free growth of metrical laws, and bud from them as unerringly and loosely as lilacs and roses on a bush, and take shapes as compact as the shapes of chestnuts and oranges, and melons and pears, and shed the perfume impalpable to form. The fluency and ornaments of the finest poems or music or orations or recitations, are not independent but dependent." Henri, in turn, asserted that "a thing that has the greatest expression of life itself, however roughly it may be expressed, is in reality the most finished work of art." [30]

Henri illustrated, by an analogy drawn from nature, his belief that to some degree every person is an artist: "It comes inevitably as the tree from the root, the branch from the trunk, the blossom from the twig. None of these forget the present in looking backward or forward. They are occupied wholly with the fulfillment of their own existence. The branch does not pose on the relation it bears to its great ancestor the trunk, and does not claim attention to itself for this honor, nor does it call your attention to the magnificent red apple it is about to bear. Because it is engaged in the full play of its own existence because it is full in its own growth, its fruit is inevitable." [31]

Variations on the theme of the organic principle run through *The Art Spirit*, a volume which presented Henri's mature reflections. "The great masters in all the arts," Henri wrote, "have been whole men, not half men. They have had marvelous fullness in all human directions, have been intensely humane in themselves and in their interests." Since the artist's skill was of subordinate interest for Henri, the fundamental questions for any artist are philosophical rather than technical: "What do you get out of nature? Why do you paint this subject? What is life to you? What reasons and what principles have you found? What are your deductions? What projections have you made? What excitement, what pleasure do you get out of it? Your skill is the thing of least interest to me." A good painting, Henri insisted, is primarily "a remarkable feat of organization" in which "every part of it is wonderful in itself because it seems so alive in its share in the making of the unity of the whole, and the whole is so definitely one thing." [32]

Closely related to Henri's conception of the correspondence between art and nature was his belief in the fundamental relationship between the various manifestations of intellectual and artistic activities. One of his students has recalled the broad cultural sweep of his teaching: "In the Henri classes painting was revealed to the pre-war generation for the first time as only another medium whereby the emotions of everyday life could be expressed. All the arts were discovered as kindred and relevant to painting. Isadora Duncan, Wagner, Dostoievski were discussed with Manet, Daumier, Eakins and Courbet. . . . He also taught us to appreciate the native genius. He was the first teacher to point out Eakins' rugged integrity and Ryder's romanticism as being distinctly American in quality. In the Henri class I heard Walt Whitman for the first time unblushingly discussed in a mixed gathering." [33]

It was within the general framework of this idea, also, that Henri reconciled the desirability of maintaining one's individuality and of retaining an awareness of the value of tradition. "Are there," he asked, "any artists in all the world who matter who have not been influenced by important predecessors, one one way, one another? Is there any art in the world, music, sculpture, architecture, anything that is permanent and beautiful, that does not accept and embody past greatness, and influence greatness to come?" [34] Compare this, then, with Emerson's statement in his first essay on "Art": "Thus the new in art is always formed out of the old. . . . No man can quite emancipate himself from his age and country, or produce a model in which the education, the religion, the politics, usages, and arts, of his times shall have no share. . . . Now that which is inevitable in the work has a higher charm than individual talent can ever give, inasmuch as the artist's pen or chisel seems to have been held and guided by a gigantic hand to inscribe a line in the history of the human race." And we hear a familiar echo of this in Whitman:

> Dead poets, philosophs, priests,
> Martyrs, artists, inventors, governments long since,
> Language-shapers on other shores,
> Nations once powerful, now reduced, withdrawn, or desolate,
> I dare not proceed till I respectfully credit what you have
>     left wafted hither . . .

Furthermore, Henri insisted that if the genuine art spirit "could but prevail in all our arts, in music, in painting, in sculpture, in writing, we would have a fundamentally greater and more interesting expression, a fundamentally greater appreciation." [35] He attempted to illustrate his thesis that "everything that is beautiful is orderly, and there can be no order unless things are in their right relation to each other." Ironically, he selected figures from the various arts (Whitman, Ibsen, Shelley, Wagner, Donatello) who, for the most part, were considered to be anything but beautiful or orderly in their own time. The "true artist" is one who breaks through conventional boundaries, he said, and cited representative "revolutionary" artists from music, sculpture, poetry, and painting: "Wagner can break through every musical limitation ever established, Rodin can mold his own outline of the universe, Whitman can utter truths so burning that the edge of the sonnet, roundelay, or epic is destroyed, Millet meets his peasant in the field and the Academy forgets to order his method of telling the world of this immemorial encounter." [36] Finally, Henri stated Emerson's and Whitman's idea that the American artist should be a "tremendously important and human creature": "His interests drive him into many important directions, into sociology, philosophy, religion, humanity. He is a man of all-round understanding of life. . . ." [37]

Henri had expressed his attitudes toward various social, economic, political, and artistic issues as early as his student days in Philadelphia. One might even say that the young man was temperamentally inclined to side with the "liberal" ideas which prevailed in American life toward the end of the century.[38] But his readings in Emerson during his student years in Europe crystallized and gave direction to what was perhaps a native tendency in his responses toward the world, toward art, and toward himself.

Many of Emerson's ideas bolstered Henri's driving desire for a vital and individual conception of art which would contribute toward the emancipation of American culture from the enervating grasp of the Academy and the Genteel Tradition. For the mature Henri, however, Walt Whitman was even more influential than Emerson in strengthening his appreciation and understanding of individuality. Whitman's special sigificance as "a force for freedom" is evident in Henri's parallel views on many problems — artistic, social, political, and cultural.

The movement which culminated in the early twentieth-century revolt in the arts in America owes a great deal, more than has heretofore been recognized, to Henri's liberal artistic theory. As we have seen, Emerson and Whitman loom large in the background of his thought. Henri's aesthetic theory is, for the most part, concerned with the nature of the artist, the artist as a spectator and recorder of life, the social responsibilities of the artist, and the artistic responsibilities of the artist. It is quite beside the point, however, to claim that Henri was a systematic aesthetician interested in erecting a pretentious aesthetic system based upon the doctrines of Emerson and Whitman. Rather, Henri, was an intelligent, serious, and energetic practicing artist and spokesman for a group of artists; at the same time, he and his fellow-artists had a capacity for being interested in and excited by those ideas which seemed to clarify their own personal and historical position. It is the fact that Henri found the center for these ideas in the utterances of Emerson and Whitman that commands our attention.

Now both Emerson and Whitman profoundly influenced Henri's views on the inevitable relationship between the artist and his work. The genuine artist is, for Emerson, a man of character and learning who discovers his greatest power in responding to his instinct and in following his intuition. Thus emerges the doctrine of self-reliance and reverence for one's own individuality, a doctrine, incidentally, which Emerson himself applied to the creative artist and to his image of the ideal observer of the art object. Whitman's emphasis, in turn, upon the artist's integrity over against mere traditionalism or cleverness results in his conception of individual self-reliance and the doctrine of "personalism."From these two roughly similar attitudes, Henri developed his own idea of the true artist as a person of character who values his independence, sincerity, truthfulness, and integrity. He stated his dissatisfaction with mere technical facility as contrasted with genuine insight and an honest expression

166

of the emotions. The artist, then, is more than an ordinary craftsman for Emerson, Whitman, and Henri; he is that sublime individual, a knower and a doer.

When Henri pronounced that any significant art must deal with *every* aspect of life, that art itself is a record of life, that the art work is a revelation of a life's experience, and that the artist's ability to approximate and penetrate the quality of life itself determines his greatness, he was restating for a later generation of Americans some of Emerson's and Whitman's more basic principles in their conception of the function of art. Thus we have Emerson's emancipated attitude toward the portrayal of the human body in sculpture, and Whitman's "unabashed" treatment of the power of sex. Or Emerson's feeling that he is near the very source of art in his enjoyment of the spectacle of men and women in the informal attitudes of work and play in common life, and Whitman's image of himself as the poet both of the city and of nature, his belief that the final decisions of language are made "by the masses, people nearest the concrete, having most to do with actual land or sea," and his reverence for "the deep silent mysterious . . . quality of life itself." Emerson's hope that the *Dial* would "go straight into life" and that it would catch into symbols the excitement of American life are reflected in Henri's own appreciation of Whitman's catalogue of that life. This is, as Henri put it, the attempt to attain "the reality of beauty in matter as it is."

Preoccupied with his own country, first of all, Henri indicated how necessary it is for the American artist to find universal meaning in life, to realize the essential beauty of his own country, and to express an "American" point of view. Similarly, Emerson voiced a fervent desire to make known the best art, literary and in every other form, for his country since he was convinced that art nourishes men's spirits. Although he realized that a knowledge of the best that the world has to offer is a rare privilege that the American artist can ill afford to ignore, he warned against the dangers of mere imitation of foreign models. For Whitman, the Americans "have probably the fullest poetical nature" and the United States themselves "are essentially the greatest poem." Henri, furthermore, envisioned the true artist as a social critic, and he judged art as successful when the artist's humanitarian convictions are finally aroused and when he identifies himself with the masses of the people in their struggles. Emerson's own enduring conviction that art is made for man, not man for art, led to his recognition of the place of the common man in his aesthetic theory. Whitman also recognized the poet's ethical influence on society, and he preached a religion of humanity. His faith in the "divine-average" rested upon his faith in social progress; and he found it impossible to overstate the poet's role in bringing about the brave new world.

Finally, Henri attempted to grapple with the nature of the artistic process. He discussed this problem largely in terms of the organic principle of art as he learned it from Emerson and Whitman. All three, then — Emerson, Whitman, and Henri — were aware of the intrinsic correspondence between art and nature and the artist and nature, and of the integral relationship between form and content and the artist's responsibility to intuit a form as close as possible to organic growth. All three minimized "finish" in the work of art since it tends to lead toward artificiality and useless ornamentation, and they found it possible to reconcile the useful and fine arts. Similarly, all three recognized the potentially beautiful character of the commonplace and the unpleasant, the importance of maintaining a balance between the past and present, and the value of preserving the benefits of tradition without sacrificing either the expression of one's individuality or the possibilities of innovation.

If called upon to express his intellectual and artistic indebtedness to the thought of Emerson and Whitman, there is no doubt that Henri would have subscribed to Whitman's own personal tribute to Emerson. "The best part of Emersonianism is," Whitman wrote, "it breeds the giant that destroys itself. Who wants to be any man's mere follower? lurks behind every page. No teacher ever taught, that has so provided for his pupil's setting up independently — no truer evolutionist." Even in this preliminary study, Henri's importance in the story of American culture must be seen in a new light. He must be recognized as one of the leading representatives of the continuity of the "liberal tradition" in American intellectual and cultural thought in the early years of the twentieth century. For Henri did even more than to establish a link with the rich and persistent values of the American past. He also functioned as a major seminal influence for his contemporaries, as well as succeeding generations, because of the breadth, vigor, and essential humanity of his views. But this is another chapter that must be told on another occasion.

### NOTES

[1] Robert Henri was born in 1865 and died in 1929. Quotations from these unpublished letters and journal are reproduced here through the courtesy and generosity

of Henri's sister-in-law, Miss Violet Organ. Hereinafter they will be cited as Henri Journal or Henri Letters.

² Henri Journal, February 18, 1890. He was also reading, among others, Ruskin, Paine, Browning, Daudet, and Tolstoy. Emerson, however, was the strongest influence at this time.

³ *Ibid.*, April 6, 1890.

⁴ *Ibid.*, February 22, March 14, April 25, June 22, and July 28, 1890.

⁵ Henri, "Progress in Our National Art Must Spring from the Development of Individuality of Ideas and Freedom of Expression: A Suggestion for a New Art School," *Craftsman*, xv (January 1909), 389.

⁶ Henri, *The Art Spirit* (Philadelphia: Lippincott, 1939), p. 86.

⁷ "Progress in Our National Art," *Craftsman*, xv, 390.

⁸ Henri, "What about Art in America?" *Arts and Decoration*, xxiv (November 1925), 35.

⁹ *The Art Spirit*, pp. 126–127.

¹⁰ Henri, "My People," *Craftsman*, xxvii (February 1915), 467–468.

¹¹ Quoted from "Only Out of Home's Narrow Confines Is Full Growth Possible for Children, Says Robert Henri," *New York Tribune*, January 25, 1915.

¹² *The Art Spirit*, pp. 7, 116, 80.

¹³ Quoted in Giles Edgerton, "The Younger American Painters," *Craftsman*, xiii (February 1908), 524.

¹⁴ Henri, "The New York Exhibition of Independent Artists," *Craftsman*, xviii (May 1910), 162.

¹⁵ "My People," *Craftsman*, xxvii, 467.

¹⁶ Quoted in "W. J. Glackens: His Significance to the Art of His Day," *Touchstone*, vii (June 1920), 192.

¹⁷ *The Art Spirit*, p. 221.

¹⁸ *Robert Henri: His Life and Works*, eds. William Yarrow and Louis Bouché (New York: Boni and Liveright, 1921), p. 24.

¹⁹ S. H., "Studio-Talk," *International Studio*, xxx (December 1906), 183. The Henri circle is reminiscent, in many ways, of Whitman's relationship to his followers.

²⁰ Quoted in Edgerton, "The Younger American Painters," *Craftsman*, xiii, 524.

²¹ Guy Pène du Bois, *Artists Say the Silliest Things* (New York: Duell, Sloan and Pearce, 1940), pp. 82, 84.

²² Quoted in *New York Realists, 1900–1914* (New York: Whitney Museum of American Art, 1937), p. 6.

²³ "Progress in Our National Art," *Craftsman*, xv, 387–388.

²⁴ "The New York Exhibition of Independent Artists," *Craftsman*, xviii, 161.

²⁵ Henri Letters, February 14, 1915.

²⁶ *Ibid.*, August 27, 1916.

²⁷ Henri, "The 'Big Exhibition,' the Artist and the Public," *Touchstone*, i (June 1917), 174, 216.

²⁸ *The Art Spirit*, p. 9.

²⁹ F. O. Matthiessen, *American Renaissance: Art and Expression in the Age of Emerson and Whitman* (London and New York: Oxford University Press, 1941), pp. 144, 592. In addition, see Vivian C. Hopkins, *Spires of Form: A Study of Emerson's Aesthetic Theory* (Cambridge, Mass.: Harvard University Press, 1951), pp. 78–104, for a comprehensive discussion of Emerson's conception of organic form in the fine arts.

³⁰ "The New York Exhibition of Independent Artists," *Craftsman*, xviii, 167.

³¹ Henri, "What Is Art?" *Arts and Decoration*, vii (April 1917), 324.

³² *The Art Spirit*, pp. 91–92, 125, 20.

³³ Helen Appleton Read, *Robert Henri* (New York: Whitney Museum of American Art, 1931), p. 10.

³⁴ Quoted in "W. J. Glackens," *Touchstone*, vii, 192.

[35] "Progress in Our National Art," *Craftsman*, xv, 391.

[36] "My People," *Craftsman*, xxvii, 459–460, 461–462.

[37] "What about Art in America?" *Arts and Decoration*, xxiv, 75.

[38] In Henri's early unpublished letters and journal we find a forecast of many of the "liberal" views which characterized his more mature thought. He expressed sympathy for a Negro who was not permitted to enter Jefferson Medical College in 1886 because of his color. After attending a lecture on women's rights in Philadelphia in 1887, he wrote: "At last the age of reason, the kindling of a spark that will grow to enlighten the world." Several years later, he expressed indignation at the plight of still another underprivileged group, the American Indian. Significantly, he opposed the argument for capital punishment and the hanging of the Chicago anarchists, and he was stirred by the Homestead Riots. A defender, even during this formative period, of the rights of all mankind on the fundamental ground that if injustice is tolerated for a minority then all men are in potential danger of losing their precious heritage of freedom, Henri is a worthy representative of the liberal position in America during a period of acute social and economic tension.

❧ THEODORE C. BLEGEN

# Singing Immigrants and Pioneers

THANKS to the ballad collectors, we know about the singing cowboy — his troubles on the old Chisholm trail and his horror of being buried on the lone prairie, "where the rattlesnakes hiss, and the crow flies free." We have heard his grim warning that Comanche Bill "will lift off your hair on the dreary Black Hills," and we are familiar with his efforts to whoop, yell, and drive his "little dogies" from Texas to Wyoming.

So also we know of the singing French-Canadian voyageur, whose favorite chanson tells of crystal fountains, roundelays, nightingales, and a love lost all for an undelivered bunch of roses, and who, when not re-calling those luckless roses, might recite, in rhythm with the strokes of his paddle, the glories of his bark canoe and of the rivers he traveled. We even know of the singing shanty boy whose ballads record lumbering in its golden age, the advance of the army of axes, the crash of falling pine, and the exploits of red-sashed lumberjacks.

The songs of cowboys, canoemen, and lumberjacks have been col-lected and made available to students of history and folklore. There has also been a wide interest in sailor chanteys, mountain minstrelsy, Ameri-can survivals of English and Scottish popular ballads, the songs of the Negroes, and the ballads of broad sections, notably the South.

But what of the singing immigrant? And the singing pioneer migrating to the West? The ballads of certain great popular movements, notably immigration and the American westward migration, have not attracted the attention they deserve. In both these fields song materials are as exten-sive in quantity as they are diverse and rich in content.

The songs and ballads of migration present two contrasting themes: on the one side, hope, the promise of the West, the glory of the fresh start, romance, triumph; on the other, deprivation, loneliness, futility, spiritual loss. The same contrast stands out in the fiction of pioneering. One school of writers portrays the westward movement as a glorious triumphant crusade, and another, probing into its psychological aspects, pictures loss as well as gain. Both the hope and courage and the tragedy of spirit that so often accompanied pioneering are depicted by O. E. Rölvaag in *Giants in the Earth*; and a parallel from real life is presented in *A Son of the Middle Border*. Hamlin Garland's father was a Per Hansa in the flesh, his mother a Beret.

The theme of the elder Garland was a brave western marching song that catches up the buoyancy of the early West:

> Cheer up, brothers, as we go,
> O'er the mountains, westward ho,
> Where herds of deer and buffalo
> Furnish the fare.
>
> CHORUS: Then o'er the hills in legions, boys,
> Fair freedom's star
> Points to the sunset regions, boys,
> Ha, ha, ha-ha!
>
> When we've wood and prairie land,
> Won by our toil,
> We'll reign like kings in fairy land,
> Lords of the soil!

That song, writes Garland, was "a directing force in the lives of at least three generations of my pioneering race," and its call continued to entice his father until, after ceaseless journeys, he found himself an old man, "snowbound on a trackless plain," his hopes frustrated, but still in spirit "the tiller of broad acres, the speculator hoping for a boom."

But the mother of the son of the Middle Border preferred a plaintive, questioning ballad in the form of a dialogue between husband and wife. The husband is ready to migrate:

> Away to Wisconsin a journey I'll go,
> For to double my fortune as other men do,
> While here I must labor each day in the field
> And the winter consumes all the summer doth yield.

But the wife does not agree:

> Dear husband, I've noticed with a sorrowful heart
> That you long have neglected your plow and your cart,
> Your horses, sheep, cattle at random do run,
> And your new Sunday jacket goes every day on.
> Oh, stay on your farm and you'll suffer no loss,
> For the stone that keeps rolling will gather no moss.

The husband is not convinced. He pleads with his wife to go and holds out alluring prospects:

> While you some fair lady and who knows but I
> May be some rich governor long 'fore I die.

But the wife reminds him of realities — the labor that awaits them, and the heavy expense,

> Your horses, sheep, cattle will all be to buy,
> You will hardly get settled before you must die.

When the husband again promises riches and tries to tempt his wife by adding, "We will feast on fat venison one half of the year," she advances an argument he cannot meet,

> Oh, husband, remember those lands of delight
> Are surrounded by Indians who murder by night.
> Your house will be plundered and burnt to the ground
> While your wife and your children lie mangled around.

The husband gives in:

> Oh, wife, you've convinced me, I'll argue no more,
> I never once thought of your dying before,
> I love my dear children although they are small,
> And you, my dear wife, I love greatest of all.

And they both join in a final refrain,

> We'll stay on the farm and we'll suffer no loss,
> For the stone that keeps rolling will gather no moss.

Such ballads the elder Garland did not like, and we can readily understand why. The men of the westward movement preferred robust, optimistic songs, with challenges to the venturesome:

> Come, all you young men, who have a mind for to range,
> Into the western country, your station for to change;
> For seeking some new pleasure we'll all together go,
> And we'll settle on the banks of the pleasant Ohio.

This Ohio ballad pictures good lands, rivers full of fish, lofty sugar trees, bountiful wild game, a Garden of Eden. It discounts the Indian menace and closes with a hopeful appeal:

> Come all you fair maidens wherever you be,
> Come, join in with us, and rewarded you shall be;
> Girls, if you'll card, knit, and spin, we'll plough,
>     reap, and sow,
> And we'll settle on the banks of the pleasant Ohio.

> Girls, if you'll card, knit, and spin, we'll plough,
>   reap, and sow,
> And we'll fold you in our arms while the stormy wind
>   doth blow.

Not less persuasive or insistent in its claims for an Eden was the early booster ballad "El-a-noy":

> 'Way down upon the Wabash,
> Sich land was never known;
> If Adam had passed over it,
> The soil he'd surely own;
> He'd think it was the garden
> He'd played in when a boy,
> And straight pronounce it Eden,
> In the State of El-a-noy.
>
> CHORUS: Then move your family westward,
> Good health you will enjoy,
> And rise to wealth and honor
> In the State of El-a-noy.
>
> 'Twas here the Queen of Sheba came,
> With Solomon of old,
> With an ass load of spices,
> Pomegranates and fine gold;
> And when she saw this lovely land,
> Her heart was filled with joy,
> Straightway she said, "I'd like to be
> A Queen in El-a-noy."

Sometimes the praise of a region is satirical, as in "Dakota Land":

> We've reached the land of desert sweet,
> Where nothing grows for man to eat.
>
> Oh! Dakota land, sweet Dakota land,
> As on thy fiery soil I stand,
> I look across the plains
> And wonder why it never rains
> Till Gabriel blows his trumpet sound
> And says the rain's just gone around.

Or in the ballad tribute to a county in Nebraska:

> Hurrah for Lane County, the land of the free,
> The home of the grasshopper, bed-bug and flea,
> I'll holler its praises, and sing of its fame,
> While starving to death on a government claim.

How happy I am as I crawl into bed,
The rattle-snakes rattling a tune at my head,
While the gay little centipede, so void of all fear,
Crawls over my neck and into my ear.
And the gay little bed-bug so cheerful and bright,
He keeps me a-going two-thirds of the night.

The choicest of the booster ballads is "Michigania," in which New England was invited to move to the West:

Come all ye Yankee farmers who wish to change your lot,
Who've spunk enough to travel beyond your native spot,
And leave behind the village where Pa and Ma do stay,
Come follow me, and settle in Michigania, —
    Yea, yea, yea, in Michigania.

Then there's old Varmount, well, what d'ye think of that?
To be sure, the gals are handsome, and the cattle very fat;
But who among the mountains, 'mid clouds and snow,
        would stay;
When he can buy a prairie in Michigania? —
    Yea, yea, yea, in Michigania.

Then there's the State of New York, where some are
        very rich;
Themselves and a few others have dug a mighty ditch,
To render it more easy for us to find the way,
And sail upon the waters to Michigania, —
    Yea, yea, yea, in Michigania.

The ballad passes in review the claims of Ohio, Indiana, and Illinois and grants that these states are very good, but concludes that they fall far below Michigania. It proceeds to chant the praises of particular Michigan localities, issues directions after the fashion of a guidebook, and at the end reiterates its friendly, if selective, invitations to the East:

Then come, ye Yankee farmers, who've mettle hearts
        like me,
And elbow grease in plenty, to bow the forest tree,
Come, take a quarter section, and I'll be bound
        you'll say,
This country takes the rag off, this Michigania,
    Yea, yea, yea, this Michigania.

The lumberjacks, singing "Michigan-I-O," were less enthusiastic than the settlers who chanted "Michigania." The shanty boys, in ballads of a kind familiar among railroad workers and cowboys, sang,

> The grub the dogs would laugh at. Our beds were
>    on the snow,
> We'll see our wives and sweethearts, and tell them
>    not to go
> To that God-forsaken country called Michigan-I-O.

A ballad from pioneer times called "The Beauty of the West" celebrates the attractions of the North Star State. It tells of an Ohioan who sets out for the West in search of the Promised Land:

> When first I left old Buckeye
> Location for to find,
> I heard of a distant country
> In language most divine,
> A land of milk and honey
> And water of the best,
> They called it Minnesota,
> The Beauty of the West.
>
> And when I came to Galena
> I didn't like the town.
> The streets they were too narrow,
> And winding was the ground.
> I stepped up to my tavern
> And wrote upon my chest,
> "I'm bound for Minnesota,
> The Beauty of the West."

He tells of boarding a steamer, the *Northern Belle*, which ascended the Mississippi and landed him at Winona. "And when I got recruited," he sings, "A'rambling I did go, I wandered the state all over, I trailed it through and through." In the course of his wanderings he came to have a warm admiration for the girls of Minnesota, and he closes with a tribute:

> The Gopher girls are cunning,
> The Gopher girls are shy.
> I'll marry me a Gopher girl
> Or a bachelor I'll die.
> I'll wear a stand-up collar,
> Support a handsome wife,
> And live in Minnesota
> The balance of my life.

Among many versions of this ballad is one called "The Lily of the West." It too tells of a traveler in search of lands in the West:

> In Eighteen hundred and fifty-four, I left my
>    native shore,
> My worthy friends and native home, never to see
>    them more.

The singer is emphatic in his advice:

> Come all ye noble emigrants that are inclined to roam
> Into this Western Country, to seek you out a home,
> If you will be advised by me, I'll tell you what's
>    the best,
> Come settle in Minnesota, the Lily of the West.

While native Americans were singing of the beauties and lilies of the West, the magic of the inland empire was making itself felt in every part of Europe. There was in process a new discovery of America brought home to the consciousness of the humblest farmer and laborer. This accompanied a mass migration, a phenomenon recorded and reflected in sources of great variety.

Official statistics have been much used, not to say abused, by students, often with little awareness of the simple truth that immigrants were people. Impressive as the statistics are, they do not open doors to understanding of the human interest and significance of the migration of millions of human beings. It is time for us to read the letters and narratives of the immigrant himself — to understand the impact of America upon European minds and of immigrants upon American life. Statistics may be eloquent, but they cannot sing. If we would probe the inner history of the immigrant, we should not neglect the ballads and songs and poems of the movement in which he centrally figured. How rich such sources are may be suggested by a few selections from the ballads and songs of the migration.

To go or not to go was the question the European mulled over as he thought about his future and looked westward. His perplexity is mirrored in dialogue ballads not unlike those sung by Hamlin Garland's mother. Sometimes these songs were obviously touched with satire, evidencing an origin in the camp of the enemies of emigration. In a Norwegian ballad of 1844, for instance, the first singer voices discontent:

> When pointed icicles cling to eaves
> And snow goes whirling above the leaves,
> When through my kitchen the cold winds blow,
> To the Mississippi I fain would go.

177

For a half-dozen stanzas he tells of empty granaries, stony meadows, and early frosts, and sighs for the delights of America, where

> The grass springs up, turning into hay,
> Your crop you cut in a single day,
> Enough to last all the winter through —
> America is the land for you!

But a second singer takes up the song, points out that there are two sides to everything on this earth, insists that

> An Eden means more than lovely woods,
> And more than stores filled with earthly goods,

and suggests that there is such a thing as unhappiness amid abundance. He inquires, Will American prosperity last?

> The land you seek with a hopeful heart —
> Its smiling Fortune may soon depart
> And famine stalk through the countryside.
> Alas, your Eden may not abide.

The singing debater snaps his fingers at the rigors of Norse winters, explains that, with mountainsides covered with birch, there is no difficulty about getting wood for the home fires, and says,

> I find no reason why I should roam,
> I make my climate in this, my home.

In a similar dialogue from 1846, one singer launches a song debate by declaring,

> I'll not stay on in this northern valley,
> I'll journey west to America,
> My strength and will I shall have to rally
> And go where best I can make my way.

Cheap land, light taxes, a chance to make a living with his hands: this is America to him. He warms to his theme as he criticizes his own country:

> Of precious freedom they like to prattle,
> How we the people control the purse!
> But bureaucrats treat us like cattle,
> They fatten — we bear the poor man's curse.

Finally he is answered by a philosophical comrade, who explains that the indictment is sound in part, but that things are getting better, and then asks, somewhat plaintively,

178

If in Wisconsin old worries languish,
If fortune rolls all my debts away,
What's the good, if my mind's in anguish?
If longing gnaws me each bitter day?

As such debates went forward, many a song was written sternly adjuring people to remain at home. One from the 1860's asks the emigrant if he expects to find in America the same sun, the same summer, the same music in the streams:

Nay, you will not find it so,
This, your fate, you've bidden:
Sun shut out by clouds below,
Stars by black night hidden;
Speech and custom of your past
From your life you sever,
Exiled you will be at last,
Down the years forever.

Others took up the challenge, however:

I'm moving west, come with me, you,
Don't sit at home and wait;
Come, let us bid this toil adieu,
This grinding work we hate.
For some, I know, it wins rich gains,
The Philistine, of course,
But we get nothing for our pains,
Save only grim remorse.

Pilgrim ballads promptly answered the singers who gloomily foretold disillusionment and an end to blessed sun and summer. Sometimes, as in a Swedish "America ballad" from the 1850's, the songs were marked by a gay irony that did not mask the essential truth underlying their lines:

Brothers, we have far to go,
O'er the salty waters,
There we'll find America —
Far across the ocean.
  Isn't that impossible?
  Ah, but it is wonderful!
  Pity that America
  Is so far away!

Trees that strike their roots in earth
Sweet they are as sugar,

Country full of maidens —
Lovely dolls they are, Sir.

Chicks and ducks come raining down,
Steaming hot and tender,
Fly upon your table,
Knives and forks in place, Sir.

The shining sun goes never down,
Everyone's your friend there,
Drinks your health in wine, Sir,
Takes you out to dine, Sir.
    Isn't that impossible?
    Ah, but it is wonderful!
    Pity that America
    Is so far away!

There was no stopping the movement. People went, in ever-increasing thousands, until a noted poet could say, in plaintive tone,

Now with horror we recall
Scourge of Black Death reaping.
Over valley hangs a pall,
Through it fevers sweeping.
Gone the folk, the hearth is cold,
Desolate the farms of old.

But the victims of the "America fever" did not abandon hearth and home without singing farewells to friends and things familiar:

Farewell, valley that I cherish,
Farewell, church and trees and home,
Farewell parson, farewell parish,
Farewell kith and kin, my own,
Lovely gardens, walks of beauty, —
Would to God this were undone! —
Home, you stay me in my duty,
Calling, "Leave me not, my son!"

From the deep woods of Wisconsin in the 1840's came this goodbye, with a bitter undertone:

Blessed land, farewell forever,
Stern thy ways, severe thy hand,
Bread denied to fair endeavor,
Still I honor Motherland.
All things vanish — care and sorrow
Pass, their marks engraved on me,

Yet my soul fronts each tomorrow
Glad, refreshed with thought of thee.

And an emigrant woman found it hard to leave her spinning wheel:

Goodbye, my old comrade,
As now I must leave you,
My heart, it is breaking,
My going will grieve you.
No longer at night,
By the glow of the fire,
Shall we sit and gossip,
And know heart's desire.

These things all about us
Had roots in my heart,
Ah, now it is bleeding
And torn as we part.
But if I must choose
From these home things I cherish,
Ah, give me my cradle
To have till I perish.

Such doleful farewells are common to all the Old World countries that contributed to the nineteenth-century stream of migration, and the Norse lament reminds one of a song of the Irish emigrants:

Tears from their eyes are falling like rain,
Horses are trotting, going off for the train,
Their hearts they are breaking for leaving the shore,
Their friends and green Erin they ne'er may see more.

And a Finnish ballad pictures the parting in only a few stark phrases:

A letter came, a steamship ticket,
A bitter cup of coffee drunk in parting.
The emigrant left,
The home folks wept.

In the ballads one can follow the emigrants to the waiting vessel and see them go aboard amid a "confusion of speech, song, laughter, weeping, and music."

The flapping sails swell with the breeze,
The ship glides out upon the seas,
Its pennons proudly flying.
Dim eyes the fading woodlands seek,
As valleys and the highest peak
Sink down, dissolving, dying.

And there are ballads celebrating the emigrant brigs, proud vessels bearing such names as the *Valhalla*, the *Achilles*, the *Preciosa*, and the *Superb*. Across the sea they went, to New York, to Quebec, to the West Indies, then back across the Atlantic by way of England, to start the triangle once again.

While emigrants sailed to the West, many people somehow managed to resist the lure, but not without singing their explanations of why they stayed at home. One Norseman refused to join a party of prospective gold hunters who bought a vessel and sailed from western Norway for California by way of South America — sailed, be it noted, only after the entire party had joined in two songs, one of hope and anticipation, one of farewell to snow-capped mountains and the beauty and music of native waterfalls. The stay-at-home did not deny that California was a land of glory:

> O El Dorado! Lovely, golden name!
> It rings upon the ears like ducats clinking!
> Search all the world, no country, to my thinking,
> Will yield such peace, such happiness, such fame.
> Ah, there the very trees bear fruit of gold,
> And golden doubloons fill the mouths of fishes,
> The ears of corn are golden, too, I'm told,
> One gathers golden flowers, if one wishes.

He appreciated the ease of getting supplies for one's table in the Far West, where, he sang,

> The fields yield crops without a touch of rake,
> Don't doubt my word, you know I'd never lie, son.
> Suppose you'd like to eat a juicy steak —
> That's easy, hurl your lasso at a bison.

But there were disadvantages, and these the singer points out:

> It's true you're more than apt to lose your life,
> The Redskins, they will scalp you if they catch you,
> And if they don't a Yankee's sure to snatch you
> And neatly carve you with his bowie knife.

And at the end he gives his final judgment:

> So let the West retain its precious gold,
> In this, my hut, contentment casts no shadow,
> In peace and song I find a joy untold,
> This haven is my lasting El Dorado.

182

Others remained behind in a long wait, among them Wergeland's Sigrid, a prototype of Solveig in Ibsen's *Peer Gynt*:

> Here mid these bleak walls,
> Where yet I see him everywhere,
> Here will I live,
> Here will I cherish my love,
> Here will I pledge each day
> My faith to my beloved.
>
> Here will I wait for him
> Till I am old and wrinkled:
> For he will come.
> The wild winds carried him away,
> The winds will bring him back.

Yet others, also remaining behind, flung ironical taunts at the emigrants in such songs as this:

> O many a fool sailed across the sea
> To Yankeeland to seek for riches,
> But back he came full of misery,
> With nary a shilling in his breeches.
>     For go you East, Sir, or go you West,
>     Your northland home still will be the best.
> There is my pride
> And there with my bride
> In peace I want to live forever.

Meanwhile, fools or not, taunts notwithstanding, the emigrants sailed out into what a poet called the "wilderness of waters," pausing even in mid-ocean to sing of hopes tempered with a strain of melancholy. The nostalgic notes are sounded over and over again in the songs and ballads, and they remind one of the forlorn Beret in *Giants in the Earth*, homesick on the treeless plains of Dakota. Sometimes the songs tell of strength hard won from pain, as in an evening meditation on the Atlantic:

> The night has fallen, and breezes of evening
> Hurry our ship toward its westerly goal,
> But the ties that bind me to home and to homeland
> Fire my courage and strengthen my soul.

A Swedish emigrant ballad from the 1850's found no similar consolation as it told of the breaking of home ties:

> We sold our home and then we started
>     On our journey far,

> Like birds that fly away
>    Under summer's waning star.
> Oh, they'll come flying back
>    When the spring is in the air,
> But we shall never see again
>    Our native land so fair.

Less disconsolate is the Irish emigrant who sails away to America and promises to "fill his purse with golden coins,"

> And then for dear old Ireland
> My passage I will take
> To end my course in Briarfield
> By the lovely Shad Lough lake.

Nostalgia lessened with time. The songs told of experiences in America — hardships, suffering, frustration, yes, but also achievement, rewards, success. A ballad from the 1870's reviews the whole story, opening with the traditional "Come, Norwegians from hilltops and valleys," and rehearsing difficulties of language, land selection, and adjustment to a new life. It was no easy thing for the immigrant to learn English:

> At the start we had troubles a-plenty
> When we stepped on this far-away strand;
> We heard only a meaningless babble
> When our ears caught the speech of the land.

And in the matter of choosing land there was much to learn:

> We had known just the rock slopes of Norway,
> Gave the Yankees the best of the land;
> We were seeking for woods and for water,
> And the prairie was not in demand.

But the general tone of this homely ballad is one of satisfaction as it tells of friendly neighbors, farms, children, schools, churches, and a gradual adjustment to the new life:

> Now the years are commencing to lengthen,
> We are living right royally here;
> And although we have had our reverses,
> We look forward without any fear.

A colorful aspect of the emigrant ballads is their reflection of special trends and episodes, such as the adventures of immigrants who sought fortunes in the gold mines of the West and the story of the paternalistic colony founded by violinist Ole Bull in Pennsylvania in the early 1850's.

The idealistic Ole Bull stunned his countrymen when he bought, or thought he bought, a hundred and twenty thousand acres of land in Potter County, Pennsylvania, and projected the colony of New Norway, centered about the town of Oleana. He invited settlers and busied himself with a dozen magnificent schemes. Naturally there was a burst of songs and ballads about this marvelous development. Jubilant songs they were:

> Come, hail the Music Master,
> Hurrah for Ole Bull!
> To cheats he's brought disaster,
> Their cup of woe is full.
> New Norway he is founding,
> A gift to every man,
> So come, your shouts resounding,
> With freedom in the van.

Another ballad praised Ole Bull as a friend of the working class:

> Good men of Norway, strong of arm,
> If fortune's barbs have torn you,
> Behold a friend whose heart is warm,
> A man who will not scorn you.
> Better he than gold or fame!
> Ole Bull — yes, that's his name!

Alas, Oleana proved a bubble. The violinist had fallen into the hands of land speculators; cheats brought disaster to him, not he to them; the colonists knew nothing but disillusionment; and the whole grand scheme went to pieces. Precisely at the climax, in 1853, the rollicking ballad of "Oleana," by Ditmar Meidell, appeared. It was a satirical song, with Land-of-Cockaigne stanzas, that was sung for two generations on both sides of the Atlantic. Here are a few of its twenty-two stanzas:

> I'm off to Oleana, I'm turning from my doorway
> No chains for me, I'll say goodbye to slavery in Norway.
> > Ole — Ole — Ole — oh! Oleana!
> > Ole — Ole — Ole — oh! Oleana!

> They give you land for nothing in jolly Oleana,
> And grain comes leaping from the ground in floods of golden manna.

> The grain it does the threshing, it pours into the sack, Sir,
> And so you take a quiet nap a-stretching on your back, Sir.

The crops they are gigantic, potatoes are immense, Sir,
You make a quart of whisky from each one without expense, Sir.

And ale as strong and sweet as the best you've ever tasted,
It's running in the foamy creek, where most of it is wasted.

The salmon they are playing, and leaping in the brook, Sir,
They hop into the kettle, put the cover on and cook, Sir.

And little roasted piggies, with manners quite demure, Sir,
They ask you, Will you have some ham? And then you say,
    Why, sure, Sir.

And cakes come raining down, Sir, with cholera frosting coated,
They're nice and rich and sweet, good Lord, you eat them till
    you're bloated.

Two dollars for carousing they give each day, and more, Sir,
For if you're good and lazy, they will even give you four, Sir.

And so we play the fiddle, and all of us are glad, Sir,
We dance a merry polka, boys, and that is not so bad, Sir.

I'm off to Oleana, to lead a life of pleasure,
A beggar here, a count out there, with riches in full measure.

I'm coming, Oleana, I've left my native doorway,
I've made my choice, I've said goodbye to slavery in Norway.

        Ole — Ole — Ole — oh! Oleana!
        Ole — Ole — Ole — oh! Oleana!

A Danish emigrant ballad resembles "Oleana" in its fanciful picture
of the glories of America, though it is perhaps a trifle gentler in its irony:

        Raisins and almonds they grow on the trees,
        The clusters hang heavy and many;
        Picking them off with the greatest of ease,
        You eat them for never a penny.

        Horses with silver are shod over there,
        The carriage wheels all silver mounted;
        Gold on the street is as free as the air,
        You pick up a fortune uncounted.

        Sugar lumps look like a big loaf of bread
        And chocolate is served every hour;
        Biscuits and cookies rain down on your head,
        And lemonade pours in a shower.

Such ballads provoked folk laughter, but their satire would have had no sting if it had punctured merely false or empty hopes and claims. In the end the laughter was rueful, for underlying the absurd exaggerations was a solid element of truth that accounted for the mounting tides of migration.

The words, in Walt Whitman's phrase, are as "simple as grass," and the melodies, for the most part, are familiar folk songs. But, like the millions of "letters home" telling of the European migration and the westward advance of the American frontier, these songs record and accompany a major folk movement — one of many and diverse strains and of such a magnitude that the people who took part in it have become lines in a graph.

The songs and ballads are of everyday folk and, to a large extent, by them. They come close to the soil and to those who work on the soil; and they touch upon the feelings of people who have made a fateful decision involving adventure and ordeal. Alongside their earthy tang, the verses betray an unmistakable authenticity. They are sources basic to and contemporary with the movement they illuminate. Their domain is social and cultural history in a transatlantic sweep — emigration, immigrant transition, the frontier story, folk culture, folk literature. And this is a domain in which the historian, seeking to interpret a many-faceted human movement, can make common cause with scholars of literature, language, folklore, anthropology and sociology, economics, music, and, in general, American culture in its full encompassment of things human and humane.

The illustrations here presented are only a few from a vast international body of sources, but it may fairly be said that they shed light on various aspects of the major movement that gave them birth and with which they deal. They reflect immigrant dreams, if not of an agrarian utopia, yet of land ownership, of abundant crops, and of ambitions that look beyond their own generation. They present some of the arguments, pro and con, that were employed in fervid old-country debates about the merits of America. The songs celebrate such basic themes as freedom, democratic choice, and open doors of opportunity. They chant hope of American tomorrows brighter than European yesterdays. But they also reveal the torn and troubled emotions of the uprooted — of those who say a final goodbye to home and country.

From these sources one can gain insight into the meaning of the emigrant crossing from the Old World to the New, and some conception of the difficulties of pioneering; but one can also share the feeling of immigrant triumph as rewards repay effort and endurance. Nostalgia is universal, but it is tempered by time and by the inevitable process of adjustment to new, and American, ways of living. The songs reflect shifts from scene to scene, state to state, decade to decade, and often from initial reverses to a measure of success. They reveal the sharp sting of satire directed against the supposed folly of abandoning the known for the uncertain, but they also touch social and economic ills at home that time would ease or correct in the light of America's experience and example. As one reviews many emigrant songs and ballads, one finds ample evidence of abiding affection for the home country alongside the building of new loyalties through the American acculturation. The stories of episodes of special interest, such as Oleana and California gold, could be multiplied many-fold if the wealth of songs and ballads from all the streams of migration were tapped.

Recent years have witnessed a rising historical interest in the use of such folk materials, but much remains to be done. We still lack a representative anthology of songs and ballads drawing upon the migration from all the countries of Europe, and we need a comprehensive collection of the ballads of the American westward movement. Perhaps the chief need, however, is that of expanding the multidisciplinary approach to the study and understanding of our national culture. Folk culture, with sources appalling in their extent and diversity, is at the grass roots of our history and life, so fundamental and all-embracing that its study invites not only individual scholarly effort but planned cooperation by students representing various fields of specialization.

To echo one of the ballads, we have far to go. We need conference and discussion on the garnering of sources and on fruitful subjects for their shared use. We can learn much by carrying forward American studies that reach across traditional boundaries. The time has surely come to lay our departmental pistols down. And among many subjects that invite related and cooperative scholarly attention are the songs and ballads of such great movements as immigration and the winning of the West.

❈ CHARLES H. FOSTER

# The "Theonomous Analysis" of American Culture

O<small>N</small> A material plane the development of the United States is the greatest rags to riches story in history. The achievement must be graphed by a steadily rising line: the foothold on a virgin continent; political independence; the conquest of the frontier; the triumph of the federal power; the building of the world's largest industrial plant; the assumption of status as a world power. But I should argue that the ascending line reports only the outer history of American society and that a line representing its inner history would diverge from it markedly, at no point so widely, perhaps, as in our own day when it is equally appropriate to entitle books on American culture *People of Plenty* and *The Lonely Crowd*. How shall we explain this divergence? Mr. Potter and Mr. Riesman have found the clue to our inner life in our materialistic goals and developments. But is it not possible that the materialistic formula explaining soul in terms of body has obscured quite as much as it has disclosed about American culture? I believe that it has and that to an extent generally unrecognized American culture like other cultures past and present can be freshly and perceptively viewed in terms of a thoroughly nonmaterialistic theory such as that animating Paul Tillich's "theonomous analysis of culture."

Tillich's theory, as advanced in *The Protestant Era* (1948), rests on the conviction that "Religion is the substance of culture, culture is the expression of religion." [1] He contends that in its ideal form a culture is a "theonomy," but that in the procession of history, "theonomy" decays into "heteronomy," and "heteronomy," in turn, decays into "autonomy." [2] The clue to Tillich's meaning would seem to lie in "the *nomos* or law of life" operating in each. Thus in theonomy "the superior law is, at the same time, the innermost law of man himself, rooted in the divine ground which is man's own ground: the law of life transcends man, although it is, at the same time, his own." [3] Since all the forms of life are "open to and directed toward the divine" in a purely voluntary spirit, "merely individual religion, individual culture, individual emotional life, and individual economic interests are impossible." [4] In heteronomy, on the other hand, the law is imposed from without: "the forms and laws of thinking and acting" are subject "to authoritative criteria of an ecclesiastical religion or a political quasi-religion, even at the price of destroying the structures of rationality." [5] "Autonomy asserts that man as the bearer of universal reason is the source and measure of culture and religion — that he is his own law." [6]

Particularly pertinent, I believe, are Tillich's extensive comments on autonomy, which he uses to describe the secular, rationalistic, individualistic cultures of the Enlightenment and the twentieth century. As we might expect in a Christian existentialist, he does not favor autonomy; it constitutes for him, in fact, the negation of culture in the ideal sense. He supposes that "Autonomy is able to live as long as it can draw from the religious tradition of the past . . . But more and more it loses this spiritual foundation. It becomes emptier, more formalistic, or more factual and is driven toward skepticism and cynicism, toward the loss of meaning and purpose. The history of autonomous cultures is the history of a continuous waste of spiritual substance." [7] For Tillich there is, however, in "the depth of every autonomous culture an ultimate concern, something unconditional and holy" implied. [8] He believes, for example, that in the late nineteenth century in Europe when culture was "in an advanced state of disintegration," "the religious reference was effective in the movements which protested — often with a prophetic passion — against this situation." Theonomous analysis, he goes on to tell us, "was able to decipher puzzling experiences, such as the visionary destruction of bourgeois idealism and naturalism in art and literature by expressionism and surrealism; it was able to show the religious background of the rebellion of the vital and unconscious side of man's personality against the moral and intellectual tyranny of consciousness. . . . It was able to do all this without special reference to organized religion, the churches being only a part of the whole picture, but with a decisive reference to the religious element which was and is hidden in all these antireligious and anti-Christian movements." [9]

As the final key term in Tillich's theory, we have "kairos," that fullness of time when history outwardly and inwardly gathers to a crisis and there is a possibility that with God's help men may make the decisions which will lead to a new period of culture in the most meaningful sense. Tillich finds that the kairos in our time has been most clearly perceived by the socialists in that they have sensed most critically the aridities and dislocations of bourgeois capitalism in art, politics, ethics, education, and other fields.[10] Their fault, however, is that they have sought to "exclude the unconditional from the spheres of thought and action and accordingly to create the new epoch merely through technology and strategy." [11] If, in short, the socialists would only respond to our epochal moment of history in a profoundly religious fashion, become, that is, religious socialists, we might well be moving toward a theonomy.

On first glance this theory looks more like a challenge to American culture than a possible perspective on it; our response is likely to be irritation. We have all been influenced far more than we imagine by the liberal interpretation of American culture which views our inner history as a series of emancipations from the tyranny and superstitions of New England Puritanism. We assume with our deistic Founding Fathers that secularism and rationalism are the distinctive ways in which American subjective experience is organized. We assume that American culture means the culture of Paine, Jefferson, and Franklin and that autonomy is the American cultural norm.

We should not, however, leap to the conclusion that religious freedom freed us from religion. Quite the reverse would seem to be the case. The challenge of religious freedom shook the established churches into new life in revivals, particularly those inspired by Charles Grandison Finney in the 1820's and 1830's, and outside the churches there developed in the 1840's a bewildering variety of new sects, private religions, religious communities and religious crusades which would have dismayed and confused Thomas Paine and Thomas Jefferson, had they been alive.

In 1822 Jefferson had supposed: "The pure and simple unity of the Creator of the universe, is now all but ascendant in the Eastern States; it is dawning in the West, and advancing towards the South; and I confidently expect that the present generation will see Unitarianism become the general religion of the United States." [12] Eight years later, however, Joseph Smith published *The Book of Mormon* and converts gathered rapidly to a sect which was virtually a negation of Jefferson's prophecy. Shortly thereafter Margaret Fuller was responding to the rationalistic

Unitarian ministers in this fashion: "For one I would now preach the Holy Ghost as zealously as they have been preaching Man, and faith instead of the understanding, and mysticism instead, etc." [13] Also pertinent is Perry Miller's observation that the Unitarian leaders Andrews Norton and Francis Bowen regarded Emerson and Parker as "throwbacks to the messy emotionalism and the dangerous mysticism that 'Liberal Christianity' had striven for a century to exorcise. To sober, judicious, rational Brattle Street and Harvard College, Transcendentalism was really 'infidelity'; it was betrayal of the citadel from within, it was a rebellion against the fathers." [14] I think Tillich furnishes an important clue to understanding this phenomenon with his phrase describing the hidden life in an autonomy: "the rebellion of the vital and unconscious side of man's personality against the moral and intellectual tyranny of consciousness."

We should not, however, describe nineteenth-century American culture simply as a revolt against deism and rationalistic Unitarianism. It was not only destruction; it was also construction, a whole series of attempts to fill the spiritual void created by the Enlightenment with new religions and even new scriptures. In the very year 1782 in which Hector St. John de Crèvecœur's *Letters from an American Farmer* appeared in London informing the world that America was a land where sects evaporated leaving a residue of universal natural religion, Mother Ann Lee, Ann the Word, as her followers called her, was touring New England with her elders winning converts to the Shakers.[15] By 1823 this sect had not only established itself in communities but had developed a body of belief, even a theology, as we can see in Calvin Green and Seth Y. Wells's *A Summary View of the Millennial Church . . . Commonly Called Shakers*, which should, I think, be catalogued as the first in a series of American scriptures. Certainly scripture is the term we must use for Joseph Smith's *The Book of Mormon* (1830) and his far more impressive *A Book of Commandments*, eventually to be titled *The Doctrines and Covenants*, which was published at Jackson, Missouri, in 1833.

Joseph Smith was a forerunner of new patterns in American culture in declaring that American persons and places were subjects of divine attention and that Hill Cumorah, near Palmyra, New York, and the Middle West had been scenes in sacred history quite as much as ancient Palestine. But his was a purely indigenous response to the spiritual void. The more significant response came with the conjunction of the native impulse and the foreign impulse in German, French, and English romanticism combined with enthusiasm for Plato, the Neoplatonists, and Swedenborg. That more culturally significant response found its first major expression six years after *The Book of Mormon* when Emerson asked on the first page of *Nature*: "The foregoing generations beheld God and nature face to face; we, through their eyes. Why should not we also enjoy an original relation to the universe? Why should not we have a poetry and philosophy of insight and not of tradition, and a religion by revelation to us, and not the history of theirs? . . . why should we grope among the dry bones of the past, or put the living generation into masquerade out of its faded wardrobe? The sun shines to-day also."[16]

It was Walt Whitman, of course, in *Leaves of Grass* (including the magnificent 1855 preface) who most clearly responded to this challenge, converting the prosaic details of American life and its political principles into scriptural terms. But Whitman was not alone. We should also name Emerson's friend Jones Very, who believed his exquisite and profound religious sonnets were dictated by the Holy Spirit. Certainly we find an obviously scriptural undertaking in Amos Bronson Alcott's enigmatic "Orphic Sayings,"[17] and though we may wish to acknowledge Lawrance Thompson's thesis that Melville did in a fashion have a quarrel with God, I think we can still detect an impulse toward scripture in many of the epical interruptions in *Moby Dick*. Some chapters in Thoreau's *A Week on the Concord and Merrimack Rivers* and *Walden* seem to me justifiably brought under the same heading, American Scripture; and though the elder Henry James would doubtless have found the suggestion blasphemous, I think we may even call his profound Fourieristic-Swedenborgian speculations, particularly *Substance and Shadow* (1863) and *Society the Redeemed Form of Man* (1879), not simply theological but also scriptural works. In some at least of its most articulate and beautiful organizations of subjective experience American nineteenth-century culture is aptly and precisely described in Tillich's terms: "culture is the expression of religion."

We must also note the religious element in the communities. In many instances they were not merely odd secular organizations in a day of experiments but in their confused and generally unsuccessful fashion attempts to recreate American society in a counterimage to the America of Franklin's "The Way to Wealth." The communities (more than one hundred and seventy-five of them) were, again and again, attempts to recreate America as a theonomy in which "merely individual religion, individual culture, individual emotional life, and individual economic interests are impossible" since all life would be divinely oriented. I think we may see the pattern even in Brook Farm.

Brook Farm was established, of course, almost in exact contradiction to Mr. Tillich's formula for theonomy. Beyond certain not clearly defined notions about combining menial and intellectual labor in a joint-stock company, the basic aim was self-fulfillment and it was assumed that if everyone went his own way in conscience everyone would move in the same direction and community would result. The conversion in the winter of 1843–1844 of this Association of Individuals into a Fourieristic Community takes status with most commentators as a repudiation of the Faith, that is, the Transcendental Faith, a giant apostasy. In his charming book on Brook Farm, Lindsay Swift goes so far as to characterize Albert Brisbane in the last sentence as the "evil genius of Brook Farm." [18] But it is more accurate, I believe, to view the conversion not as a corruption and conspiracy engineered by Albert Brisbane, Horace Greeley, and William H. Channing but as a development of the religious impulse toward theonomy. The terms in which George Ripley, Minot Pratt, and Charles Dana describe the change in the preamble to the community's new constitution, January 18, 1844, seem to me significant: "Meanwhile every step has strengthened the faith with which we set out; our belief in a divine order of human society, has in our minds become an absolute certainty. . . ." [19] I find also extremely significant the fact that William H. Channing, a chief proponent of the change to Fourierism, should in 1846 tell the Brook Farmers that "the great problem and movement of this day" was "that of realizing a unitary church." [20] Finally we have the fact noted by John Humphrey Noyes that Brook Farm "brought upon the public mind, not only a new socialism but a new religion, and that religion was *Swedenborgianism*." [21]

But Brook Farm did not, of course, endure in the manner of some religious socialist communities such as John Humphrey Noyes' Oneida. I suspect that Noyes, who was a notable precursor of Tillich in theonomous analysis, supplies us with the fundamental explanation: the weakness was not the socialism but "the character of the afflatus" which organized Brook Farm. Ripley and Channing might feel deep longings for a theonomous community but they were essentially Transcendentalists: "The original afflatus carried them to the verge of Communism; but 'their gift of tongues' prevailed and spoiled them. And the tendency to literature, as represented by Emerson, is the farthest opposite to Communism, finding its *summmum bonum* in individualism and incoherent instead of organic inspiration." [22] Of this we have a symbol in the fact that in 1844 Channing brought to a close his extraordinary Christian Socialist journal, the *Present*, so that he might work on the memoirs of his uncle, William Ellery Channing.[23]

Not only do we find at Brook Farm elements of theonomy. We also find them, I believe, in the departure of many communities from conventional attitudes and practices in sexual relations. It may seem that here no generalization is possible since we are faced with opposing and contradictory phenomena: celibacy among the Shakers, polygamy among the Mormons, community of wives at Oneida, and "the dear love of comrades" in Whitman's democratic mystique, which called for a transcendental community of the whole United States. But Charles Lane, who had lived through the failure of Alcott's Fruitlands Community, gives us justification, I believe, for generalizing about these programs. He sensed a crucial difficulty in focusing man's attention at one and the same time equally on private love in the family and universal love in the community, and he declared: "The question of association and of marriage are one. If, as we have been popularly led to believe, the individual or separate family is in the true order of Providence, then the associative life is a false effort. If the associative life is true, then is the separate family a false arrangement. . . . That the affections can be divided or bent with equal ardor on two objects, so opposed as universal and individual love, may at least be rationally doubted. History has not yet exhibited such phenomena in an associate body, and scarcely in any individual. The monasteries and convents, which have existed in all ages, have been maintained solely by the annihilation of that peculiar affection on which the separate family is based." [24] A similar recognition, sometimes only half-conscious, rather than any interest in sex or lack of sex per se seems to me basic in these sexual programs. They were all attempts — even Whitman's vaguely homosexual program of adhesiveness — to replace private love by universal love, thus linking not pairs but multitudes in a religious union.

But what of our modern period? If we are going to deal, as Henry Nash Smith supposes we should in American Studies, with "the investigation of American culture, past and present, as a whole," [25] we cannot rest our case on such facts as nineteenth-century American scriptures and religious-socialist communities. If American culture in the nineteenth century was on close inspection religious, must we not say that in our time the American mind and heart broke free of that "messy emotionalism and dangerous mysticism" which Norton and Bowen found so regrettable in the Transcendentalists? Looking over the cultural landscape in 1925, we should have found good reason for supposing that liberation had at last arrived. In *Main Street*, *Babbitt*, and *Arrowsmith*, Sinclair Lewis was bringing a superbly rationalistic almost eighteenth-century mind to the criticism of American life; H. L. Mencken was laughing down even faith in democracy and the common man; F. Scott Fitzgerald was apparently proclaiming a philosophy of complete moral irresponsibility; young Ernest Hemingway was apparently viewing life in completely nihilistic terms; T. S. Eliot was denouncing and mocking conventional values; a young Mississippi writer named William Faulkner was just about to add his voice in *Soldiers' Pay* to the chorus denouncing the old ways of feeling and saying.

Modern American culture in retrospect seems, however, a very different matter from what it seemed in prospect a quarter-century ago. However much we may still value Mencken and Lewis for their wit and their hard-hitting criticism of the banal and moribund aspects of American society, they do not seem quite the spokesmen of American culture they once appeared to be; and as we have come to a clearer understanding of Hemingway, Eliot, and Faulkner, to take the most obvious examples, we have been obliged to make major revisions in our initial judgments. I do not mean to imply that we should blend Hemingway and Faulkner into some composite image of the religious artist comparable, let us say, to Walt Whitman. Rather, we have been obliged to recognize that Hemingway, Eliot, Faulkner, and the mature F. Scott Fitzgerald were engaged not in expressing a secular and rationalistic organization of subjective experience but in depicting and criticizing with the most serious moral concern the spiritual emptiness, the emotional aridity of the human condition in our America. I think we must say the same thing of Robinson Jeffers, however limited and destructive we may suppose his combination of nihilism and primitivism to be.

Admittedly, our modern American artists exhibit a sensibility different in important ways from their nineteenth-century predecessors, but it is notable that again and again our critics have coupled Hemingway with Hawthorne, Faulkner with Melville, Sherwood Anderson with the

196

Transcendentalists. Is there, then, after all a family likeness among the major figures in our two most articulate cultural moments? I think we must say that there is and that the likeness consists not in lines of influence but in a common dissatisfaction with materialism and secularity.

This modern dissatisfaction may be described as the reverse of the Puritan-Transcendental coin. If modern American culture is not precisely religious, it is rather clearly not secular and rationalistic, and we have only to imagine Thomas Jefferson's trying to work his way through Faulkner's religious and social meditations in Section IV of "The Bear" or Benjamin Franklin's dipping into Warren's *Brother to Dragons* to realize, once again, that even in our time religion, as Tillich holds, has been "the substance of culture" and culture "the expression of religion" to a degree that would have struck our deistic Founding Fathers with astonishment.

This is true not only of the American writers who came to major notice in the 1930's, 40's, and 50's such as Eliot, Hemingway, Faulkner, and Warren, but also of the earlier writers who claimed attention in the 1920's. Waldo Frank has noted perceptively, for example, in commenting on *Winesburg, Ohio*, that the Bible and a "Testamental accent and vision modulate every page of Anderson's great story," [26] and Edgar Lee Masters has called attention to the Swedenborgian mysticism in Vachel Lindsay's early poems such as "Johnny Appleseed's Hymn to the Sun." [27] Nor should we overlook Hart Crane. In *The Bridge*, he was almost Whitman reborn in his magnificent if chaotic effort to make "the curveship" of Brooklyn Bridge and other American particulars "lend a myth to God." [28]

It can be argued, of course, that Anderson, Lindsay, and Crane spoke more for themselves than for the multitude, that any religious impulse we may be able to discover in them proves very little about the general cultural situation. But their impulses, their attitudes, were shared by a figure whose every work in the 1920's took status as a cultural event. In such plays as *Desire under the Elms* and *Strange Interlude*, Eugene O'Neill dramatized to the full the contemporary disenchantment and pessimism and seemed to propose more insistently than any other American writer the id rather than the soul as the main mover in human life. Privately, however, O'Neill was far from a thoroughgoing naturalist. He told Joseph Wood Krutch: "Most modern plays are concerned with the relation between man and man, but that does not interest me at all. I am interested only in the relation between man and God."[29] To George Jean Nathan he wrote: "The playwright today must dig at the roots of the sickness of today as he feels it — the death of the old God and the failure of science and materialism to give any satisfying new one for the surviving primitive religious instinct to find a meaning for life in, and to comfort its fears of death with. It seems to me that anyone trying to do big work nowadays must have this big subject behind all the little subjects of his plays or novels, or he is simply scribbling around the surface of things and has no more real status than a parlor entertainer." [30]

I think we may even discover a deeply religious impulse in Robert Frost, who is often regarded as a purely humanistic spokesman, largely, I suspect, because he has been so successful in mixing the scent as critics and readers have tried to track him down to some trite and fixed attitude:

> Some people want you not to understand them,
> But I want you to understand me wrong.[31]

The game, however, is to understand Frost right, and to understand him right means in part, I think, that we notice that his two long poems, *A Masque of Reason* and *A Masque of Mercy*, are embodiments of his theory that "to be at all charming or even bearable, the way is almost rigidly prescribed. If it is with outer seriousness, it must be with inner humor. If it is with outer humor, it must be with inner seriousness." [32] I think we must suspect a play on "masque" and read these poems as masks of outer humor hiding a religious seriousness.

I find significant in these poems not the often noticed approaches to Emerson but the approaches to the paradoxes of religion less Transcendentally conceived. Undoubtedly Frost does mean Emerson's "Uriel" in *A Masque of Reason* when he quotes "the greatest Western poem yet," [33] but Frost's point in the dialogue between Job and God is not that

> Evil will bless, and ice will burn [34]

but the insight God and Job groped out together that

> . . . the discipline man needed most
> Was to learn his submission to unreason . . .[35]

Similarly, the play in *A Masque of Mercy* is not deeply Emersonian. Note the interpretation of the Sermon on the Mount:

> . . . just a frame-up to insure the failure
> Of all of us, so all of us will be

Thrown prostrate at the Mercy Seat for Mercy.[36]

. . . . . . . . . . . . . . . . . .

An irresistible impossibility.
A lofty beauty no one can live up to
Yet no one turn from trying to live up to.[37]

Frost here almost versifies Emerson's opposite, the elder Henry James, who ultimately saw the Spiritual Law as "a ministry of death, *to convince those who stood approved by it of SIN*, thereby shutting up all men, good and evil alike, but especially the good, to unlimited dependence upon the sheer and mere mercy of God."[38]

I do not imply influence here. The similarity may be nothing more than Frost's own sharp insight or simply an ultimate flowering of his rearing in a Swedenborgian home. But the elder Henry James, in any case, seems to me a good name to remember in dealing with Frost in his attitude of one step forward and two steps backward in the matter of religion, indeed, I should suppose, in dealing with most major American artists in their attitude toward the Protestant Church. It is, I am convinced, in addition to the factors I have already noticed, the very religiousness of the American artist that makes him say in his various tones with Emerson in "The Problem"

I like a church; I like a cowl;
I love a prophet of the soul . . .
Yet not for all his faith can see
Would I that cowlèd churchman be.[39]

An important clue to why the American intellectual should have this troubled response I find in James' *Substance and Shadow*: "Protestant men and women, those who have any official or social consequence in the church, are apt to exhibit a high-flown religious pride, a spiritual flatulence and sourness of stomach, which you do not find under the Catholic administration . . . But our conspicuous Protestant religiosities male and female — such of them as are really animated by the spirit of Protestantism — are sweeter on the surface than in the depths. Their moral fine-linen disguises any amount of spiritual squalor. For they believe themselves personally appreciable of the Lord's heart; make the culmination of their faith to consist in 'a personal assurance' towards God or confidence of acceptance at His hands, which is proof against all adverse probabilities, and therefore intensely insulting to more modest natures."[40]

Frost speaks the same sentiment firmly at the close of *A Masque of Mercy*:

> But I'm too much afraid of God to claim
> I have been fighting on the angels' side.
> That is for Him and not for me to say.
> For me to say it would be irreligious.[41]

This same distaste for what James called "the high-flown religious pride" of the Protestant has been, I suspect, a major element in the almost universal dissociation of the Protestant American artist and intellectual from the Protestant churches, and it may do much to explain the apparently paradoxical countermovement away from Protestantism toward Anglicanism and Roman Catholicism. Theonomous analysis of American culture certainly must confront the fact that in the last century and a half the most vital expressions of American Protestantism, with a few exceptions such as the contributions of William Ellery Channing, Theodore Parker, and Horace Bushnell, have been made by persons *outside* rather than *inside* any American Protestant church. The nonmembers and particularly the ex-members culturally speaking have counted for more than the members, and in consequence we make only the most superficial appraisal of American culture when we suppose American religion is the faith and practice we discover in the Protestant churches.

In any attempt to try out Tillich's theonomous analysis as a possible avenue to new methods in American Studies, we must recognize not only the religious and social concern uniting the bearers and expressors of our culture, but the inconsistent manifestations in our theonomic periods. American culture, more insistently I am confident than other cultures, takes the form in its greatest moments of debate, of dialectic, and this debate, it seems to me, amounts, abstractly considered, to a competition between champions of theonomy, heteronomy, and autonomy: John Winthrop and the Reverend John Wilson versus Anne Hutchinson and John Wheelwright; Jonathan Edwards versus that critic of the Great Awakening, Charles Chauncy; William H. Channing and John Humphrey Noyes versus Emerson and Thoreau; T. S. Eliot versus Irving Babbitt and Norman Foerster. Not only would this seem to be so: there would seem to be dialectics within the notable personalities themselves, even, for example, within Emerson, as Stephen E. Whicher has recently demonstrated in his remarkable anthology of Emerson's writings. And the Civil War itself viewed in cultural terms seems to me not only a conflict of regions and economies but an immense series of dialectics within the American mind. I find the essence of our cultural situation penetratingly summarized by Lionel Trilling: "A culture is not a flow, nor even a confluence; the form of its existence is struggle, or at least debate — it is nothing if not a dialectic. And in any culture there are likely to be certain artists who contain a large part of the dialectic within themselves, their meaning and power lying in their contradictions; they contain within themselves, it may be said, the very essence of the culture, and the sign of this is that they do not submit to serve the ends of any one ideological group or tendency . . . they contained both the yes and no of culture, and by that token they were prophetic of the future."[42]

Tillich's triad of theonomy, heteronomy, and autonomy has operated not only in public and private debate but, from the Civil War period to the period of World War I, constitutes almost exactly the historical procession. What I have in mind is the transition from the Transcendentalists to Mark Twain and Howells and finally to the Darwinists and Pragmatists. Mark Twain, whose works Henry Nash Smith has perceived "were impaired before they were written, and by forces that were in large part internalized in the author,"[43] perfectly illustrates the major artist responding to the heteronomy of Victorian conventions and to his own compulsion to a commercial and worldly rather than to an artistic and spiritual success; and the bitterness, the disillusion, the attempts at self-justification in his late works such as "The Man That Corrupted Hadleyburg" and *The Mysterious Stranger*, all indicate that a new and disheartening stage had been reached in American culture. But in Mark Twain we have remnants of idealism which vanish completely in those representing the next cultural step.

In William Graham Sumner, Brooks Adams, Mr. Justice Holmes, and Theodore Roosevelt, autonomy, we may say, has set in, in earnest. Man is now completely a law unto himself in a world of ruthless economic rivalry, imperialism, verbal sops to the masses, and brute power, and even some churches seem to have preached the Law of the Jungle. Of this acutely autonomous moment Theodore Dreiser was, of course, the major spokesman, but he was more.

In an introduction to *Sister Carrie* Kenneth S. Lynn has quite properly emphasized that the materialistic yearnings in Carrie, Drouet, and Hurstwood represent Dreiser's own worldly aspirations, and these aspirations certainly are the main burden of the novel. But we must not neglect the concluding pages. There Carrie is not "bored" after having achieved materialistic success, as Mr. Lynn contends.[44] On the contrary she now yearns for those higher things of which Ames had given her a glimpse earlier. She is for Dreiser the type of the artist, and the metaphor he employs at this point is significant: "As harps in the wind, the latter [that is, the artists] respond to every breath of fancy, voicing in their moods all the ebb and flow of the ideal." [45] Here, obviously, we are not so close to Zola's naturalism as to Emerson's Transcendental aeolian harp or Thoreau's humming telegraph wire. Looking back through the novel in the light of this metaphor and, indeed, of the whole concluding section, we find good reason for Dreiser's having tentatively entitled *Sister Carrie, The Flesh and the Spirit*.

I believe we have made too much of Dreiser's own statements that he found life confused and meaningless. In Dreiser as in that applewood table Thoreau described in the concluding paragraph of *Walden* there was a winged life slowly working its way out through the "many concentric layers of woodenness in the dead dry life of society." I find stages of this development not only in the early novels and in a short story such as "The Lost Phoebe," written in 1912, but in Dreiser's usually neglected book of poems, *Moods Cadenced & Declaimed* (1926, enlarged 1928), where he often tentatively questions his own materialism and naturalism, as for example in "Protoplast," which begins

> My error consists
> If at all,
> In seeking in mortal flesh
> The likeness
> Of what
> Perhaps
> Is Eternal.[46]

Yet another sign of his emergence from materialism is the introduction to *The Living Thoughts of Thoreau* (1939), where he declared he was more impressed by Thoreau's sense of "a superior and pervasive something" directing "the conscious mechanisms" of the universe than by "all my philosophic and scientific reading of recent years from Democritus to Einstein . . ." [47]

In Dreiser, we can discern, I believe, a lifelong struggle in the midst of autonomy toward theonomous values. This struggle eventually would lead him from an essentially nonreformist position to deep sympathy with socialism and communism, which he gave in *America Is Worth Saving* (1941) religious overtones, faint indeed, but enough, I think, to suggest some remote kinship between him and such nineteenth-century Christian socialists as Ripley and William H. Channing. It is also significant that Dreiser should conclude his career with *The Bulwark* where in the person of Solon Barnes he dramatizes the deep and beautiful possibility that the Quaker faith might triumph over all manner of worldly disillusion and disappointment. There was more than "failure of nerve" in the fact that shortly before his death Dreiser should take Communion in the Congregational Church. More than any other writer of the early twentieth century Dreiser marks the transition from autonomy to the theonomic concerns, if not certainties, expressed finally by Anderson, Eliot, Faulkner, and Warren.

Does Tillich's "theonomous analysis" then work so well as provocation to new perspectives, new insights, and new methods in the study of American culture that we can apply it to all periods of our development? I think we must hesitate to say so. One of our greatest periods of cultural expression would seem comprehended only with ingenuity by any of Tillich's terms. I mean the late eighteenth century, the Enlightenment. In terms of social vision, the Enlightenment would seem our most intense, our most articulate dedication to "Society the Redeemed Form of Man," but religiously it would seem so attenuated (I am thinking, of course, of the deism of Paine, Jefferson, and even Franklin) as to be a quite different phenomenon from the Union as interpreted by Lincoln in his sublime Proclamation Appointing a National Fast Day, 1863, his Gettysburg Address, and his Second Inaugural. Applying Tillich's scheme mechanically, the Enlightenment might be made to fall into the triad theonomy, heteronomy, autonomy as the last term of the series, the theonomy having been the Great Awakening of the 1740's and the heteronomy the attempts of the Edwardsians and Hopkinsians to panic and logic-chop their congregations back into ecstatic closeness to "the unconditional and holy." But we sense immediately, I think, that the Enlightenment is in no true sense comparable to what Tillich finds characteristic of an autonomy, its spiritual waste; certainly, no just-minded student of the Enlightenment would call it exhausted and spiritually empty.

Shall we, then, say that in view of the obvious magnificence of our Enlightenment Tillich's perception of culture at one important moment not only proves inadequate but strikes on the rocks of fact and actually goes to pieces? This may be the conclusion to which we are forced; and we should certainly feel, I believe, no obligation to go down with the theory. But I suspect that "theonomous analysis" may even prove useful in reading our Enlightenment. Is it not possible that we have all too easily glossed over the spiritual thinness of the Founding Fathers and that a truly critical appraisal of American culture must face the issue of cultural naiveté in, for example, Jefferson with the candor Robert Penn Warren has employed in *Brother to Dragons*? None of Tillich's terms may be appropriate but they still may serve to remind us that our late eighteenth-century American culture was incomplete, a making, as it were, of the bricks of civilization without sufficient spiritual straw.

Ultimately, however, I think we must say that useful and provocative as Tillich's theonomous analysis proves in understanding major patterns in American culture it does not supply the ultimate clue. That ultimate clue, I believe, lies in the fact that the spiritual naiveté, the emotional and imaginative thinness, the very secularity of the eighteenth-century American mind was the necessary prelude to the rich and various cultural expressions of the American mind and heart in the nineteenth and twentieth centuries. We must finally call our Enlightenment if not a theonomy at least an "Infidel Church" making our patches of theonomy possible. I borrow that phrase from the Shaker elder F. W. Evans, who in his theonomous analysis of history in the light of the symbols and images in the Revelation of St. John the Divine, saw the function of the Enlightenment as a necessary prelude to the growth of his own Millennial Church:

*Sixth Church*, — the Infidel Church of America, which excludes the clergy of Babylon — Christendom — from Civil power; declaring that all human beings are born equal, possessing an inherent right to land; and that, in religion, there being no Inquisition, all may believe what they please. This prepared the way for the

*Seventh Church*, — the Shaker Church of Christ's Second Appearing, in which *Revelation*, Celibacy, Oral Confession, Community, Non-Resistance, Peace, Gift of Healing, Miracles, Physical Health, and Separation from the World, are the foundations of the "new heavens . . ." [48]

Admittedly Tillich's theory does not work completely in the American situation. Still the report must be that there are, generally speaking, remarkable insights to be gained from looking at American culture in terms of his theonomous analysis. I should not wish to be misunderstood as suggesting that Tillich as a distinguished existentialist philosopher is the man "to redesign the whole enterprise" of American Studies.[49] We are still quite emphatically at the stage in which our method is growing out of our repeated criticism of practice, and in which the inadequacies of our answers lead to "the reformulation of the questions, and the re-formulated questions in turn suggest new ways of finding answers." But I am not quite so confident as Henry Nash Smith that "a new method will have to come piecemeal, through a kind of principled opportunism, in the course of daily struggles with our various tasks."[50] I suggest that the tentative, pragmatic, "piecemeal" approach to method in American Studies is only one of the ways open to us and that another may well lie in trying out various theories of culture such as that of Paul Tillich. I think the theory, the generalization, may well throw unexpected light on the particulars and indicate new ways of pertinently analyzing them.

In any case, it seems to me that if our subject matter in American Studies is "American culture, past and present, as a whole," we should interest ourselves particularly in encompassing and provocative views of the whole problem of culture, and even dare to venture into the dark woods of existentialism.

### NOTES

[1] The quotations are taken from the Phoenix edition of *The Protestant Era* (Chicago: University of Chicago Press, 1957), p. xiii.

[2] *Ibid.*, pp. 44, 45.

[3] *Ibid.*, pp. 56, 57.

[4] *Ibid.*, p. 44.

[5] *Ibid.*, p. 57.

[6] *Ibid.*, p. 56.

[7] *Ibid.*, p. 46.

[8] *Ibid.*, p. 58.

[9] *Ibid.*

[10] *Ibid.*, p. 49.

[11] *Ibid.*

[12] Adrienne Koch and William Peden, eds., *The Life and Selected Writings of Thomas Jefferson* (New York: Modern Library, 1944), pp. 703–704.

[13] Perry Miller, ed., *The Transcendentalists: An Anthology* (Cambridge, Mass.: Harvard University Press, 1950), p. 8.

[14] *Ibid.*, p. 11.

[15] Calvin Green and Seth Y. Wells, *A Summary View of the Millennial Church or United Society of Believers Commonly Called Shakers*, 2nd ed. (Albany: C. Van Benthuysen, 1848), pp. 28–29.

[16] Ralph Waldo Emerson, *Nature*, in *The Complete Works of Ralph Waldo Emerson*, ed. Edward Waldo Emerson (Boston and New York: Houghton Mifflin, 1903), I, 3.

[17] I have in mind Alcott's "Orphic Sayings" not only in their original form in the

*Dial* in 1840–1841 but as a lifelong work appearing in various radical journals and in *Tablets* (1868), *Concord Days* (1872), and *Table Talk* (1877).

[18] Lindsay Swift, *Brook Farm: Its Members, Scholars, and Visitors* (New York and London: Macmillan, 1900), p. 281.

[19] John Humphrey Noyes, *History of American Socialisms* (Philadelphia: Lippincott, 1870), p. 523.

[20] *Ibid.*, p. 533.

[21] *Ibid.*, p. 539. Noyes had in mind the many articles on Swedenborg appearing in the *Harbinger*, the Fourieristic journal edited by George Ripley, which from 1845 to 1847 was the official organ of Brook Farm.

[22] *Ibid.*, pp. 561–562.

[23] W. H. Channing, "Closing of the Volume," *Present*, xi and xii (April 1844), 431–432.

[24] Charles Lane, "Brook Farm," *Dial*, iv (January 1844), 356.

[25] Henry Nash Smith, "Can 'American Studies' Develop a Method?" p. 3 in this book.

[26] Waldo Frank, "Winesburg, Ohio, after Twenty Years," *Story*, xix (September–October 1941), 32.

[27] Edgar Lee Masters, "The Tragedy of Vachel Lindsay," *American Mercury*, xxix (July 1933), 357–369.

[28] Hart Crane, *The Bridge*, in *The Complete Poems of Hart Crane*, ed. Waldo Frank (Garden City, N.Y.: Doubleday Anchor Books, 1958), p. 4.

[29] Joseph Wood Krutch, "Introduction" to Eugene O'Neill, *Nine Plays Selected by the Author* (New York: Liveright, 1932), p. xvii.

[30] *Ibid.*

[31] Robert Frost, *A Masque of Mercy* (New York: Henry Holt, 1947), p. 25.

[32] Frost, "Introduction" to Edwin Arlington Robinson, *King Jasper: A Poem* (New York: Macmillan, 1935), p. xiii.

[33] Frost, *A Masque of Reason* (New York: Henry Holt, 1945), p. 17.

[34] Emerson, "Uriel," *The Complete Works*, ix, 27.

[35] Frost, *A Masque of Reason*, p. 12.

[36] Frost, *A Masque of Mercy*, p. 26.

[37] *Ibid.*, p. 27.

[38] Henry James, *Society the Redeemed Form of Man, and the Earnest of God's Omnipotence in Human Nature* (Boston: Houghton, Osgood, 1879), p. 74.

[39] Emerson, "The Problem," *The Complete Works*, ix, 6.

[40] Henry James, *Substance and Shadow: or, Morality and Religion in Their Relation to Life: An Essay upon the Physics of Creation* (Boston: Ticknor and Fields, 1863), pp. 213–214.

[41] Frost, *A Masque of Mercy*, p. 38.

[42] Lionel Trilling, *The Liberal Imagination: Essays on Literature and Society* (Garden City, N.Y.: Doubleday Anchor Books, 1953), pp. 20–21.

[43] Henry Nash Smith, "Can 'American Studies' Develop a Method?" p. 5 in this book.

[44] Kenneth S. Lynn, "Introduction to Theodore Dreiser," *Sister Carrie* (New York and Toronto: Rinehart, 1957), p. xv.

[45] *Ibid.*, p. 452.

[46] Theodore Dreiser, *Moods Cadenced & Declaimed* (New York: Boni and Liveright, 1928), p. 247.

[47] Theodore Dreiser, "Presenting Thoreau," *The Living Thoughts of Thoreau* (New York and Toronto: Longmans, Green and Co., 1939), pp. 9–10.

[48] F. W. Evans, *Autobiography of a Shaker and Revelation of the Apocalypse with an Appendix* (Mt. Lebanon, N.Y.: F. W. Evans, 1869), p. 99.

[49] Henry Nash Smith, "Can 'American Studies' Develop a Method?" p. 15 in this book.

[50] *Ibid.*

# American Studies, Past, Present, and Future

Iɴ ʜɪѕ 1948 survey of American Studies in the universities and colleges of the United States, Tremaine McDowell set forth as the first principle of such programs the discovery in them of "the complex design of American life" in which "may be seen the fundamental diversity of human experience within which the student should eventually find a fundamental unity." [1] Doubtless the reader of the present volume up to this point has been impressed by the diversity of its contents. It is the purpose of this concluding chapter to attempt to discover what fundamental unity there may be in the movement which these essays have illustrated rather than described. To do so, we must borrow another of Mr. McDowell's principles and attempt "that reconciliation of the *then* and *now* which makes the future possible." [2] The movement must reveal both a history and a rationale before an analysis of its accomplishments and its prospects is possible.

As Mr. McDowell and others have frequently pointed out, American Studies as a separate academic program began as a series of rebellions in the various established disciplines. In departments of English, discontent was three-pronged: against the assumption that American literature, because it is largely written in the English language, is merely an inferior branch of English literature; against the assumption that serious research can be done only in literature predating 1800; and against the domination of historical philology in literary study to the detriment of sociological, psychological, philosophical, and aesthetic approaches. In 1948 William G. Crane, reporting to the National Council of Teachers of English, found that the college teaching of American literature could be traced back to 1890 and before, but that the subject did not begin to have a place of its own in the curriculum until after 1918 and was not generally recognized for at least another decade. [3] The American Literature Group of the Modern Language Association was founded after World War I and *American Literature* as a separate scholarly journal began publication in 1929.

The reasons for the steady growth of this movement in literary study are complex, but an examination of the scholarly books and articles of the period shows a close relationship between it and the shift of emphasis from linguistic and belletristic approaches to those of cultural and intellectual history. Vernon L. Parrington's *Main Currents in American Thought* appeared in 1927, ten years after the first volumes of the *Cambridge History of American Literature*. The growing influence of such radicals in the philosophy and method of literary study as Babbitt, Lovejoy, Manly, and Lowes was reflected in re-examinations of the ideas and backgrounds of American as well as English authors. Even more important, scholars in American literature began to show a heretical interest in such historians as Turner, Beard, McMaster, and Schlesinger and to reshape their literary interpretations around dynamic theories of historical evolution in both the individual and the group. A theory of literary history which was based mainly on a linguistic tradition and which sought to explain a work of literary art by reference solely to its "sources" in other works of literature began to give way to a theory which saw literature as the direct product of the circumstances, both within and without the experience of the writer, that had brought his artistic expression to fulfillment. This new approach sharply distinguished those works which were the productions of artists who had participated in the shaping of a civilization on the North American continent from those of artists who had remained in the British Isles. American literature in itself and in relation to its culture suddenly became a legitimate field for scholarly devotion.

This shift of emphasis was greatly aided, if not actually caused, by basic shifts in scientific thinking from the systems of analysis and classification of data current in the nineteenth century and earlier to the organic systems developed mainly by modern physics and biology. New theories about the character and functions of nature itself began to be reflected in theories of literary production, and students of American literature, partly because they were exploring a virtually new culture, were perhaps more generally adventurous in their speculations and their methods than most scholars in fields where historical philology had for so long held undisputed sway. Literary Americanists needed a new orientation for their thinking in order to justify their very existence. Scholars like Norman Foerster, H. L. Mencken, Van Wyck Brooks, V. L. Parrington, and F. O. Matthiessen were too independent and original for the ranks of the Modern Language Association, while scholars who remained within the guild but fought for the new dispensation — men like Arthur H. Quinn, Jay B. Hubbell, Stanley Williams, Kenneth Murdock, Sculley Bradley, and Ralph L. Rusk — developed needed agencies and instruments and produced major works in literary history in the new idioms. The appearance of the *Literary History of the United States* and the founding of the *American Quarterly* and the American Studies Association were almost simultaneous at mid-century.

The contribution of general historians to the American Studies movement followed similar lines and was, in somewhat the same fashion, a by-product of the new science. Scholars in general American history had, however, one advantage over their literary brethren: American history had been recognized from the start as a legitimate field for special research. The narrative historians, Bancroft, Parkman, Prescott, and Motley, told the American story for itself and without apology even though they saw it chiefly in the context of the expansion of European power, and the "objective" constitutional and military historians like Adams, Channing, and Hildreth applied the new German documentary techniques to American sources without inhibition. The revolution was apparent more in changing theories and methods of historiography than in a shift to the American field as such.

It was important, however, in both ways. Frederick Jackson Turner's frontier theory explained American development as an indigenous growth rather than as an importation, but it also pioneered in the application of economic determinism to historical data. Schlesinger's study of immigration, Beard's work on the framing of the Constitution, Becker's analysis of the Declaration of Independence, and the surveys of Morison, Commager, Nevins, and others were only a few of the many reinterpretations of old facts in terms of immediate environmental causation. To these men, literature was one of the many sources of documentation for movements which embraced the entire human experience in any given time and place. They were drawn to the literary historians at about the same time that the literary historians were turning to them and for much the same reason, a desire to broaden their field of inquiry, their methods, and their range of usable data.

Meanwhile parallel revolutions were taking place in the scholarly study of the other arts and of the social sciences, revolutions which are still in progress and which need not be discussed at length here. The general historians were soon aware of sources of fresh and dynamic thought among their colleagues in economics, political science, and sociology, whereas the literary historians found their interest in environmental causation echoed among the historians of painting, sculpture, architecture, and the minor and "useful" arts. Both groups found the philosophers turning from the classical forms of their subject to pragmatism and experimentalism and from traditional histories of pure philosophy to a type of intellectual history which was firmly anchored to the time, the place, the group, and the thinker.

American Studies as a movement caused none of these trends, but by 1935 it was providing a convenient point of focus for all of them. The prestige of the United States as a world power encouraged the study of its culture, and the strong movements away from overspecialization and toward cooperation among the academic disciplines made the creation of interdepartmental programs in this and similar fields virtually inevitable. Harvard led the way in 1936 with a graduate program in the History of American Civilization, and Pennsylvania, Yale, Minnesota, and other universities followed.

At first these alliances could be described as little more than loose confederations or extensions of the programs of single departments, usually literature or history. There was little if any feeling that a new subject or a new discipline was in the making. Courses were often grouped merely because they could be described as "American" and their synthesis was left wholly to the student. Administrative committees seldom met and often took little responsibility for either the program or its students. Doctors of Philosophy were thrown out into the academic world without status or job and usually drifted back into conventional channels for their careers. There were few new journals ready to publish experimental scholarship in interdisciplinary problems and the established journals were largely inhospitable and suspicious. The movement needed a rationale as well as a history.

Again progress toward integrity as well as originality came from general trends in the scholarly world rather than from within the American Studies movement itself. As modern science learned to deal with problems of human nature and human culture rather than merely with the physical world and its biological and economic manifestations, the study of American civilization gradually began to develop meanings and methods of its own. It is still far from the goal of systematic research to which all scholarship tends to aspire, but it has made great progress in the past decade, as the essays in this volume will testify.

Some of the trends which began to bear directly on the problem of understanding American or any other modern culture were to be found in the so-called behavioral sciences — sociology, cultural anthropology, and both social and individual psychology. Other contributions to understanding were found in the new analytical methods of criticizing sophisticated works of art and literature and the new techniques for analyzing and interpreting mass or popular culture, many of them developed by the folklorists and by the students of linguistic analysis and semantics. Cross-cultural indexing of artifacts and documents, psychological analysis of group and individual motivation, content analysis of communication documents, studies in myth and symbol as basic rather than idiosyncratic formulations of experience — these approaches began to supplement the older methods of the physical and social scientists and of the general and art historians. Again, American Studies, by offering a limited body of closely related data on the cultural history of a nation which had developed wholly in the modern era, provided a convenient focus for research and teaching. Modern scholarship was regaining slowly the conception of total cultures which had inspired humanistic scholarship from classical times through the Renaissance but which had been lost in the disintegrative tendencies of modern scientific research; and, even more important, it was learning to apply this conception to modern cultures. American humanistic scholars began to realize that an immediate culture of recent development and a high degree of sophistication as well as complexity was available to them for examination: the culture of the United States as a political unit, of the North American continent as a geographical unit, and of the people who settled and developed this area as a cultural group. In spite of the difficulties inherent in the problem and the variety among the proposed methods of dealing with it, there seemed at last to be recognition that here was a single and legitimate field for scholarly research as well as a convenient pedagogical device for liberalizing higher education.

The problem of developing suitable methods for such research was, however, very far from solved. In fact, the failure of the movement to settle on a generally accepted method of dealing with its diversified materials instead of being a weakness appeared as one of its major strengths. It could remain experimental and exploratory; it could still act as the yeast rather than the dough of research, the academic staff of life. American Studies still could, and should, be thought of in the plural, as a mixture of different ways of dealing with the same material, but the mixture had tended to become chemical rather than mechanical; that is, its components could now merge in a more integrated whole because each gave up a part of its own identity in becoming a facet of the general enterprise. Since about 1945, the study of American civilization has become not so much a new discipline as a new focus for the investigation of human habits, ideals, and achievements. As a branch of humanistic scholarship it is learning to apply the principles and methods of traditional humanism to modern problems and thus to answer in part the criticism that the humanities, alone of the great divisions of learning, are wholly lost in the past.

Most of the essays in this book could not have been written before 1945, and the book itself, if undertaken at all, would have been held together mainly because its contents dealt with things American. As it is, anyone who starts with the assumption that there may be un underlying unity will soon discover in the separate essays organic relationships with each other and with the book as a whole. Since only a few of them were primarily planned for this volume, the existence of such unity, if it can be discovered, can only in part be attributed to skillful editing. The unity now exists in the field of American Studies itself.

Henry Nash Smith quite properly opens the discussion as perhaps the oldest scholar to hold a doctorate in the history of American civilization as such. Even so, he speaks as youth to a youthful enterprise. A few of the other contributors — among them Mr. Tate, Mr. Blegen, and myself — may be older in years, but must remain, in a sense, fellow travelers lacking the badge of the order. Only those who, like Mr. Smith, have committed themselves professionally by taking a higher degree in American Studies can realize the full urgency of the problem of unity; and there is a constantly increasing number of brilliant young scholars who are so committed. Whatever the value of loose organization in a curriculum, the human spirit to its credit will always demand an organizing principle and a unity of goal in its thinking and in its action. When the first Ph.D. in American Studies or American Civilization was awarded, the happy days of intellectual anarchy and free adventure were over. A moral commitment had been made.

That commitment is deeply evident in Mr. Smith's clear presentation of the central problem of the book and the movement. To him, "American Studies" means one thing only, a concern for an increased understanding of American culture. The existence of such a culture is assumed. If culture is defined as the way in which subjective experience is organized, there remains only to discover who has done the organizing, exactly what components have been organized into a single whole, and how to study the result.

The tacit assumption in this essay that a single method, although not yet in sight, would be desirable for research in American Studies springs from the desire to find an organic unity in the subject itself rather than merely a synthesis in the mind of the student. To appreciate the difference in attitude of the scholar trained in one of the older disciplines and of the product of the new program, one need only turn to Mr. McDowell's statement of a decade ago: "The discipline of American Studies is the intellectual process whereby a student assimilates the complicated and often contradictory details of American civilization . . . whereby he fashions out of them a picture of these United States. In doing so, he reduces diversity to some degree of unity." [4] Compare this descriptive procedure with the effort of Mr. Smith to understand Mark Twain through his writing and in the context of his culture and with the suggestion that "it may turn out that one of the distinctive fields of American Studies is precisely this ambiguous relation between works of art and the culture in which they occur." The difference is not so much that between two scholar-colleagues as between the devoted pioneer of a movement and its committed product, a difference between 1948 and 1958. This difference is roughly reflected in the essays in this book: those which are based in the older disciplines but use methods or materials borrowed from others, and those which focus on a central problem of the culture itself.

Even though Mr. Smith's findings are, at least for the present, largely negative, his basic but unanswered question provides a plan for the volume which follows and perhaps for the movement as well: "To find out what was happening to the man and to the society we have to ask questions which lead simultaneously to literary analysis and to analysis of social change." And he recognizes that "the development of a method for American Studies is bound up with an effort to resolve the dilemma posed by the dualism which separates social facts from aesthetic values." This is where the movement started, with history as the spokesman for the social approach moving toward literature as the spokesman for the aesthetic, but now they have met, they are engaged in a common enterprise, and they are faced with a tough and resistant inner dualism.

Whether or not this dualism can or should be resolved, it provides a framework for the following essays. The first four are unified in that they seek in historical and social data the evidences for cultural definition. The methods of the behavioral sciences in analyzing the controlling ideas and habits of the American people are here used to discover, in Mr. Denney's phrase, "how Americans see themselves." The national character, if it exists, is expressed in the ideas, artifacts, and institutions which the society as a whole generates. The scholar can isolate and define the elements thus reflected from the total culture and approach an understanding of both its facts and its values. An event such as the Lindbergh flight and institutions such as a communitarian society or a labor organization can serve as evidences of what the people think and therefore what the culture is. The validity of the data derived from the process of group image-making is tested in a variety of ways, but in accepting the image as a social fact, a long step has been taken by these scholars from the impersonal realm of pure science into the subjective realm of the humanist.

The continuity of the volume suddenly breaks with Mr. O'Connor's essay which asks a different but closely related question. This and most of the following papers proceed from a base in literature and the other arts rather than from one in history and the social sciences. Within this grouping there are sub-classifications. The other arts present slightly different problems from those of literature, and the problems of mass communication are not those of the individual artist, but these essays have in common an inquiry into the relation of artistic expression of some kind to the culture which produces it. This is the other face of the coin. Mr. Smith's dualism is maintained throughout even though a literary critic like Mr. Tate here addresses himself to a problem of social causation and a historian like Mr. Blegen is concerned with popular balladry. The main issue in all the essays of this second group is that of aesthetic value.

Robert E. Spiller

In Mr. O'Connor's statement of the difference between the reality of art and that of life — a problem which much concerned Henry James but is implicit in all aesthetic theory — he brings no new light to students of literature, but he exposes with devastating emphasis the fallacy of those workers in the social sciences who would use literature as merely one more form of documentation without distinguishing between the realm of fact and that of idea, symbol, and value. Literature and the other arts create their own world of reality on the level of myth and symbol, a world often unacknowledged even by the mind of the artist himself. As important to the culture as is the reality of fact and artifact, it can often be discovered only by inference and stubbornly resists the exacting methods and standards of research in the sciences.

It is at this point that an effort at cooperation between literary scholars Bowron and Marx and sociologist Rose opens a possible new avenue to understanding. The rhetorical and dialectical traditions of Mr. Tate and the vernacular tradition of Mr. Marx himself are understandable only as covert culture, yet they are as real as Sherman's march to the sea. Mr. Noble's distinction between the intellectual level of Veblen's ideas and the intuitive or aesthetic level of Dreiser's is more significant than is a distinction between the relative positions of the two men on the idea of progress. Mr. Levenson uses the sensibility of the artist Henry Adams as a lens through which to examine changes in the culture of science in America. Mr. Kwiat's study of the parallels in the artistic and intellectual expression of painter Henri and writers Emerson and Whitman broadens understanding of the relations, not only between two arts, but between the arts and ideas in American culture. The essay by Mr. Blegen, which deals with popular or folk expression, demonstrates that high culture is not alone in creating a world of values and attitudes which, expressed through symbol, must be regarded for the purposes of research as cultural facts. Mr. Foster employs a concept drawn from religious and social philosophy in an attempt to arrive at an analysis of American culture in terms of both social fact and aesthetic value.

It would seem from all this evidence that American Studies may not be as far from the goal of unified methodology as Mr. Smith appears to believe. The dualism may be one of direction only. Is not the movement from the level of fact and opinion of the society as a whole, through its image-making propensity, up (or down) to the level of value and myth merely the reverse of that taken by the literary or art critic who starts

215

on the level of the imagination and moves through value and myth to the materials of actual life from which aesthetic expression is derived? Should the two not meet somewhere in a realm of images which could express both the social realities and the covert dreams of the total culture? The fact that no single essay in this volume succeeds in completely re-solving the dualism between society and art would seem to indicate that, for the present at least, Mr. Smith is correct in assuming that no solution has been found. Yet the diverse methods illustrated in this book and the syntheses which emerge, although tentative and perhaps incomplete, strongly suggest that American Studies has a future.

What, then, is the hope for the future? Perhaps it lies in the acceptance of the humanist's contention that life is and always must remain dual. Man constantly aspires to monism, whether of God or Nature, and as constantly fails. The human consciousness, to be whole, must participate in the divine and in the material, but can not identify wholly with either and remain human. As American Studies began with a flirtation between literary and historical studies, it would seem now in danger of ending in a divorce because it asks that union become total unity.

Another way of stating the problem is to think of a stereopticon viewer which achieves a three-dimensional effect by allowing two angles of vi-sion to focus simultaneously on a single object. Perhaps the two kinds of reality — that of the imagination and that of the reason — are both real, both essential to human culture in its more complex forms. Perhaps what is needed is a tolerant relationship of cooperation between the two dis-ciplines, that dealing with art and that dealing with society, and a willing-ness on the part of each to move from the level of fact to the level of value. Perhaps the limitation of scholarship in American Studies to one method and one kind of material would spell defeat, self-inflicted.

The irony of the present situation in social and humanistic scholarship is that the trend is counter to any such cooperation. The desire to achieve objective, "scientific" validity is once more separating scholars — not only in American Studies, but in other branches of research as well. The social scientist strives to isolate the social fact from its cause and its con-sequence so that it may stand up and be counted; and the literary critic strives to free the work of art from both intention and affect so that its supposed meaning may be read from its own being, the text, uncon-fused by what are considered to be extraneous circumstances. Not only is the artist once more being deliberately alienated from his society, but society is being deliberately robbed of its aesthetic experience. Values themselves, in the social science definition, are all of one level of worth although they may exist in a hierarchy of abstraction. Content, whether social or aesthetic, becomes form and form becomes content; the dialectical relationship between them is ignored or suppressed. Quantification, objectivity, and system are once more pushing the humanities and the social sciences apart, and American Studies may fall between.

Mr. Smith has thoroughly considered this problem and has provided a clear estimate of what internal analysis in literary criticism (the "New" Criticism) and quantification in social science research (content analysis) are accomplishing separately and are failing to accomplish together. William K. Wimsatt, Jr., and Monroe Beardsley make the case for literary criticism when they say, "The Intentional Fallacy is a confusion between the poem and its origins. . . . The Affective Fallacy is a confusion between the poem and its *results*. . . . The outcome of either fallacy, the Intentional or the Affective, is that the poem itself, as an object of specifically critical judgment, tends to disappear." [5] Bernard Berelson speaks similarly for the social sciences when he defines content analysis as "a research technique for the objective, systematic, and quantitative description of the manifest content of communication." [6] In both cases the process is that of arbitrarily isolating and delimiting elements of subjective experience in order to approximate the precision and accuracy demanded by science. In both, the endeavor is doomed to failure if regarded as more than a provisional operation to suggest rather than to prove hypotheses. Both are highly useful within these limits, but are misleading if strained beyond them.

The difficulty on both sides of the dilemma is, of course, that in an effort to be objective and scientific on the one hand and aesthetically pure on the other — in short, to achieve a validity above experience — both types of scholars tend to confuse means with ends. What is only a method, a provisional isolation of an entity for purposes of analysis, attains the finality of verifiable truth. The methods of content analysis can be successfully applied to elements which are not really objective and quantitative, such as values, images, and ideas, if the categories developed are recognized as quantitative only in their expression and not in any absolute sense and if the results are regarded as suggestive rather than as scientifically valid. In spite of the advances in the techniques of psychological analysis in recent years, human thinking and feeling are still very far from submitting to the conquests of exact human knowledge. In both the individual and the social mind, there are vast areas which require purely qualitative rather than logical methods of understanding and evaluation. Bernard Berelson somewhat reluctantly admits the usefulness of "qualitative" as well as quantitative analysis, especially for meanings which are largely connotative, but warns that it too has a responsibility for sharpening categories and hypotheses and for avoiding "impressionistic and ambiguous formulations." He does not, however, develop the positive usefulness of such analysis for purely speculative explorations into the realms of social metaphor, myth, and ritual. Presumably he would not approve such formulations as Malinowski's imaginative as well as scientific study of the mind and habits of the primitive Trobriand Islanders,[7] Constance Rourke's attempt to probe the roots of American culture by exposing folk elements which underlie a complex and rapidly changing modern civilization,[8] and the broad revelation of a national character in the generalization of David Riesman and his associates that modern times have witnessed a shift of emphasis from the "inner" to the "other" directed man.[9] All such speculative studies are suspect by the purists among research scholars because their hypotheses cannot be submitted to factual and quantitative validation; but it is just this quality which allows them to impinge on the realm of the human imagination and thereby provide possible meeting grounds with the students of the arts.

On the other hand, there is nothing in the procedures of the New Critics which would prevent the application of their insights to the total product of the artist, to the creative processes that underlie his work, and to his biographical and social conditioning as well as to the isolated work of art, if the fact of isolation is accepted only as a provisional condition of the analytical process and not as an end in itself. This, of course, the purists among the New Critics could not allow, but there are increasing signs of restlessness among them and of desire to relate their findings, in the way that Mr. Tate relates southern literature, to broader and deeper contexts of experience than can be found in a single poem, novel, painting, play, or composition. Their sometimes violent and unreasoning antihistoricism, as found in many of their so-called histories of criticism as well as in their individual analyses, must give way to a recognition of the validity of content study *through* as well as *in* form, and the larger relationships between life and art, experience and expression. If the doors are once more opened, as they were for Goethe, Lessing, Coleridge, and Arnold, on the speculative exploration of the realm of imagination, myth, and metaphor which exists in the creative process as well as in the work of art, the literary critic might recapture his right to conversation with the more speculative of the social scientists.

It must be admitted that the urge toward final and tenable results is today strong in all fields of scholarly research; the desire of social scientists, and even of humanists, to become as accurate and predictable as physical and natural scientists is also impelling. Hence a move in the direction of intuitive and nonquantitative methods may be increasingly unlikely. If this trend continues, American Studies may well become a branch of sociology and move with the purists in that field into severely limited and definable areas of research or it may dissolve with the New Criticism into the vacuum of pure literary analysis. But the literary, cultural, and intellectual historians, who have always had a stake in pure speculation in spite of repeated efforts, and repeated failures, to reduce their discipline to a science, are likely to protest. The latest committee attempt on their part to explore the methodology of their craft, far from reducing history to a mere analytical description of society, concludes with the suggestion that "the use of social science approaches focuses attention on the aspects of the event that reveal the major dynamics of the culture" and predicts that "When the United States is even two hundred years old instead of a hundred and seventy . . . broader and less detailed syntheses will be demanded by the exigencies of space and time, and it will be up to the historian to . . . avail himself of the aid offered by the social scientist." [10]

The scholar in American Studies, devoted as he is to a specific field of data and to a single large historical event — American civilization, both in its development and in its present status — is more free to explore and experiment with methodology than are the scholars who are committed to specific disciplines. By learning to use the techniques of both types of analysis, that of the social scientists and that of the literary and art critics, but by refusing to be confined to the ends proposed by the purists in either field, he may discover broader and deeper truths about man's experience in a single time and place than would be available to the more specialized researcher. He might also, by analogy, better understand man's experience in other times and places and, by generalization, the

219

nature of culture itself. The movement should not give in wholly to the historians and, through them, to the formalizing and limiting methods of the social sciences, nor should it renounce history and move into formal literary and art criticism. Its role is still, and probably should remain, that of the mediator; but in filling this role, it can develop even further than it has during the past decade toward self-esteem and precision in carrying out its specific if not specialized task. That task is the understanding of the culture of the United States, and there is no one research method competent to accomplish it alone. A focus on objective does not necessarily mean a limitation on method.

## NOTES

[1] Tremaine McDowell, *American Studies* (Minneapolis: University of Minnesota Press, 1948), p. 51.

[2] *Ibid.*, p. 8.

[3] Committee on the College Study of American Literature and Culture, William G. Crane, chairman, *American Literature in the College Curriculum* (Chicago: National Council of Teachers of English, 1948).

[4] McDowell, *American Studies*, p. 33.

[5] William K. Wimsatt, Jr., *The Verbal Icon* (New York: The Noonday Press, 1958), p. 21.

[6] Bernard Berelson, *Content Analysis in Communication Research* (Glencoe, Ill.: The Free Press, 1952), p. 18.

[7] Bronislaw Malinowski, *Magic, Science, and Religion* (Glencoe, Ill.: The Free Press, 1948).

[8] Constance Rourke, *The Roots of American Culture* (New York: Harcourt, Brace and Co., 1942).

[9] David Riesman and others, *The Lonely Crowd* (New Haven, Conn.: Yale University Press, 1953).

[10] Thomas C. Cochran and others, *The Social Sciences in Historical Study: A Report of the Committee on Historiography* (New York: Social Science Research Council, Bulletin No. 64, 1954), pp. 163, 171.

INDEX

# Index

Adams, Brooks: 134, 201
Adams, Charles Francis: 124, 129
Adams, Henry Brooks: and Clarence King, 130–131; and *Principles of Psychology*, 136–137; and progress, 131–133; and scientific revolution, 134–136; belief in reason, 126, 130–131, 133, 135, 137; "catastrophe," 125-126, 133–134, 136; early scientific interests, 125, 129–130; family's scientific interests, 124, 126–129; on Lee's son, 102; personal influences on ideas, 133–134; review of *Principles of Geology*, 125, 130, 133; significance in study of culture of science, 123–124, 137; mentioned, 215
Adams, Herbert Baxter: 209
Adams, John: 124, 126, 127–128, 131, 132, 134
Adams, John Quincy: 124, 127
Adler, Alfred: 19
Adolescence: 16–17, 19, 21–23, 24, 57, 60, 85–86
Adorno, T. W.: 16
Aesthetics: 10–11, 13, 15, 72, 74, 76–78, 80, 82, 83, 98, 121, 128, 154–170, 197–198, 202, 207, 211, 214–216, 217
Agassiz, Louis: 124
Agrarianism: 66, 102–105, 187
Alcock, John: 31
Alcott, Amos Bronson: 193, 195
Algren, Nelson: 81
American Federation of Labor: 64–65, 66–73
American Legion: 28
*American Literature*: 208
*American Quarterly*: 209
American Revolution: 53, 78–79, 119
"American Scholar, The": 101
American Studies: development of as separate academic program, 207–210;

future of, 216–220; method in, 3–15, 84, 195–196, 200, 205, 211–220; rationale of, 210–212; unity of as demonstrated by essays, 212–216
American Studies Association: 209
Amish Communities: 45, 57
Anarchism: 54, 56, 58, 121, 170*n*38
Anderson, Sherwood: difference between art and life, 74, 75, 78; religious tone, 196, 197, 203
Anglicanism: 200
Anschutz, Thomas: 153–154
Anthropology: 4, 14, 19, 22, 47, 86, 94*n*3, 143, 145–146, 187, 211
Aquinas, St. Thomas: 124, 140
Archimedes: 104
Architecture: 104, 163, 164, 210
Aristotle: his *Ethics, Politics,* and *Rhetoric,* 82, 98, 101, 102
Arnold, Matthew: 13, 219
*Arrowsmith*: 196
"Art": Emerson's first essay quoted, 162, 164–165; his second essay quoted, 163
"Art of Fiction, The": quoted, 78
Artist and the public: 3–8, 9, 10, 74, 75, 76, 77–78, 79, 80, 82–83, 87, 88, 91, 92, 93, 100, 106, 110, 115, 118, 154, 156–157, 161–163, 165, 197–198, 208
Artistic theory. *See* Aesthetics
Artzybasheff, Boris: 21
*As You Like It*: 83

*Babbitt*: 196
Babbitt, Irving: 200, 208
"Backward Glance o'er Travel'd Roads, A": quoted, 158
Ballads: English and Scots border, 32, 171; pioneer and immigrant, 171–188, 215
Bancroft, George: 209

223